中央民族大学青年文库

基于用法的汉语动结式研究

A Usage-Based Approach to Chinese Resultative Constructions

余烁◎著

中央民族大学出版社
China Minzu University Press

图书在版编目（CIP）数据

基于用法的汉语动结式研究 = A usage-based approach to Chinese resultative constructions / 余烁著. — 北京：中央民族大学出版社，2022.8（2023. 1重印）
ISBN 978-7-5660-2106-9

Ⅰ. ①基… Ⅱ. ①余… Ⅲ. ①汉语—语法—研究 Ⅳ. ①H14

中国版本图书馆CIP数据核字（2022）第126919号

基于用法的汉语动结式研究
A Usage-Based Approach to Chinese Resultative Constructions

著　　者　余　烁
责任编辑　戴佩丽
封面设计　舒刚卫
出版发行　中央民族大学出版社
北京市海淀区中关村南大街 27 号　　邮编：100081
电话：（010）68472815（发行部）　传真：（010）68933757（发行部）
（010）68932218（总编室）　（010）68932447（办公室）
经 销 者　全国各地新华书店
印 刷 厂　北京鑫宇图源印刷科技有限公司
开　　本　787 × 1092　1/16　印张：22.75
字　　数　310 千字
版　　次　2022 年 8 月第 1 版　2023 年 1 月第 2 次印刷
书　　号　ISBN 978-7-5660-2106-9
定　　价　98.00 元

Preface

This book provides a study with a usage-based approach to resultative constructions in Mandarin Chinese in line with construction grammar from a cognitive-typological perspective. Mainly focusing on the acceptability of Chinese resultatives formed as [subject + verb + (object) + result XP + (aspect marker 了 *le*)], the research consists of a corpus study and acceptability judgements via questionnaire surveys. As some Chinese resultatives are more acceptable with the 把 *ba*-construction whereas others are not, the questionnaires also investigate combinations of 把 *ba* and resultatives.

In the corpus study of Chinese resultatives, data are collected from the Lancaster Corpus of Mandarin Chinese (LCMC) based on the result XPs listed in the Online Database on Verb-Resultative Constructions in Contemporary Chinese (ODVRC). A result XP refers to a change of state or location of a referent of an NP caused by an action denoted by the verb, based on which two tests are proposed to identify Chinese resultatives. The tests also distinguish marginal and prototypical resultatives in Chinese. A descriptive analysis of Chinese resultatives is presented in terms of type and token frequency with regard to different classifications, namely subject- versus object-oriented, transitive- versus intransitive-based, and weak versus strong versus spurious. I propose a distinction among agent- versus patient- versus location-oriented resultatives to fully account for the properties of Chinese resultatives. In addition, the results suggest that Chinese belongs to the same type as English, permitting both strong and weak resultatives. This is different from languages which only allow weak ones (e.g. Japanese, French and Italian).

Two questionnaire surveys among Chinese college students are carried out to test the acceptability of subject– and object–oriented resultatives, as well as combinations with the 把 *ba*–construction. Magnitude estimation is adopted as a judging technique, which can detect subtle but significant differences in acceptability. The results suggest that the acceptability of subject– and object–oriented resultatives depends on whether there could be a postverbal NP in the sentence. The conditions that determine acceptability in the two types vary phonologically, syntactically and semantically.

The acceptability of 把 *ba* + resultatives forms a continuum, especially for 把 *ba* + subject–oriented patterns with significant differences. The acceptability of 把 *ba* + resultative depends on the degree of semantic transitivity expressed by a sentence. Generally, resultatives construed as having a high degree of semantic transitivity are more acceptable with 把 *ba*. The cognitive explanation I propose is that high transitivity expressed by the sentence is compatible with the function of 把 *ba* as a marker of the high transitivity. This also sheds light on the discussion of the function of the 把 *ba*–construction in scholarship for viewing it as a marker of high transitivity rather than expressing disposal or causativity.

Acknowledgements

This book grew out of my PhD. thesis, which was completed at Lancaster University. After four years, this long journey has come to an end. I express my first gratitude to my two supervisors: Dr Daniël Van Olmen and Dr Willem Bernardus Hollmann. Their rich knowledge in various linguistic areas, insights into my topics and comments on my thesis are of no question the most important in my PhD study. I would like to thank Professor Jonathan Culpeper, Dr Amanda Patten and Dr Vittorio Tantucci for their invaluable suggestions on my thesis and being supportive in the panels. My thanks also go to Dr Silke Brandt for kindly chairing my confirmation panel and Professor Panos Athanasopoulos for the Viva.

I thank Professor Xiaoqun Lu in Minzu University of China. She helped me with the data collection of my first survey, which contributes a major part to my findings. I also thank Huadong Li, Jun Zhang, and Xingxuan Shen for their suggestions of my pilot study. I sincerely appreciate the support from Professor Fengchun Zhang and Colette Webb in Confucius Institute at Lancaster University, for providing me a lot of opportunities to teach Chinese there.

Among the years in Lancaster, I am very grateful to have quite a few friends, with whom I could have fun and get refreshed for my research. They are Diansha Wang, Yifan Li, Shuangfa Huang, Jing Huang, Tanjun Liu, Bew

Charoenchaikorn, Mandy Yu, Zoe Ad, Miranda Barty–Taylor, Claire Kelly, Emily Winter, Laura Clancy, Hissah Alruwaili, Abdalkarim Zawawi and many others. I am so glad that we could have dinners together regularly, watch films, have trips in the UK, or just chat. We do need each other so as to finish the degree with colourful memories. Also I would like to thank my friends at home, those I knew in Senior High School, university and at work. Although we cannot meet often, I know you girls will be there for me.

I would also express my appreciation to my family. My grandma, aunts (especially my third aunt), the three older cousin sisters, thank you. In the end, I am deeply grateful to my parents. They respect my choices since I was in Senior High School, and always support and encourage me with great love.

Table of Contents

Table of Contents

List of Figures

List of symbols and abbreviations

*	Indicating an unacceptable example
?	Indicating a marginally acceptable example
BNC	British National Corpus
CCL	The corpus built by the Center for Chinese Linguistics in Peking University
LCMC	The Lancaster Corpus of Mandarin Chinese
ODVRC	The Online Database on Verb–Resultative Constructions in Contemporary Chinese
A	The most agent–like argument in a sentence
AP	Adjective phrase
ASP	Aspect marker 了 *le*
CL	Classifier
NP	Noun phrase
O	Object
POSS	Possessive 的 *de*
P	The most patient–like argument in a sentence
PP	Preposition phrase
VP	Verb phrase
XP	Used in 'the result XP', which denotes the result of a change of state or location of a referent of an NP

Chapter 1 Introduction

1.1 Preliminaries

1.1.1 The resultative construction in Mandarin Chinese

The resultative construction in Mandarin Chinese, exemplified by (1) and (2), is characterized by the presence of a result XP, which refers to the result of a change of state or location of a referent of an NP (cf. Li 1990, Sybesma 1992, Song 2003, Shi 2008, Zhao 2009). So (1) is interpreted as ‘he walked, and as a result he was tired’; the result XP 累 *lei* ‘tired’ refers to the result of the change of his state. (2) is understood as ‘she wiped her hair and as a result her hair was dry’, with the result XP干 *gan* ‘dry’ denoting the result of the change of her hair. Structurally, the Chinese resultative construction is formed as [subject + verb + (object) + result XP + (aspect marker 了 *le*)][1] – for instance, in (1) as

1 了 *le* as an aspect marker signals perfectivity in Mandarin. According to my corpus study of Chinese resultatives (for more information, see Chapter 4), 134 out of 500 instances take 了 *le*. In view of its optional yet not uncommon co–occurrence, I have included it here as an optional part of the construction, although one could also argue that it is best seen as (part of) another construction, which is compatible with the resultative construction.

[subject + verb + result XP + 了 *le*] and in (2) as [subject + verb + object + result XP + 了 *le*].[2]

(1)	他	走－累－了		(CCL 2.1)[b]
	ta	*zou-lei-le*		
	he	walk–tired–ASP		

'He walked and as a result he was tired.'

(2)	她	擦－干－了	头发	(CCL 89.1)
	ta	*ca-gan-le*	*toufa*	
	she	wipe–dry–ASP	hair	

'She wiped her hair dry.'

The literature, both generative (e.g. Li 1995, Gao 1997) and cognitive (e.g. Shen 2004, Shi 2008), has discussed example (3) and its alleged multiple interpretations at great length. Corpus data and native speaker judgements suggest, however, that this is a very infrequent and unacceptable construction.[4] The position taken in this book is that a discussion of resultatives in Mandarin or indeed any language should be based first and foremost not on artificial and potentially dubious examples, but instead on authentic language data.

(3)	淘淘	追－累－了	悠悠	(Li 1995: 257)
	Taotao	*zhui-lei-le*	*Youyou*	
	Taotao (name)	chase–tired–ASP	Youyou (name)	

---

2 In the thesis I will use *resultative construction* and *resultative* , *Mandarin* and *Chinese* interchangeably.

3 CCL refers to the corpus built by the Center for Chinese Linguistics PKU; see Chapter 3, Section 3.2 for more information.

4 I asked over 200 students (all native speakers) in class informally when I was teaching in Anhui University of Science and Technology in 2012, and none of them thought the sentence was good.

a. Taotao chased Youyou and as a result Youyou was tired.

b. Taotao chased Youyou and as a result Taotao was tired.

c. Youyou chased Taotao and as a result Youyou was tired.

Given that the focus of this book is on resultatives in authentic language, how resultatives are used should be considered. I consulted the Online Database on Verb–Resultative Constructions in Contemporary Chinese (ODVRC; for more information about this database see Chapter 3, Section 3.2). Although the ODVRC lists various patterns of result XPs, many of the patterns are not resultatives, at least not in my definition; see for instance (4). The first part of the collocation in (4) is an adjectival phrase (AP) 简单 *jiandan* 'simple' rather than a verb. The clause, therefore, does not express the result of an action, even though it is similar in form to a resultative. The inadequacy of the ODVRC shows that an adequate definition of resultatives in Mandarin requires consideration not only of structure but also of meaning, and furthermore suggests that some tests for judging whether a sentence is a resultative construction may be useful. I have already touched on semantics in my definition above, and I will come back to tests in Chapter 4, Section 4.2.2.2.

(4) 我们的	生活	简单–极–了	(ODVRC)
womende	*shenghuo*	*jiandan-ji-le*	
our	life	simple–extreme–ASP	

'Our life was extremely simple.'

In addition, directional verbs are also viewed as resultatives in the ODVRC. According to quite a few Chinese scholars (e.g. Wang 1999, He 2004, Yang 2004), directional verbs in Chinese form a finite set, including monosyllabic ones like 来 *lai* 'come', 去 *qu* 'go', 上 *shang* 'up' and 下 *xia* 'down', and disyllabic ones which are formed as some other directional + 来 *lai* 'come'/去 *qu* 'go', for instance 上去 *shang qu* 'up go' (go up), 过来 *guo lai* 'pass come' (come over). Verbs may precede both monosyllablic (e.g. 5a/b) and disyllabic directionals (see 5c). In other words, directional complements are in the form of verb + result XP (directional).

(5) a.

小王	爬–上	一	棵	树	(CCL 4.1)
XiaoWang	*pa-shang*	*yi*	*ke*	*shu*	
XiaoWang (name)	climb–up	one	CL	tree	

'XiaoWang climbed up a tree.'

b.

瓶子	漂–出	岩洞	(Shen 2003:18)
pingzi	*piao-chu*	*yandong*	
bottle	float–out	cave	

'The bottle floated out of the cave.'

c.

我	搬–过来	一	把	椅子 (CCL108.1)
wo	*ban-guo lai*	*yi*	*ba*	*yizi*
I	move–pass come	one	CL	chair

'I moved a chair here.'

According to Goldberg (1995) and Rappaport Hovav and Levin (2001), resultatives include a change of state or location of an NP, which suggests that examples like (5) are resultatives, since the directional denotes a change of location of an NP caused by an action. For instance, 上 *shang* 'up' in (5a) refers to the subject 小王 *XiaoWang* (name), the result 'up' being led to by the action 'climb' ; 过来 *guo lai* 'pass come' (come over) in (5c) states a change of location of the object 椅子 *yizi* 'chair', which is caused by the action 'move'. However, directionals emphasize the direction of the action in Chinese. For example, 来 *lai* 'come' indicates the direction of an action from a distant point to a nearby place, and 下 *xia* 'down' suggests the orientation of an action, from top to bottom. The movement of an action will subsequently cause a change of location of an NP, but it is not what the directional focuses on. Therefore, directionals may be viewed as resultatives in a broad sense (e.g. Shen 2003, Song 2004, Shi 2008), but I will not engage in further discussion about this here. I will mainly focus on change–of–state patterns.

A further issue worth noticing is that 'wipe clean' in (6a) is a commonly discussed example in the scholarship (e.g. Goldberg 1995, Washio 1997, Rappaport Hovav and Levin 2001, Goldberg and Jackendoff 2004, Croft 2012). Nevertheless, its literal translation into Chinese did not sound natural to native speakers, including myself, in my pilot study (see 6b).[5] (6b) would be more acceptable if it was combined with 把 ba (as in 6c). Therefore, the book also aims to test and explain the acceptability of 把 ba and resultatives. More about the 把 ba–construction will be introduced below, in Section 1.1.2.

(6) a. She wiped the table clean. (Washio 1997:10)

b. ?她 擦–干净了 桌子

ta *ca-ganjing-le* *zhuozi*

she wipe–clean–ASP table

'She wiped the table clean.'

5 A pilot study was carried out at Lancaster University with four native speakers of Chinese concerning the acceptability of 把 *ba* + resultatives. More about the pilot study will be mentioned in Chapter 3, Section 3.3.4.

c.

她	把	桌子	擦-干净了
ta	*ba*	*zhuozi*	*ca-ganjing-le*
she	*ba*	table	wipe–clean–ASP

'She wiped the table clean.'

1.1.2 The 把 *ba*-construction

The 把 *ba*–construction is formed as in (7) (e.g. Wang 2003). The 把 *ba*–construction is illustrated in (8a), with (8b) its counterpart without 把 *ba*. Similar in semantics, (8a) and (8b) differ in that the postverbal NP 苹果 *pingguo* 'apple' in (8a) is emphasized more than in (8b), and (8a) is interpreted as the subject 我 *wo* 'I' carrying out the action more intentionally, although there is no difference in acceptability between the two. Another point to be noticed is that a post–ba NP (e.g. 苹果 *pingguo* 'apple') is always required in the 把 *ba*–construction.

(7) NP_1 *ba* NP_2 V (aspect marker 了 *le*)

(8) a.

我	把	那	个	苹果	吃	了
wo	*ba*	*na*	*ge*	*pingguo*	*chi*	*le*
I	*ba*	that	CL	apple	eat	ASP

'I ate that apple.'

b.

我	吃	了	那	个	苹果
wo	*chi*	*le*	*na*	*ge*	*pingguo*
I	eat	ASP	that	CL	apple

'I ate that apple.'

Semantically, the 把 *ba*–construction has been analyzed as expressing disposal (Wang 1947, Li 1974, Wang 2003), causation (Guo 1999, Xiong 2004, Ye 2004), or high transitivity (Hopper and Thompson 1980, Sun 1995) in previous scholarship (see Han 2013 for an overview). The analysis of 把 *ba* has been widely discussed since the 1940s from various perspectives, but no agreement has been reached until now. This book aims to make a contribution to the debate, specifically from the point of view of the occurrence of 把 *ba* in resultative constructions.

1.1.3 The acceptability of resultative constructions in Mandarin

As mentioned in Section 1.1.1, some Chinese resultatives are better accepted with 把 *ba* than without 把 *ba*. Moreover, in the same form as verb + result XP, some resultatives are acceptable, whereas others are not and only good with 把 *ba*. That is, it is not the case that all resultative constructions are acceptable when combined with 把 *ba*. Therefore, the acceptability of Chinese resultatives (including with and without 把 *ba*) emerges as a question.

Chinese resultatives can be classified as subject–oriented and object–oriented, based on the distinction proposed by Rappaport Hovav and Levin (2001; for a more elaborate discussion see Chapter 2, Section 2.2.2.4), with the two differing in whether the result XP is predicated of the subject, as in (9a) or the object, as in (9b). A further difference between (9a) and (9b) is that there is a postverbal NP in the latter, but not in the former.

(9) a. 他 走–累–了 (CCL 2.1)

ta *zou-lei-le*

he walk–tired–ASP

'He walked and as a result he was tired.'

b. 她 擦–干–了 头发 (CCL 89.1)

ta *ca-gan-le* *toufa*

she wipe–dry–ASP hair

'She wiped her hair dry.'

By definition, object–oriented resultatives involve a postverbal NP. The occurrence of postverbal NPs in subject–oriented resultatives is somewhat more complex. In the Lancaster Corpus of Mandarin Chinese (LCMC; for more information see Chapter 3, Section 3.2), more than half (55.6%) of the subject–oriented resultatives do not take an object. As the change of state is related to the subject, a postverbal NP need not occur. So normally there are no combinations of 把 *ba* and subject–oriented resultatives, since the 把 *ba*–construction requires a postverbal NP, whereas subject–oriented resultative constructions do not take an object.

However, there are some subject–oriented resultatives found in the corpus with a postverbal NP (e.g. 10/11/12a). This raises a question: why can some subject–oriented resultatives not take an object, for instance (13), whereas some can, such as (10/11/12a).

(10) a. 他 想–明白–了 这 个 问题 (CCL 7.1)

ta *xiang-mingbai-le* *zhe* *ge* *wenti*

he think–understand–ASP this CL question

'He thought about this question and as a result he understood it.'

b.	他	把	这	个	问题	想–明白–了
	ta	*ba*	*zhe*	*ge*	*wenti*	*xiang-mingbai-le*
	he	*ba*	this	CL	question	think–understand–ASP

'He thought about this question and as a result he understood it.'

(11) a.	冬冬	听–懂–了	他的	话	(CCL 21.1)
	Dongdong	*ting-dong-le*	*tade*	*hua*	
	Dongdong (name)	listen–understand–ASP	his	words	

'Dongdong listened to his words and as a result Dongdong understood them.'

b.	?冬冬	把	他的	话	听–懂–了
	Dongdong	*ba*	*tade*	*hua*	*ting-dong-le*
	Dongdong (name)	*ba*	his	words	listen–understand–ASP

'Dongdong listened to his words and as a result Dongdong understood them.'

(12) a.	人们	喝–腻–了	甜的	(CCL 1.1)
	renmen	*he-ni-le*	*tiande*	
	people	drink–be tired of–ASP	sweet	

'People had drunk (the) sweet (drink) so many times that they were tired of it.'

b. *人们 把 甜的 喝–腻–了

renmen *ba* *tiande* *he-ni-le*

people *ba* sweet drink–be tired of–ASP

'People had drunk (the) sweet (drink) so many times that they were tired of it.'

(13) *他 走–累–了 山路

ta *zou-lei-le* *shanlu*

he walk–tired–ASP mountain road

'He walked on the mountain road and as a result he was tired.'

Moreover, subject–oriented resultatives with a postverbal NP provide opportunities for combining with 把 *ba*. Nevertheless, acceptability varies between sentences with and without 把 *ba* based on judgements made by participants (including myself) in my pilot study. Subject–oriented (10b) is acceptable, (11b) is marginally acceptable and (12b) is the least acceptable, whilst the examples without 把 ba (10a, 11a, 12a) are all fully acceptable. The acceptability of 把 *ba* + subject–oriented resultatives has rarely been discussed in the literature. Ye (2004) and Zhao (2009) mention some examples like (11) and (12), but no differences in the acceptability among (10)–(12) have been suggested (for more information about their discussion of (11) and (12) see Chapter 2, Section 2.4).

Similarly, combinations of 把 *ba* and object–oriented resultative constructions in Chinese also have different degrees of acceptability. Some object–oriented resultative sentences appear to be more or less equally acceptable both with and without 把 *ba* as in (15), whereas some are better with 把 *ba* than without one (e.g. 14b). There are also cases, like (16), where the variant with 把 *ba* seems to be less acceptable. Although there are discussions regarding the acceptability of 把 *ba* and object–oriented resultative constructions in previous scholarship (e.g. Huang 1996, Wang 2001, Song 2004, and Li 2008), differences in acceptability among such examples as (14)–(16) are not mentioned. All the issues concerning (10)–(16) will be discussed and I will attempt to explain them.

(14) a. ?她 擦–干净了 桌子

ta *ca-ganjing-le* *zhuozi*

she wipe–clean–ASP table

'She wiped the table clean.'

b. 她 把 桌子 擦–干净了

ta *ba* *zhuozi* *ca-ganjing-le*

she *ba* table wipe–clean–ASP

'She wiped the table clean.'

(15) a. 他 擦–干–了 头发 (CCL89.1)

ta *ca-gan-le* *toufa*

he wipe–dry–ASP hair

'He wiped his hair dry.'

b. 他 把 头发 擦–干了

ta *ba* *toufa* *ca-gan-le*

he *ba* hair wipe–dry–ASP

'He wiped his hair dry.'

(16) a. 妹妹 哭-湿-了 手绢 (CCL 1.1)

meimei *ku-shi-le* *shoujuan*

younger sister cry–wet–ASP handkerchief

'The younger sister cried and as a result the handkerchief was wet.' ('The younger sister cried the handkerchief wet.')

b. ?妹妹 把 手绢 哭-湿-了

meimei *ba* *shoujuan* *ku-shi-le*

younger sister *ba* handkerchief cry–wet–ASP

'The younger sister cried and as a result the handkerchief was wet.'('The younger sister cried the handkerchief wet.')

Taking into account all the aforementioned, this book aims to answer the following questions:

1. What qualifies as a Chinese resultative construction have? (cf. Chapter 4)

2. What do Chinese resultatives look like in actual usage? (cf. Chapter 4)

3. How can Chinese resultatives be viewed from a typological perspective? (cf. Chapter 4)

4. What determines the capacity of subject/agent–oriented resultatives to take a postverbal NP?[6] (cf. Chapter 5)

---

6 Based on examples in the CCL, it is not always the case that the subject in a subject–oriented resultative is the agent. Instead, it could be the patient, as in (i). This research question mainly focuses on the typical subject/agent–oriented type as in (10a).

(i) 衣服 洗-干净-了 (CCL 5.1)

yifu *xi-ganjing-le*

clothes wash–clean–ASP

'The clothes were washed clean.'

5. What determines the acceptability of subject/agent–oriented resultatives with and without 把 *ba*? (cf. Chapter 5)

6. What determines the acceptability of object–oriented resultatives with and without 把 *ba*? (cf. Chapter 6)

7. What is the function of 把 *ba* in a resultative construction? (cf. Chapters 5 and 6)

1.2 Theoretical framework

This book adopts the frameworks of cognitive linguistics and construction grammar from the usage–based and typological perspectives (cf. Langacker 1987, Lakoff 1987, Goldberg 1995, Croft and Cruse 2004). According to Hollmann (2003:17), cognitive linguistics and construction grammar are not the same. For instance, some linguists who study head–driven phrase structure grammar (HPSG, e.g. Pollard and Sag 1994) consider themselves construction grammarians, whereas in many respects HPSG is more in line with structuralist and generative approaches than with cognitive linguistics. Some cognitive topics are sometimes discussed without any explicit commitment to a construction–based view, for instance cognitive lexical semantics (cf. Croft and Cruse 2004: 109), which often does not touch on the notion of construction.

As a nonderivational model (Croft and Cruse 2004: 257), construction grammar views constructions as form–meaning pairs, which is in contrast to the analysis of syntax in terms of Phonetic Form, Logical Form and transformational rules suggested by generative linguists (e.g. Haegeman 1994, Chomsky1995). Construction grammar views constructions as symbolic units in terms of structure and semantics. Argument structure constructions, for instance, are independent of verbs and express meaning themselves. For instance, let us consider, with Goldberg (1995: 9), the example "Dan talked himself blue in the face". As regards the meaning of the verb, a non–constructional theory would need to propose a sense of TALK like 'X causes Y to become Z by talking', which would make the verb ambiguous between its basic sense and its sense in this sentence, and cause the semantics of the verb to be more complicated, even implausible. However, from a constructional perspective, the example could be analyzed as caused result with that interpretation being contributed by the resultative construction itself.[7]

In addition, according to Croft and Cruse (2004: 292), many cognitive linguists take the usage–based model for language investigations. Two usage–based properties are proposed to affect grammatical representation, namely the frequency of occurrence of the grammatical forms (e.g. constructions), and the meaning of the words and constructions in use. Viewed in this way, frequency plays an important role in acceptability of constructions, and contributes to understanding grammatical units. Regarding the usage–based model in syntax, constructions are instances of schemas rather than output of rules. Therefore, syntactic construction schemas are viewed as product–oriented, which have a coherent syntactic structure and different rules for each 'input construction' (Croft and Cruse, 2004: 313).

7 More about the relation and interaction of meanings between verbs and constructions will be discussed in Chapter 2, Section 2.2.2.1.

This is an appealing virtue of construction grammar for the analysis of resultative constructions. The Chinese resultative construction is formally defined as [subject+ verb + (object) + result XP + (了 *le*)], with the result XP semantically referring to the result of a change of state of an NP (either the subject or the object) caused by the action denoted by the main verb. Meanwhile, as the constructionist view is most prominent in cognitive linguistics, and as cognitive linguistics offers a usage-based perspective that is especially helpful for the interpretation of my corpus data, the book is based on the two theoretical backgrounds.

Regarding typology, Croft (2002: 1) proposes three linguistic definitions of typology. First, it can refer to a classification of structural types across languages (i.e. typological classification). Thus a language is viewed as belonging to a single type in this definition. A simple example is that English belongs to Germantic languages, whereas French is a Romance type. Second, typology means the study of patterns that appear across languages systematically (typological generalization). Cross-linguistic patterns are language universals, for instance "all languages have oral vowels" (Croft 2002: 52). Third, it represents a methodology for linguistic analysis, namely a functional-typological approach, in contrast to generative grammar (e.g. Chomsky 1981). The typological method provides explanations of the language universals. The typological view in this book mainly focuses on type of Chinese resultatives and an analytical method for data (cf. Chapter 4), which correspond to the first and the third concept defined by Croft respectively.

1.3 Structure of the book

The remainder of the book is composed of the following parts. Chapter 2 is a literature review, about resultative constructions, the 把 ba–construction, the combination of 把 *ba* and resultatives, and corpus studies on Chinese resultatives.

In Chapter 3 I will discuss my two–fold methodology, namely a corpus–based approach, and an acceptability judgement approach. In line with the usage–based model, the two methods complement each other and provide plausible answers to the research questions.

In Chapter 4 I will conduct a corpus study of Chinese resultatives, which aims to answer Questions 1–3. An accurate definition with two tests for the identification of Chinese resultatives will be proposed. This also leads to distinguishing marginal and prototypical resultatives in Mandarin. The usage of Chinese resultatives will be analyzed in terms of type and token frequency. The properties of Chinese resultatives will be further investigated from a typological point of view.

Chapter 5 will focus on subject/agent–oriented resultatives. The factors which affect the capacity of subject/agent–oriented resultatives to take a postverbal NP will be discussed. The acceptability of subject/agent–oriented resultatives with and without 把 *ba* will also be studied through questionnaire surveys. I will argue that subject–oriented resultatives either formed with transitive verbs and a two–place result–XP, or interpreted as repeated actions, can take a postverbal NP. Sentences with the interpretation that the subject is able to achieve something thoroughly are acceptable with 把 *ba*. The degree of acceptability of 把 *ba* + subject–oriented resultative varies with respect to the interpretation of resultatives, which forms a continuum.

In Chapter 6 I will investigate the acceptability of object-oriented resultatives with and without 把 *ba*, relying on the method of questionnaire surveys. I will suggest that the acceptability of object-oriented resultatives without 把 *ba* is dependent on whether there is a postverbal NP, which is determined by the number of the syllables of the pattern 'verb + result XP', as well as on the conception of the action (concrete or abstract). The acceptability of 把 *ba* + object-oriented resultatives is generally high, though small differences exist, these being caused by the status of the main verb (syntactically transitive or intransitive). Meanwhile, together with Chapter 5, the function of 把 *ba* is discussed, which gives a consistent account of 把 *ba* semantically. This answers Question 7.

In Chapter 7 I will conclude the book, indicate the limitations of my study, and propose further research concerning resultatives in Mandarin Chinese and across languages from a typological perspective.

Chapter 2 Literature review

2.1 Introduction and structure of the chapter

Resultative constructions have been widely discussed in the scholarship, from the perspectives of formal/generative approach (e.g. Simpson 1983, Williams 1983, Hoekstra 1988, Sybesma 1992, Levin and Rappaport Hovav 1995, Neeleman and Van de Koot 2002, among others) and functional–cognitive linguistics (Goldberg 1995, Talmy 2000, Boas 2003, Broccias 2003, to name but a few). Most analyses are based on English (e.g. Simpson 1983, Hoekstra 1988, Goldberg 1995, Levin and Rappaport Hovav 1995/ 2001, Broccias 2003), though a few people have looked at Dutch (Williams 1983, Neeleman and Van de Koot 2002) and German (Boas 2003) too, and resultatives have been examined from a typological point of view as well (Washio 1997). Likewise, the literature on Chinese resultatives includes generative and cognitive approaches. The same holds for discussion of the 把 *ba*–construction, including the combination of the resultative construction and the 把 *ba*–construction.

This chapter consists of the following parts: Section 2.2 is about the resultative construction. Section 2.3 focuses on the 把 *ba*–construction.

In Section 2.4, the combination of the resultative construction and other constructions including the 把 *ba*–construction is examined.[1] Section 2.5 summarizes corpus studies of the Chinese resultative construction in the literature. Section 2.6 is the conclusion.

2.2 Resultative constructions

Resultative constructions have been discussed within the formal (e.g. Simpson 1983, Williams 1983, Hoekstra 1988, Levin and Rappaport Hovav 1995, Neeleman and Van de Koot 2002) and functional literature (e.g. Goldberg 1995, Washio 2001, Levin and Rappaport Hovav 2001).

2.2.1 Formal approach

2.2.1.1 Lexical–functional grammar

Simpson (1983) views English resultatives as complex verbs formed by a matrix verb and a resultative attribute, the latter describing the state of an argument resulting from an action denoted by the verb. She suggests two types of verbs that take resultative attributes, namely verbs of contact (e.g. 1a) and verbs referring to a change of state (e.g. 1b, 1c). The former is transitive (1a),

1 In the Chinese tradition, resultative constructions have been discussed not only with the 把 *ba*–construction, but also with other constructions, as there are differences in acceptability among sentences. This will be illustrated further in Section 2.4.

and the latter can be transitive (1b) or intransitive (1c). In addition, (1a) can be passivized as in (1d).

(1) a. I painted the car yellow. Simpson (1983: 143)

b. I froze the ice cream solid.

c. The ice cream froze solid.

d. The car was painted yellow.

Simpson (1983) argues that the resultative attribute in the transitive pattern like (1a) is always predicated of the object, while in the intransitive pattern it refers to the subject (e.g. 1c). As the passivized counterpart of (1a), the resultative attribute in (1d) is predicated of the subject. Based on lexical–functional grammar (LFG), the passive is a lexical rule which converts an object into a subject (Bresnan 1982, cited by Simpson 1983: 144). Therefore, the controller of the resultative *yellow* in (1d) is an underlying object *the car*.[2]

Regarding the intransitive patterns to which result XPs are added, Simpson suggests two types of resultatives, namely those formed with unergative verbs (e.g. 2a) and those with unaccusative verbs (see 2b). According to Simpson (1983: 145), an unergative verb is named as such because the subject is an underlying subject similar to the subject of a transitive clause. An unaccusative verb, on the other hand, takes a subject that has properties in common with the object of a transitive verb. In (2a), the subject *I* is the subject of the unergative verb *danced*. (2b), in contrast, is formed with an unaccusative verb (also intransitive in 2b) *froze*. Although *the pond* is the subject, as discussed above,

2 According to Chomsky (1986: 124), *control* indicates the relation between subject and predicate. For instance, in *John decided to vote twice*, *John* controls *vote*, which is subject control, and *John* is the controller of *vote*. However, in *John persuaded Bill to vote twice*, *Bill* controls *vote*, and it is object control, with *Bill* the controller of *vote*.

it behaves as an underlying object of the verb (e.g. transitive in 1b). That is, it is interpreted as 'the pond was frozen solid' without any difference in meaning. The unergative verb could take a reflexive as in (2a), which is called a fake reflexive by Simpson. The verb is controlled by the object *myself* co–indexed with the subject *I*, hence referring to the subject indirectly, and *dance* is still predicated of the object (the reflexive).

(2) a. I danced myself tired. Simpson (1983: 145)

b. The pond froze solid.

c. I danced.

Therefore, Simpson (1983: 148) argues that the syntactic constraint on English resultatives is such that they must be controlled by an object, whether in an underlying form as in (1d) or in a surface form (e.g. 1a/b, 2a).

However, this analysis is challenged by Rappaport Hovav and Levin (2001: 774). Consider the minimal pair *kick free* (see 3a) and *kick himself free* (e.g. 3b) as an example (both are taken from Rappaport Hovav and Levin 2001: 774). (3a) contains a bare result XP and (3b) a reflexive resultative, both of which share the same verb and result XP going beyond syntactic analysis. That is, the resultative construction *kick ... free* could occur on its own (see 3a) or take a reflexive as in (3b). So, it is inadequate to account for such a phenomenon based merely on the syntactic differences in verbs (e.g. transitive vs. intransitive, unaccusative or unergative), as suggested by Simpson.

(3) a. A man grabbed and groped her and tried to get under her clothing, but she kicked free and fled.

b. Laughing uproariously, Beckett lunged around the office with one leg.

Furthermore, according to Rappaport Hovav and Levin (2001: 770), there are some resultatives in English where the result XP is predicated of the subject, as in (4), which are defined as subject–oriented resultatives. These constructions violate the assumption made by Simpson (1983) that English resultatives can only be controlled by objects, but are still acceptable, which casts doubt on her analysis. Rappaport Hovav and Levin (2001) analyze this type of resultative which will be discussed in Section 2.2.2.4.

(4) The wise men followed the star out of Bethlehem. (Rappaport Hovav and Levin 2001:770)

2.2.1.2 Small clause theory

Stowell (1981) first proposes the concept of the Small Clause (SC), which is defined as a constituent formed by an NP and a predicate functioning as an argument of a verb (cf. Hoekstra 1988: 106). Hoekstra (1988) adopts the theory and extends it to the resultative construction. To begin with, it is argued that the subject should be generalized across categories (Hoekstra 1988: 106). That is, the subject is not necessarily an NP of which a main verb is predicated in a clause. It can also be the semantic subject of a predicate in a clausal complement. For instance, the structure of *I consider John foolish* is analyzed in (5). Since *foolish* is predicated of *John* semantically, the latter is the subject of the former. Viewed in this way, *John* and *foolish* form a clausal element, namely a small clause.

(5) I consider [SC John foolish]. (Hoekstra 1988: 107)

Furthermore, two types of small clauses are suggested, as in (6a/b). The first type (e.g. 6a) does not have a PRO subject; the second (e.g. 6b) can have one, but does not need to.[3] In (6a) *John* and *tired* form a SC, which is a complement of the verb *found*. Regarding (6b), PRO is only allowed in a non–finite clause and cannot be governed (Chomsky 1981: 6).[4] In (6b), *John* is coindexed with PRO. As *left* is intransitive, PRO and *tired* form an SC predicative adjunct of *left*. The SC is outside of the VP, hence not governed by the verb *left*. Therefore (6b) is grammatical.

In contrast, in (6c) the subject *I* and the PRO are coindexed. If [PRO dead] is a projection of *dead*, the unit is headed by the main verb *want* which is finite. Then, PRO is governed. This is forbidden according to the definition of PRO. So (6c) is ungrammatical.

(6) a. I found [$_{SC}$ John [tired]] (Hoekstra 1988: 122)

b. John left [$_{SC}$ PRO [tired]]

c. * I wanted [$_{SC}$ PRO dead].

Hoekstra (1988) and Sybesma (1992) apply SC theory to the resultative construction. Hoekstra (1988: 115) argues that the resultative [NP AP/PP] is a small clause which forms the complement of the matrix verb. The structure of the resultative sentence is (7).

(7) NP $_{SUBJ}$ [$_{VP}$ V [$_{SC}$ NP AP/PP]]

According to Hoekstra (1988), there is no thematic relation between the verb and the subject of a small clause.[5] This can be illustrated with the Dutch

---

3 PRO is an abstract pronominal element which is coindexed (i.e. having the same referentiality) of its antecedent (Chomsky 1981: 6).

4 According to Chomsky (1981: 5), government theory is “the relation between the head of a construction and categories dependent on it”. For instance, in the verb phrase (VP) *help him*, the verb *help* is the head of the phrase, and governs the object *him*.

5 Thematic equals semantic (Haegeman 1994: 49).

examples as (8). In (8a) the subject *zich* 'himself' in the small clause and the main verb *werkte* 'worked' do not form a relation semantically. Rather, *zich* 'himself' and *suf* 'full' form a subject–predicate relation in the SC, while *zich* 'himself' and the subject of the matrix clause *hij* 'him' are coindexed.[6] As for (8b), however, the subject *het huis* 'the house' of the small clause is interpreted as the object of the verb, which contradicts the previous claim that there is no semantic relation between the main verb and the subject of a small clause. Hoekstra (1988: 117) explains this problem away as a "shadow interpretation"; the knowledge we have of the world tells us that if a house ends up green as a result of painting, the house has to be painted.

(8) a. Hij [$_{VP}$werkte [$_{SC}$ zich suf]] (Hoekstra 1988: 115)
He worked himself full
'He worked himself full.'

b. Hij [$_{VP}$ verft [$_{SC}$ het huis groen]] (Sybesma 1992: 13)
He paints the house green
'He paints the house green.'

Neeleman and Van de Koot (2002) rightly point out that the SC approach is problematic. First, the alleged resultative small clause fails to meet standard constituency tests. For instance, in (9a) *Frank to win* forms a small clause as a complement of the matrix verb and behaves like a constituent. Substitution by the pronoun *it* is possible here, as (9a) shows. The resultative in (9b), by contrast, fails this constituency test, which suggests *himself silly* does not constitute a small clause.

---

6 The translation of *suf*, however, is not correct. Via personal communication with Willem Hollmann, a translation of *suf* as 'drowsy' or 'senseless' would be far more accurate.

(9) a. Bill expected *Frank to win* and Peter expected *it*, too. (Neeleman & Van de Koot 2002: 392)

b. *Bill laughed *himself silly* and Peter laughed *it*, too.

Second, since the resultative small clause is a complement of the verb, the verb should theta–mark it, but no thematic role (θ–role; cf. Chomsky 1981: 5) seems to be available for it with intransitive verbs. In (10), for example, the one–place verb *miaowe*d could only assign an external θ–role to the subject *the cat*. As a complement of the verb, the resultative SC *Frank awake* should receive an internal θ–role. Yet, none is available.

(10) The cat miaowed Frank awake. (Neeleman and Van de Koot 2002: 358)

SC theory has also been applied to Chinese resultatives by Sybesma (1992) and Zou (1994). It is argued that the NP–complement is the semantic subject of the predicate in a clausal complement (small clause) and that verb–movement is involved. (11a) is analyzed as in (11b). 头发 *toufa* 'hair' is the subject in the small clause, where 干 *gan* 'dry' is predicated. Then 干 *gan* 'dry' moves from the small clause to the position adjacent to the verb 擦 *ca* 'wipe'.

(11) a. 他 擦–干–了 头发
ta *ca-gan-le* *toufa*
he wipe–dry–ASP hair
'He wiped his hair dry.'

↓ ↑ (Sybesma 1992: 178)

b. *ta* $[_{VP}[_{V'}V_1$ *ca* $[_{VP/SC}$ [NP *toufa* $[_{V'}[V_2$ gan-le]]]]]]
he wipe hair dry–ASP
'He wiped his hair and as a result his hair was dry.'

However, SC theory is problematic for two reasons. First, as suggested by Neeleman and Van de Koot (2002) opposing Hoekstra's analysis, if the resultative small clause is a complement of the main verb, the verb should theta-mark it, but no θ-role seems to be available for it with intransitive verbs, such as 哭 *ku* in (12a). 哭 *ku* 'cry' is intransitive and SC analysis would give "cry + NP complement". This makes no sense since 'cry' cannot take an object. However, (12a) is grammatical. Second, SC theory cannot account for sentences where no semantic relation can be found between the postverbal NP and the result predicate. For instance, if analyzed in line with SC theory, (12b) should be 'his words understand'. Yet, there is no subject–predicate relation between 话 *hua* 'words' and 懂 *dong* 'understand', so the analysis does not work. But (12b) is fully acceptable.

(12) a. 妹妹 哭-湿-了 手绢

meimei *ku-shi-le* *shoujuan*

younger sister cry–wet–ASP handkerchief

'The younger sister cried and as a result the handkerchief was wet.'

('The younger sister cried the handkerchief wet.')

b. 我 听-懂-了 他的 话

wo *ting-dong-le* *tade* *Hua*

I listen–understand–ASP his words

'I listened to his words and as a result I understood them.'

2.2.1.3 Predication theory

An alternative to Stowell (1981) has been proposed by Williams (1983), namely Predication theory. He defines subjects as "external arguments" with the statement in (13).

(13) *Subject as external argument*

The subject of a predicative phrase XP is the single argument of X that is located outside of the maximal projection of X. (Williams 1983: 287)

Predication theory assumes that the subject and predicate are coindexed. According to the definition in (13), *John* in (14a) is the subject of *sick*, in contrast with SC theory which views PRO as the subject of *sick*. That is, in Predication theory, the two no longer form a clause. (14b) is ungrammatical because *John* is coindexed with two predicates, namely *want* and *dead*, and is assigned two θ–roles, namely the external θ–role of each predicate. This violates the so–called theta criterion, which states that each argument receives a unique θ–role, and each θ–role is assigned to one and only one argument (Chomsky 1981: 36).

(14) a. $John_i$ [$seems_0$ $[sick]_{APi}]_{VPi}$.[7] (Williams 1983: 16)

b. * $John_i$ [wants $dead_i]_i$.

Within the framework of Predication theory, Neeleman and Van de Koot (2002) argue that the verb and the resultative form a complex predicate which selects the object. The structure of *the cat miaowed Frank awake* is exemplified in (15), which has a notable distinction from SC analysis.

(15) The cat [*v* miaowed–*v* [$_V$ Frank [$_V$ t_V $awake_A$]]]. (Neeleman and Van de Koot 2002: 358)

The contrast between (10) and (15) hinges on whether the resultative forms a constituent with its subject or with the verb at the deep structure. Recall the constituency test mentioned in Section 2.2.1.2 as in (16a): *himself* and

7 According to Williams, *seem* has no external θ–role, hence it is assigned index 0.

silly cannot form a constituent as an SC. Hence the ungrammaticality of (16a) provides evidence in favour of treating the verb and resultative as a complex predicate. In addition, the main verb and the result XP cannot be separated by an adverbial, as in (16c). That is, *cut* and *open* in (16b) should be viewed as a whole and adjacent to each other. The adjacency effect (i.e. two elements stay near to each other) in (16b) indicates a close relation between the two. These suggest the verb–resultative combination is compatible with the complex–predicate viewpoint, rather than SC theory.

(16) a. *Bill laughed *himself silly* and Peter laughed it, too.

b. John quickly cut open the box. (Neeleman and Van de Koot 2002: 388)

c. *John cut quickly open the box.

Boas (2002) argues against Predication theory regarding the types of postverbal NPs. He suggests that NPs are restricted to a set of nouns which are related to the activity denoted by the matrix verb. For instance, in (17) *John* can *paint* objects such as *the house* and *the dog*, but cannot paint *beer* or *sky* because the scenario of painting liquid or untouchable objects like sky goes against our life experience. If the resultatives in (17) are all analyzed based on their form in terms of Predication theory (or any other syntactic perspective), the differences in acceptability in (17) cannot be explained. These differences suggest that there is more to resultatives than their pure syntactic make–up. Therefore, the syntactic analysis of resultative constructions is not felicitous. Further semantic restrictions should be proposed.

(17) John painted {the house/?his dog/*his beer/*the sky}$_i$ green$_i$

With respect to Predication theory and Chinese resultatives, no further analysis has been done. Following Simpson (1983), Neeleman and Van de Koot

(2002: 384) argue that resultatives must be object–oriented. However, as stated throughout this chapter as well as the whole book there are subject–oriented resultatives that take postverbal NPs in Chinese (e.g. 18). Thus, Predication theory as it stands is not applicable to all Chinese resultatives, which weakens the theory in terms of descriptive adequacy and explanatory power.

(18)	我	听–懂–了	他的	话
	wo	*ting-dong-le*	*tade*	*hua*
	I	listen–understand–ASP	his	words

'I listened to his words and as a result I understood them.'

2.2.2 Functional-cognitive analysis

2.2.2.1 Goldberg (1995): Construction Grammar

Goldberg (1995) discusses English resultatives from a constructional approach. Based on cognitive linguistics, she treats constructions as form–meaning pairs existing independently of verbs, which is in contrast with the traditional view that the verb bears the central role. She analyzes resultatives in terms of relations with other constructions, argument structure and constraints on resultative constructions.

To begin with, within the framework of Construction Grammar, a construction is defined as "existing if one or more of its properties are not strictly predictable from knowledge of other constructions existing in the grammar" (Goldberg 1995: 4). Therefore, constructions are regarded as the basic units of language. Later, Goldberg and Jackendoff (2004: 533) updated the definition of constructions as any pairing (very frequent) of meaning and function that is sufficiently frequent to be stored as a unit.

Since constructions exist to some extent independently of verbs, they provide an independent sense of the interpretation of a sentence. According to Goldberg (1995: 43), verbs are associated with frame-specific participant roles, whereas constructions bear argument roles, such as agent, patient. Participant roles are instances of general argument roles. The number and type of participant roles involved in a sentence correspond to the number and type of participant roles profiled by the verb in frame semantics.

For instance, the verb *hand* involves three profiled participants, which is illustrated as hand <hander, handee, handed>. The ditransitive construction is stated as CAUSE–RECEIVE <age pat rec>, which specifies three argument roles, namely agent, participant and recipient. Constructions also specify which roles are profiled in the following statement (19).

(19) Every argument role linked to a direct grammatical relation (SUBJ, OBJ, OR OBJ_2) is constructionally profiled. (Goldberg 1995: 48)

Verbs and constructions are independent from, though connected with, each other. Then, Goldberg argues that the participant role of a verb may be semantically fused with the argument role of the argument structure construction. Hence, two principles are proposed, namely the Semantic Coherence Principle (as in 20a) and the Correspondence Principle (see 20b). The first principle states that only compatible roles can be fused. Two roles are compatible if one can be construed as an instance of the other, which depends on general categorization. The second principle addresses that each participant role must be fused with an argument role. That is, each participant role has to be fused semantically and bear an argument role of the construction.

(20) a. The Semantic Coherence Principle: Only roles which are semantically compatible can be fused. (Goldberg 1995:50)

b. The Correspondence Principle: Each participant role that is lexically profiled and expressed must be fused with a profiled argument role.

c. He handed me the book.

To be specific, as mentioned above, the verb *hand* has three participant roles, and the ditransitive construction contains three argument roles. Regarding example (20c), the participant roles of the verb and the argument roles of the construction are fused, as in Figure 2.1. The hander *he* is compatible with the agent role since the hander can be construed as an instance of the agent role. So it is fused with the latter in the subject position. Likewise, the handee *me* is fused with the recipient role in the object position and handed *the book* with the patient in the object2 position. Each participant role of the verb is compatible with the argument role of the construction, therefore fusion and argument realization are achieved, with the two principles fulfilled as well.

Composite Fused Structure: Diransitive+*hand*

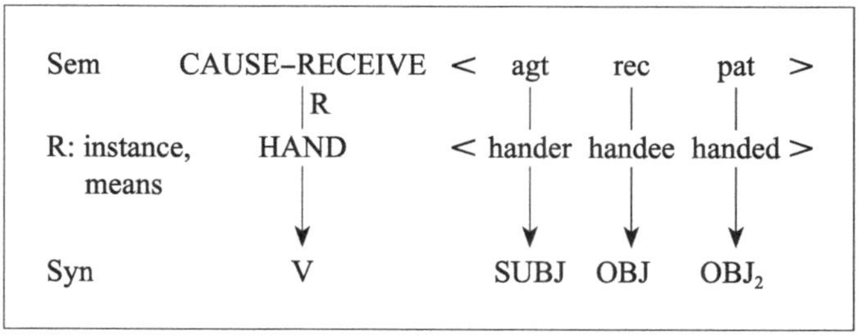

Figure 2.1 Composited fused structure: Ditransitive + *hand* (Goldberg 1995:53)

With regard to English resultative constructions, Goldberg (1995: 81) argues that the resultative construction is a metaphorical extension of the caused–motion construction. The result XP (change of state; e.g. 21a, a target domain) is a metaphorical change of location in the caused–motion construction (see 21b, a source domain).[8] That is, the change of location of the NP in (21b) *off the table* can be construed metaphorically as coding a change of state as in (21a). Resultatives can only refer to arguments that can be categorized as patient arguments. This constraint distinguishes resultatives from caused–motion expressions. Directionals do not require that the argument they predicate is a patient, only that it is a theme. For instance, the NP *napkin* in (21c) is the theme of the verb *sneeze*, not the patient. Moreover, Goldberg (1995: 182) suggests that resultatives with a postverbal NP are transitive, for instance (21a). Those without an object are intransitive, such as (21e).

(21) a. Pat hammered the metal flat. (Goldberg 1995: 81)

b. Pat threw the metal off the table.

c. He sneezed the napkin off the table.

d. He cried himself asleep.

e. The pond froze solid.

Since the notion of *fusion* and the two principles form a crucial part of Goldberg's Construction Grammar theory, the next step is the fusion of participant roles of a verb with the argument roles of a resultative construction. For instance, in (21a), the participant roles of the verb *hammer* <hammerer, hammered> are fused with the argument roles of the resultative construction

8 According to the theory of metaphor proposed by Lakoff& Johnson (1980), the source domain is about the literal meaning if an expression, whereas the target domain is what the sentence is actually about.

<agent, patient>. *Pat* is mapped onto the subject position as the agent of the resultative construction since *Pat* can be interpreted as an instance of an agent role. Similarly, *metal* fuses with the patient role of the construction in the object position, the former construed as an instance of the latter. Then, the Semantic Coherence Principle is satisfied. Moreover, since both participant roles of the verb are fused with the argument roles of the construction, the Correspondence Principle is also met.

Recall the inadequacy of the generative approach with respect to the resultatives formed with intransitive verbs and postverbal NP, as in (21d); this is explained by Goldberg (1995) in line with the constructional perspective. The participant role of the verb is fused with the agent argument of the construction in the subject position. Since the intransitive verb only has one participant, the element in the object position is fused with the patient role provided by the resultative construction. That is, the postverbal NP, such as the reflexive *himself*, is an argument of the construction, although not necessarily that of the main verb cry (Goldberg 1995: 189). Since the NP is compatible with the patient role, fusion is plausible. Then, the two arguments expressed in the sentence are fused with roles provided by the verb/construction and realized syntactically, with the two principles satisfied.

Generally, Goldberg proposes analyses of English resultatives from a constructional perspective. As discussed before, a number of other approaches (e.g. SC theory) cannot account for the argument realization of examples formed with intransitive verbs plus postverbal NP. Goldberg provides plausible explanations for such patterns by using fusion as well as the Semantic Coherence Principle and the Correspondence Principle.

However, viewing resultative constructions as a metaphorical extension of caused–motion constructions is questionable. If there is a metaphorical mapping from caused–motion constructions to resultative constructions, the former should come before the latter. But there is an absence of evidence that the latter comes from the former diachronically. In addition, Goldberg and Jackendoff (2004) argue that English resultative constructions form a family cognitively. They suggest that there could be idiosyncrasy involved in resultatives, which are to be considered individually. For instance, they argue that the subject–oriented resultatives mentioned in Chapter 1, Section 1.1.3 (i.e. the result XP predicated of the subject; cf. Rappaport Hovav and Levin 2001) are marginal resultatives.[9] Goldberg and Jackendoff (2004) state that the principles and properties they suggest for English resultatives are language–specific, but they do not illustrate how the principles work for examples like (22). As will be elaborated in the following part, the Semantic Coherence principle does not work for subject–oriented resultatives like (22), although it is marginal in Goldberg and Jackendoff's view.

(22) Martha danced mazurkas across the room. (Goldberg and Jackendoff 2004: 556)

In line with the construction grammar developed by Goldberg (1995), some linguists discuss Chinese resultatives based on the form V + AP (e.g. Luo 2009, Zhao 2009a, b). As mentioned above, the semantic frame of a verb has participant roles, whereas a construction bears argument roles. Zhao (2009a,

9 Goldberg and Jackendoff (2004: 556) argue that subject–oriented resultatives as in (22) are less acceptable than (ii) below, which points to the marginality of this type.

(ii) Martha waltzed across the room. (Goldberg and Jackendoff 2004: 556)

b) analyzes Chinese resultatives in this regard. She suggests that the semantic roles of the verb in (23) are compatible with the argument roles of the argument structure construction, hence the participant roles of the verb 唱 *chang* 'sing', namely 她 *ta* 'she' and 歌 *ge* 'song', are fused with the agent and patient roles of the construction, respectively. Therefore, fusion is complete, and the Semantic Coherence Principle and the Correspondence Principle are satisfied.

(23)	她	唱–红–了	那	首	歌
	ta	*chang-hong-le*	*na*	*shou*	*ge*
	she	sing–popular–ASP	that	CL	song

'She sang that song and as a result the song was popular.'

The Semantic Coherence Principle works well with English resultatives as well as Chinese examples like (23). However, a problem emerges when it is applied to the subject–oriented type (e.g. 24 and the English example 'dance mazurkas' in 22). In (24), since the verb走 *zou* 'walk' is intransitive, it profiles only one participant role, walker. The intransitive resultative construction, on the other hand, requires a patient in the subject position (Goldberg 1995: 191). If we apply the process of fusion to (24), the participant role of the verb will be fused with the argument role of the construction. However, the role of the verb *walker* cannot be an instance of the *patient* role, so the Semantic Coherence Principle is violated, and fusion cannot be achieved. But (24) is good. Similarly, in (22) the role of the verb *danced* is not semantically compatible with the *patient* role of the resultative construction, which violates the Semantic Coherence Principle. But (22) is acceptable.

(24) 他 走－累－了

ta *zou-lei-le*

he walk–tired–ASP

'He walked and as a result he was tired.'

Although incorporating Goldberg's theory with Chinese resultatives is plausible, revisions may be needed. Then the theory will be changed from various perspectives, and the results will be uncertain or still unsatisfactory. All these make the construction–grammar approach proposed by Goldberg (1995) not preferable for Chinese resultatives.

Zhao (2009a) provides possible solutions to this problem. As another example of subject–oriented resultatives, in (25), the result 烦 *fan* 'bored with' is predicated of the subject 他 *ta* 'he'. According to Zhao (2009a), one of the semantic roles of the verb 听 *ting* 'listen', namely the *listener* 他 *ta* 'he', is fused with the agent role of the construction as the subject. Meanwhile, the patient role of the construction is also assigned to 'he', as it is 'he' that undergoes a change of state. The NP 'words' (the *listened* of the verb) is fused with the theme role of the construction in the object position. However, there are two problems with this analysis. One, as mentioned above, is that the *listener* role of the verb is not compatible with the *patient* role of the construction, hence it cannot be fused with the latter. The other is: can two roles (agent and patient) of the construction be assigned to one NP (i.e. 他 *ta* 'he' in 25)?

(25) 他 听－烦－了 妈妈 的 话 (Zhao 2009a:261)

ta *ting-fan-le* *mama* *de* *hua*

he listen– bored with –ASP mother POSS words

'He listened to his mother's words and as a result he was bored with them. ('He was bored with his mother's words.')

Zhao (2009a) argues that argument realization in Chinese resultative constructions is rather loose and not restricted by the Semantic Coherence Principle, which happens when the semantic role of the verb is incompatible with the argument role of the construction. So, the fusion of the verb's *listener* role with the construction's patient role in (25) is plausible. However, the notion of 'loose argument realization' is vague, and there does not seem to be any empirical evidence as to the location of the threshold between what is and is not acceptable.

She further states that "the patient of the construction is compatible with the agent role of the verb, which are both in the subject position" (Zhao 2009a: 261). Accordingly, although the object of a verb is affected the most by the action denoted by the verb, other entities under the scope of the influence of the action may also undergo a change of state and be construed as patients, such as the agent of the action. In other words, "it is possible that an entity undergoes a change of state as a result of its own action" (Zhao 2009b: 106). Thus, the subject is also construed as a patient in (25). This argument seems to provide an explanation for the subject being construed as patient; however, it cannot solve the problem of 他 *ta* 'he' in (25) being assigned both agent and patient roles. So Zhao's analysis cannot account for the Chinese resultatives in (24) and (25).

2.2.2.2 Washio (1997): a typological perspective

Washio (1997) distinguishes two types of resultatives, namely strong and weak. According to him, English resultatives take the form S–V–O–AP. In a strong resultative the AP adds a piece of information to the verb and this information is not predictable from the basic sense of the verb. That is, the meaning of the verb and adjective are independent of each other. So some transitive resultatives (the main verb is transitive, as in 26a), and all intransitive ones (the main verb is intransitive; see 26b) are strong resultatives. In (26a), the sense of the AP *flat* is independent of the action *pound*, which makes it a strong resultative. Similarly, in (26b), since the result AP *thin* is not a predictable result of the action *running*, it adds information to the verb, hence it is construed as a strong resultative.

(26) a. They pounded the metal flat. (Washio 1997: 7)

b. The joggers ran the pavement thin.

On the other hand, in weak resultatives, the semantics of AP is related to that of the verb but does not repeat the verb's meaning. That is, the resultative implies the state of the patient resulting from the verb. In (27a) the AP *solid* is predictable from the action *freeze*, so it is construed as a weak resultative. In (27b), the AP *clean* is a potential result caused by the action *wipe*, hence it is weak.

(27) a. The river froze solid. (Washio 1997: 10)

b. She wiped the table clean.

Washio (1997) points out that there are both strong and weak resultatives in English, whereas only weak resultatives are allowed in Japanese, French and Italian. Moreover, he introduces a third type of spurious resultative, which denotes a state resulting from a manner of action. The adjective specifying the result state can be replaced by the corresponding adverb with little change in meaning; see (28). In (28a), the AP *loose* could refer to the object *shoelaces* or the action *tied*, therefore it can be replaced by its adverbial *loosely* with more or less the same interpretation of the sentence. The same situation occurs in (28b): *thick and thickly* are interchangeable with little difference in meaning.

(28) a. He tied his shoelaces loose/loosely. (Washio 1997: 17)

b. He cut the meat thick/thickly.

Washio's classifications of resultatives form one domain for the corpus study of Chinese resultatives from a typological perspective (see Chapter 4). Since he does not mention any Chinese examples, my study will refine our understanding of resultatives in Chinese and in general. For instance, Chinese corresponds to the same type as English (i.e. permits both strong and weak resultatives). Resultative constructions in the field of typology will be discussed further in Chapter 4, Section 4.4.1.

2.2.2.3 Talmy (2000): motion event

According to Talmy (2000), a motion event (macro–event) comprises two subevents, namely a Frame (Main) event and a Co–event, the latter bearing the relation of Manner or Cause to the former, while accompanying it. Moreover, Talmy (2000) argues that a motion event can be classified as a self–contained motion and a causative event. There is an agent involved in the latter, but not in the former. For a nonagentive (self–contained) event, a Frame event involves four cognitive components: Figure (F), Ground (G), Motion (M) and Path (P). Figure is a moving entity, Ground is a reference entity, Motion means the action and Path refers to the way the Figure moves in relation to the Ground (Talmy 2000: 25). If an event is agentive, a fifth element is proposed, namely Agent, with the motion marked as $_{A}$MOVE (i.e. CAUSE to MOVE). To be specific, in (29a) as a nonagentive event, *the rock* is Figure, *the hill* is Ground, *down* is

Path and *roll* is Motion. Meanwhile the motion event is composed of *the rock MOVED down the hill* as a Frame event and *the rock rolled* as a Co–event.

(29) a. The rock rolled down the hill. (Talmy 2000b: 30)

[the rock MOVED down the hill] + [the rock rolled]$_{\text{Manner}}$

b. I kicked the keg into the storeroom.

[I $_{\text{A}}$MOVED the keg into the storeroom] + [I kicked the keg]$_{\text{Cause}}$

With respect to an agentive event as in (29b), I is Agent, *the keg* is Figure, *the storeroom* is Ground, *into* is Path and *kick* is Motion. The Main event is *I* $_{A}$*MOVE the keg into the storeroom* and the Co–event is *I kicked the keg* form a macro–event.

Resultative constructions indicate a change of state of a property caused by an action, which can also be viewed as a macro–event. Therefore, motion–event analysis can also be applied to resultatives. Talmy (2000) proposes state–change constructions which correspond to resultative constructions in English, with the schema illustrated in (30a). For instance, in (30b) I is Agent, *the fence* is Figure, *blue* is Ground, *TO* is Path (since there is a change of state involved, TO indicates Path metaphorically) and *paint* is Motion. The change event consists of a Frame event (I MOVED the fence to blue) and Co–event *I painted it.*

(30) a. V NP Adj 'make NP Adj by Ving' (Talmy 2000: 251)

b. I painted the fence blue.

c. [I $_{\text{A}}$MOVED the fence TO a STATE [BEING blue]]+ [I painted it]$_{\text{Cause}}$

Based on how manner and path are expressed in a motion event, Talmy (2000) classifies languages into two types: satellite framing languages (e.g. English, Chinese) and verb framing languages (e.g. Spanish). The two differ in whether the frame event is expressed by the satellite (path) or the main verb: the former by the satellite (e.g. 31a), the latter by the verb (e.g. 31b). For instance, in (31a) the manner 'run' is expressed by the main verb, and the path in the satellite, so English is a satellite framing language. By contrast, in (31b) the path *entró* 'enter' rather than manner *corriendo* 'running' is integrated into the main verb, so Spanish is a verb framing language.

(31) a. He ran into the cave.

b. *Entró*	*corriendo*	*a*	*la*	*cueva*
enter.3SG.PST	running	to	the	cave

'He ran into the cave.'

Talmy's discussion based on motion events sheds light on the relation between cognition and language. From the theory he presents, we can see how events are integrated cognitively and represented linguistically. However, although he focuses on event integration and the representation of motion events across languages, when his analyses are extended to Chinese, some problems arise, which will be explained below.

Within the framework of motion events proposed by Talmy (2000), scholars discuss Chinese resultatives in a broad sense. As discussed in Chapter 1, the result XP refers to AP or directional verbs (cf. Shen 2003, Song 2003, 2004). Based on Talmy's (2000) analysis, Song (2004) provides an analysis of (32a) as in (32b): 我 *wo* 'I' is the Agent, 蜡烛 *lazhu* 'candle' is Figure and 灭 *mie* 'quench' is Ground. The causative event is interpreted as "I blew the candle and caused the candle to quench". The motion 'blow' in the co-event "I blow candle" is integrated with $_{A}$MOVE into the frame event "I AMOVE candle INTO quench", hence one motion, namely 吹 *chui* 'blow'.

(32) a. 我 吹–灭–了 蜡烛

wo *chui-mie-le* *lazhu*

I blow–quench–ASP candle

'I blew out the candle.'

b. [*wo* 'I' $_{A}$MOVE *lazhu*'candle' INTO *mie*'quench'] $_{\text{frame event}}$ + [*wo* *chui* lazhu'I blow candle'] $_{\text{co-event}}$

Song (2004) further argues that examples like (33a) can be analyzed as (33b). According to him, there are two events in (33a), a Frame event *he was tired* and a Co–event *he walked*. He suggests that (33a) be viewed as an autonomous event, since the Figure 他 *ta* 'he' moved on its own and became tired on its own, which means there is no agent involved. The Co–event is low in prominence, so it is integrated with the Frame event conceptually and is expressed together with the Frame event. However, Song's argument that there is no agent involved in (33a) is problematic, since 他 *ta* 'he' is the agent of walking, whereas the result of being tired does not entail an agent, but an experiencer. Therefore Song's analysis of subject–oriented resultatives like (33a) casts doubt on a motion–event theory for resultative constructions.

(33) a. 他 走–累–了

ta *zou-lei-le*

he walk–tired–ASP

'He walked and as a result he was tired.'

b. [*ta*'he'MOVE INTO*lei* 'tired'] $_{\text{Frame event}}$ + [*ta zou* 'he walk'] $_{\text{Co-event}}$

2.2.2.4 Rappaport Hovav and Levin (2001): event structure

Rappaport Hovav and Levin (2001) analyze resultatives from an event–

structure perspective. According to them (p.775), the English resultative construction describes a complex event which consists of two subevents, an action subevent denoted by the main verb, and a result subevent denoted by the result XP, presenting a change of state or location caused by the main verb (cf. Boas 2003, Goldberg & Jackendoff 2004, Croft 2012). For instance, in (34) there is a subevent of singing and a subevent of becoming hoarse, with the two forming a complex event structure in the resultative.

(34) She sang herself hoarse.

As mentioned in Section 2.2.1.1, and first observed by Simpson (1983), result XPs can only be predicated of the object in English. Based on this, Levin and Rappaport Hovav (1995: 34) propose the Direct Object Restriction (DOR). That is, resultatives must refer to an object, and cannot be predicated of an oblique object or a transitive subject. (35b) is unacceptable since the resultative *flat* is predicated of the oblique *on the metal* rather than the direct object *metal* as in (35a). (35c) is also unacceptable as the adjective *dirty* cannot relate to the direct object (the cookies) or the subject. This also explains why a reflexive is needed in a resultative construction like (35d). Since a resultative cannot be related to the subject, a reflexive coindexed with the subject must be present after the main verb to express the meaning 'he sang and as a result he became hoarse'. In contrast, there is no such a reflexive in (35e), which makes it unacceptable.

(35) a. Bill hammered the metal flat.

b. *Bill hammered on the metal flat.

c. *Polly cooked the cookies dirty.

d. He sang himself hoarse.

e. *He sang hoarse.

Rappaport Hovav and Levin (2001: 770) point out that although DOR is appealing and can account for most of the resultative data in English, there are, nevertheless, some examples suggested by Wechsler (1997: 313) and Verspoor (1997: 150–151) with the result XP predicated of the subject rather than the object, for example (36). In (36a), the result XP *out of Bethlehem* denotes the subject *the wise men*, and in (36b) *to exhaustion* relates to the subject *John*. Meanwhile *follow* and *swim* are transitive. The acceptability of (36) suggests the inaccuracy of DOR.

(36) a. The wise men followed the star out of Bethlehem. (Wechsler 1997:313, cited by Rappaport Hovav and Levin 2001:770)

b. John swam laps to exhaustion. (Verspoor 1997:151, cited by Rappaport Hovav and Levin 2001:770)

Based on the examples in (36), Rappaport Hovav and Levin (2001: 770) distinguish a subject–oriented transitive–based pattern and make a semantic distinction between subject–oriented and object–oriented resultatives in English. The two differ in whether the result XP is predicated of the subject (36a/b) or the object (37a/b). In (36a), the result XP *out of Bethlehem* applies to the subject and is caused by the action *follow*, which fits the definition of a resultative. In (37a) the PP *to death* relates to the object *the robber*.

(37) a. The police shot the robber to death.

b. The joggers ran the pavement thin.

In addition, Rappaport Hovav and Levin (2001:770) suggest that English resultatives should be classified in terms of verbs, namely transitive–based as in (36a) and (37a), where the verb *follow* and *shot* are used transitively, and intransitive–based in (36b) and (37b), as the verbs *swim* and *run* are normally intransitive.

Rappaport Hovav and Levin (2001) propose two types of event structure to account for various resultative patterns from a semantic point of view, namely a simple event structure and a complex one. There is only a causative relation in the latter, not in the former. For instance, with respect to intransitive–based resultative patterns, there is a causative paraphrase for the reflexive resultative (e.g. 38a) as 'Pat's *yelling* caused him to *become hoarse*'. Thereby, (38a) has a complex event structure, the yelling subevent and the becoming hoarse subevent, the latter causing the former. The two subevents do not need to be 'temporally dependent' (Rappaport Hovav and Levin 2001: 775). That is, the hoarseness can occur some time after the yelling is over. In order to realize the mapping of event–structure to syntax, (38a) has to meet the argument–per–subevent condition,[10] hence a reflexive pronoun needs to be present so that in both subevents there is an argument: Pat in *yelling* and *himself* in *becoming hoarse*.

(38) a. Pat yelled himself hoarse. (Rappaport Hovav and Levin 2001:784)

b. The truck rumbled into the driveway.

c. The pond froze solid.

According to Rappaport Hovav and Levin (2001), the bare XP resultative in (38b/c) cannot be construed with a causative interpretation. That is, it is

10 Rappaport Hovav and Levin (2001: 779) propose the argument–per–subevent condition as "there must be at least one argument XP in the syntax per subevent in the event structure".

inappropriate to interpret (38b) as 'the truck's rumbling caused it to be in the driveway'. Accordingly, the authors argue for a simple event structure for bare XP resultatives like (38b/c), which involves temporal dependence between the two subevents. That is, the subevents are temporally coextensive and unfold at the same rate. Thus, the bare XP resultative has a simple event structure, involving a form of event composition that gives rise to a single event without a causal relation. This process is achieved through conditions on event identity (Rappaport Hovav and Levin 2001: 781): the subevents must have the same location and be temporally dependent. Taking (38c) as an example, the subevent *the pond's freezing* and the subevent *becoming solid* occurred at the same time in the same place, therefore the two subevents are represented as one event and coidentified, thus forming a single event structure of (38c).

However, according to Broccias (2013: 38), the single event structure of a bare resultative as in (38c) does not hold true in some senses. He suggests that causality should be applied to (38c) as well. In his view, *freeze* in (38c) means "to become solid", and there is a tautology regarding the interpretation 'the river froze' causing 'the river became solid'. In other words, based on our world knowledge, it is reasonable to interpret (38c) as 'the pond's freezing caused it to become solid'. Viewed in this way, there could be a causal relation between the two subevents *freezing* and *becoming solid*, which casts doubt on the single-event analysis of the bare resultative as in (38c).

To sum up, the analysis of English resultatives from an event–structure viewpoint by Rappaport Hovav and Levin (2001) sheds light on syntactic–to–semantic mapping. The subject/object–oriented–resultative distinctions form a crucial part for this book regarding Chinese resultatives. The classifications of transitive/intransitive–based resultatives proposed by them are also dimensions for analyzing the corpus data in Chapter 4. As Broccias (2013) argues, simple event–structure analysis of bare resultatives is problematic. Actually, resultatives cannot be fully accounted for in terms of event structure. The event structure of resultatives will be further illustrated in Chapter 4, Section 4.2.2.2.

2.2.2.5 Boas (2003): a usage–based approach

Boas (2003) discusses the syntactic and semantic features of English resultatives from a constructional and usage–based perspective. He takes the English resultative to be formed as [NP V NP XP], where X is A/P. He then compiles a list of 51 APs and PPs that can function as resultative phrases in view of the examples discussed in the literature (e.g.. Simpson 1983, Rappaport Hovav and Levin 2001) and conducts an exhaustive search in the 100–million–word British National Corpus (BNC) for these 51 APs and PPs. The 6,000 hits in the BNC, along with several hundreds of examples from the scholarship, dictionaries, the Internet and native speaker elicitations, form the largest set of data on English resultatives for a comprehensive investigation to date (Boas 2003: 18).

Based on the sentences mentioned above, Boas (20–3: 126) observes that the question of whether a verb can occur in resultative constructions is a matter of conventionalization, which cannot be explained by general constraints. For example, the corpus data show that some verbs suggest clear tendencies for a syntactic category of resultative phrases. According to Boas, DRIVE occurs 329 times in resultative constructions in the BNC, of which 253 times with AP (e.g. DRIVE *crazy/ mad/ insane*), and 76 times with PP (e.g. DRIVE *to distraction/ to suicide*). The difference in frequency between AP and PP suggests a preference for DRIVE occurring with APs, which is related to conventionalization. By contrast, KILL has strict collocational restrictions and only *dead* is allowed as a resultative for use with it.

Accordingly, Boas (2003: 158) argues that the distribution of resultatives is largely conventionalized in terms of collocational dependencies. Some verbs are more frequently used with some resultatives, for example WIPE *clean*, which is more frequent than WIPE *dry*, so the former pair is more collocationally dependent than the latter. Each verb is used with a resultative phrase that specifies the semantic or syntactic class, for example *drive* being associated with APs more than PPs. He thus classifies English resultatives into two types, namely conventionalized resultatives (e.g. 39a) and nonconventionalized resultatives (e.g. 39c). The former are resultatives based on lexicalized event–frames (which represent the conventionalized semantic/pragmatic/syntactic information of a certain sense of a verb) with a prototypical (subcategorized) or nonsubcategorized patient (e.g. a fake object which is an object of a verb that is normally intransitive). For instance, in (39a) *water* is a prototypical patient of the verb *froze*. In (39b) *feet* is a fake object licensed by the verb ran and the two form a conventionalized resultative construction.

(39) a. They froze the water solid. (Boas 2003: 220)

b. Carol ran her feet sore. (Boas 2003: 250)

c. He sneezed the napkin off the table. (Boas 2003: 260)

On the other hand, the nonconventionalized resultative construction is defined by Boas (2003: 215) as an analogy based on current conventionalized resultatives, e.g. (39c). Since this type is not formed conventionally, it requires rich contextual information so as to be available for an analogical connection with the sentence and form a resultative construction. The process is instantiated by (39c). The resultative meaning does not describe a result of *sneezing* as expected conventionally. In order to associate *sneeze* with the resultative meaning of *blow* and further with the syntactic frame [NP V NP XP] to express a resultative semantics, additional information needs to be provided through the context, such as a patient *the napkin* with a force–dynamics procedure (Boas 2003: 279). It is reflected linguistically, such that the intransitive verb *sneeze* can take a postverbal NP. That is, according to Boas (2003: 281), as more information is required contextually, fewer collocational restrictions are imposed on the postverbal constituents in resultatives formed with intransitive verbs plus 'objects' than transitive verbs with regular objects.

Finally, Boas (2003: 282) proposes a continuum of English resultatives. At one end are totally fixed resultatives (e.g. *break into pieces*, *wipe out*), which reveal the fact that speakers have general world knowledge about these types of conventionalized expressions. At the other end lie free combinations such as *sneeze-off-the-table*, which licenses the semantics of *sneeze* with contextual information to express a resultative meaning through analogy with conventionalized event–frames (such as *blow*). In the middle of the continuum is a fuzzy area (e.g. fake objects like *run-the feet-sore*). They are not as conventionalized as the first type, since the speakers have some knowledge of the result caused by the action (e.g. feet may become sore by running); nevertheless, it is unexpected that the intransitive verb *run* can take a postverbal NP in a resultative construction.

Boas's analysis of English resultative constructions reflects the situation in use. He argues that various phenomena are caused by conventionalized syntactic, semantic and pragmatic information, as well as collocational restrictions. Viewed in this way, the frequency of resultatives could suggest a tendency between language use and cognition: we find certain resultatives more natural because they are used more frequently. The distribution of resultatives sheds light on the studies on resultatives with respect to syntactic, semantic and pragmatic perspectives from a usage–based and corpus model. However, the distinctions that he suggests between fuzzy and nonconventionalized resultatives are not clear. Both (39b) and (39c) are intransitive but the author does not clarify why *run the feet sore* is conventionalized yet fuzzy, whereas *sneeze the napkin off the table* is unconventionalized. Boas appeals to frequency but does not operationalize his distinction between conventional and non–conventional in terms of specific frequencies (e.g. expressed as a number of tokens per one million words). In addition, the conventional type in (39b) does not sound natural to native speakers. If (39b) is conventional, we may ask why it is not as acceptable as the unconventional one in (39c). This further casts doubt on the classification. So, to classify resultatives into conventionalized/ unconventionalized and conduct further analyses does not seem very tenable.

Moreover, Boas's study emphasizes resultatives in a descriptive way. Boas (2003: 318) claims that exceptions always exist, so there is no need for general syntactic rules or semantic principles to account for the acceptability of resultatives. Conventionalization may explain all instances. In my opinion, conventionalization itself requires explanation. Acceptability may be a function of frequency, but why do certain constructions become more frequent than others? So, more work should be done after description.

2.2.2.6 Broccias (2003): Cognitive Grammar

Broccias (2013) discusses the resultative construction (e.g. 40a) and the *at*–construction (e.g. 40b) in English under the framework of cognitive grammar (Langacker 1987).[11] According to Broccias (2013: 9), the *at*–construction involves an intended change of position. For instance, (40b) is interpreted as 'John tried to kick the wall', with the event of kicking taking place but not necessarily being successful (i.e. John's legs may touch the wall or not). Both constructions are related to a change of state or location possibly achieved by a participant in an event, so they are viewed as change constructions. He further classifies English resultative phrases into transitive as in (40a/d) and intransitive as in (40c), the two differing in whether they take a postverbal NP.

(40) a. John hammered the metal flat. (Broccias 2013:2)

b. John kicked at the wall.

c. The river froze solid.

d. Frank sneezed the tissue off the table.

Broccias (2013) analyzes English resultatives in terms of the following dimensions: causation, orientation of the resultative, transitivity and temporal dependency. To begin with, Broccias (2013: 28/331) looks at the causal relation in a resultative construction, which applies to both transitive and intransitive cases. For instance, in (40a) as a transitive example, *the hammering* subevent causes the 'metal became flat' subevent; therefore, resultatives like (40a) encode complex events.

Moreover, Broccias (2013: 38) suggests that causality is inherent in the

11 The *at*–construction is irrelevant to my thesis, so I will not discuss it further.

intransitive resultative (40c) as well. According to him, since *freeze* in (40c) means 'to become solid', it is acceptable to interpret the sentence as 'the river froze' causing 'the river became solid'. Viewed in this way, *solid* specifies the degree of freezing, hence construed as *completely*, which is similar to the function of an intensifier. The causative interpretation of (40c) cannot be ruled out since to ask "why is the river solid?" and to answer "Because it froze" is reasonable. Therefore, Broccias suggests that the intensifier interpretation for (40c) may be considered the default one, but a causal relation cannot be rejected a priori. So, all resultatives have a causal meaning according to Broccias (2013).

Second, regarding the temporal dependency between two subevents of a resultative construction, Broccias (2013: 32) proposes temporal generalization. That is, if the resultative phrase refers to a visible condition, there is no temporal gap between the two subevents. For instance, *clean* in (41a) is visible, hence there is no temporal gap between the event of wiping and the event of the table becoming clean. In contrast, *sore* in (41b) refers to a physical state which is invisible, therefore the two subevents *dancing* and *John's feet being sore* do not necessarily coexist.

(41) a. John wiped the table clean.

b. John danced his feet sore.

Third, in terms of transitivity, which refers to whether there is a postverbal NP in a resultative syntactically, Broccias (2013: 181) suggests that the causal relation of a resultative codes an energy–flow transfer from the agent to the patient. For example, in (41a) *wipe* is construed with energy flowing from *John* to *the table*. If the postverbal NP is not a subcategorized object of the verb, it means the cause of a change event and the verb does not code sufficient energy flow. Consequently, the action is construed as being carried out in an above–the–norm reading so that it can cause a change of state of the postverbal NP. For instance, *feet* in (41b) is an unsubcategorized object of the verb *run*, whereas the resultative sentence is acceptable. This is because it is interpreted with an above–the–norm reading such that John danced more than expected/normal and his feet were sore (Broccias 2013: 179).

With respect to the orientation of a resultative, Broccias (2003: 4) follows Rappaport Hovav and Levin's (2001) classification of subject/object–oriented resultatives and suggests more examples of the former, for instance (42). In (42a), with the transitive verb 'love', the PP 'to distraction' refers to the subject 'I'. There is a causal relation in (42a) such that 'I love you' causes 'I become distracted'. He furthermore argues that subject–oriented resultatives in English can only take prepositional phrases, which refer to a change of state (see 42a) or position (e.g. 42b). However, subject–oriented resultatives can also occur with an adjective form in Chinese, as in intransitive (43a) and transitive (43b/c).

(42) a. I love you to distraction. (Broccias 2003: 4)

b. We played leapfrog across the lawn.

(43) a. 他 走–累–了

ta *zou-lei-le*

he walk–tired–ASP

'He walked and as a result he was tired.'

b. 她 听–懂–了 小宇 的 话

ta *ting-dong-le* *Xiaoyu* *de* *hua*

she	listen–understand–ASP	Xiaoyu(name)	POSS	words

'She listened to Xiaoyu's words and as a result she understood them.'

c. 他	听–烦–了	老师	的	话
ta	*ting-fan-le*	*laoshi*	*de*	*hua*
he	listen–bored with–ASP	teacher	POSS	words

'He listened to the teacher's words and as a result he was bored with them.' ('He was bored with the teacher's words.')

To sum up, Broccias analyzes English resultative constructions as demonstrating change. He discusses subject–oriented resultatives in English, which supplements previous discussions, since that scholarship was mostly based on the object–oriented type. This sheds light on Chinese resultatives. Some concepts he proposes are worth considering for Chinese. 懂 *dong* 'understand' in (43b) and 烦 *fan* 'bored with' in (43c), for instance, are interpreted as having an invisible status. Meanwhile 累 *lei* 'tired' in (43a) and 烦 *fan* 'bored with' in (43c) are construed with an 'above–the norm' reading. It is observed that Chinese subject–oriented resultatives are largely formed with such examples. Although in Broccias's view an 'above the norm' reading is typical where the object is not subcategorized, whereas 话 *hua* 'words' is subcategorized by 听 *ting* 'listen', the concepts of invisible status and energy flow caused by the action with 'above–the norm' reading may provide possible explanations for examples like (43b/c), which will be discussed in detail in Chapter 5 (see especially Section 5.5.1).

2.2.2.7 Croft (2012): a 3D model

Croft (2012) discusses English resultatives and in particular the two types proposed by Rappaport Hovav and Levin (2001), namely bare and reflexive resultatives. He argues that there is no temporal interval between the subevents of a resultative construction. That is, the process which leads to the result state begins with the causing subevent, even though the result may be achieved at the end of the temporal interval profiled by the causing subevent (Croft 2012: 331). For instance, in a reflexive resultative (e.g. *He sang himself hoarse*), with a different intuition from Rappaport Hovav and Levin (2001), Croft claims that the result of being hoarse starts with the singing action but occurs at the end of the action. 'He' became hoarse at the end of the singing event, but only realized it later (perhaps the next day). So there is no temporal independence between the two subevents.

Croft proposes a three–dimensional (3D) model for representing causal and aspectual structure for diverse constructions and analyzes resultatives with this approach. According to Croft (2012: 53), (44) is a two–dimensional analysis of a seeing event. It is composed of a time dimension (t) and a qualitative state dimension (q). As an event unfolds over time (t), it is represented as a sequence of qualitative states on the q–axis. For instance, seeing only has two states on the *q*–axis: not seeing and seeing something. Based on the two–dimensional representation in (44), the causal chain as a third dimension is added to link the individual participant subevents.

(44)
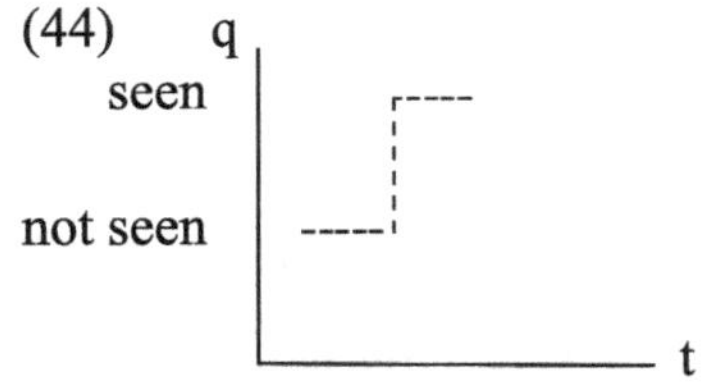

Two–dimensional representation of aspect (Croft 2012: 53)

According to Croft (2012: 328), a directed change (which designates a change being directed, including directed achievements, directed activities, incremental accomplishment and nonincremental accomplishment) is crucial in differentiating the two types of English resultatives. A directed change is represented in the geometric model such that the endpoint of the profiled phase is higher on the q dimension than the starting point of the phase, suggesting the change is scalar. To be specific, a bare resultative denotes an incremental accomplishment, which is an incremental process leading to a result. It is presented as in (45) in the 3D model. He suggests that there is temporal dependence in (45) since there is only one (causal) subevent which involves the NP undergoing change. This is in line with the analysis proposed by Rappaport Hovav and Levin (2001). In addition, the aspectual construal of *freeze* is a directed change (from not–solid to solid), as illustrated in (45).

(45) The pond froze solid.

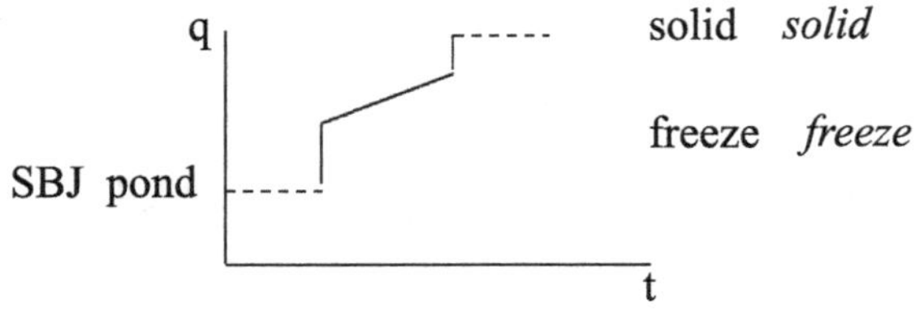

(Croft 2012: 329)

Croft (2012: 329) further argues that a reflexive resultative is a nonincremental accomplishment, which is interpreted as 'an undirected activity phase that ends in a directed achievement to the result state', as presented in (46). Moreover, Croft provides a geometrical representation of the transitive–based resultative as shown in (47), with an undirected wiping action and a directed activity of a result, which is also a nonincremental accomplishment, and hence two subevents.

(46) He sang himself hoarse.

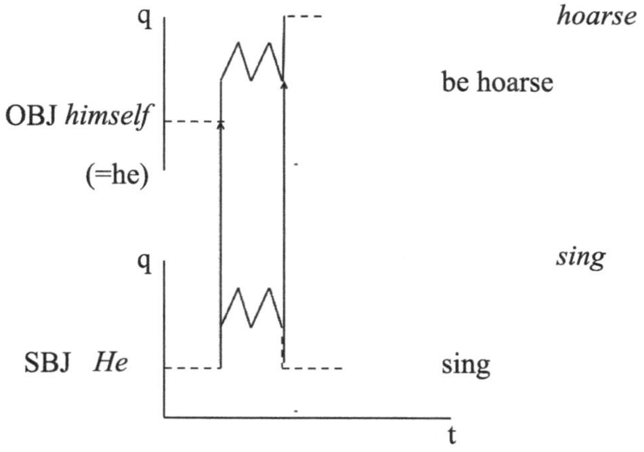

(47) Kay wiped the table clean.

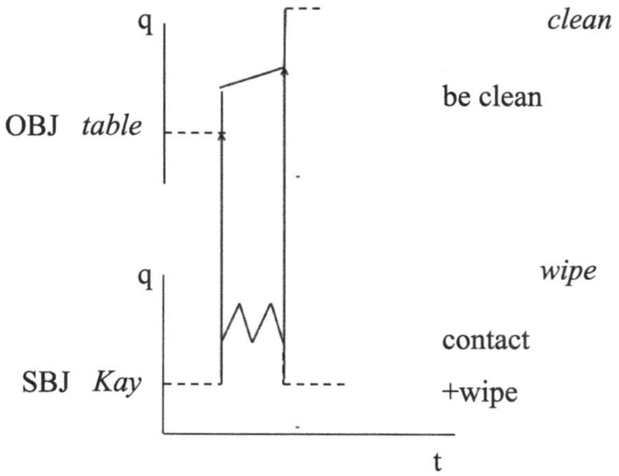

(Croft 2012: 339)

Croft (2012) demonstrates English resultatives in a 3D model that illustrates how one or two subevents of a resultative construction are processed in time. His arguments about the event structure and the temporal relation between subevents involved in resultatives suggest that the causal relation construed in a resultative is the most significant factor for defining resultatives. This sheds light on identifying Chinese resultatives, which will be discussed in Chapter 4, Section 4.2.2.2.

2.2.3 General discussion of resultatives

Generally speaking, several factors concerning resultatives have been discussed by scholars from various viewpoints, namely type (i.e. orientation, syntactic transitivity) and event structure, including temporal relations.

To begin with, with respect to orientation in type, resultatives are first argued to be object–oriented, as in (48a), such that the result XP can only be predicated of the object (see e.g. Simpson 1983, Goldberg 1995, Neeleman and Van de Koot 2002). Then, counterexamples are presented by Wechsler (1997) and Verspoor (1997), as in (48b), which are formed with a transitive result phrase predicated of the subject referent. Rappaport Hovav and Levin (2001) thereby propose the notion of a 'subject–oriented resultative'. That is, the result XP is predicated of the subject. Broccias (2003) endorses this statement. However, Goldberg and Jackendoff (2004) argue that examples like (48c) are marginal, which is not well accepted.

(48) a. I painted the car yellow.

b. John swam laps to exhaustion.

c. Martha danced mazurkas across the room.

Neeleman and Van de Koot (2002) disagree with the subject–oriented type and argue that 'to exhaustion' in (48b) is an adjunct. (48b) may seem different from the object–oriented type, as in (48a). However, (48b) can be interpreted as 'John swam and as a result he was exhausted'. In addition, as mentioned above and as will be discussed in Chapter 4, analysis of my Chinese corpus data reveals abundant examples of subject–oriented resultatives (53.4% of all resultatives), for instance (49a/b). Therefore I will maintain the subject/object–oriented classification as a fundamental distinction in my discussion of resultatives in this book. Even though the subject–oriented type is not frequent in English, it must clearly be included for the broader theoretical discussion.

(49)	a.	他	走–累–了			
		ta	*zou-lei-le*			
		he	walk–tired–ASP			
		'He walked and as a result he was tired.'				
	b.	她	听–懂–了	小宇	的	话
		ta	*ting-dong-le*	*Xiaoyu*	*de*	*hua*
		she	listen–understand–ASP	Xiaoyu(name)	POSS	words
		'She listened to Xiaoyu's words and as a result she understood them.'				

Regarding the second aspect of type, resultatives are classified into transitive and intransitive in the scholarship. However, there are distinctions among scholars. As mentioned in Section 2.2.2.1, Goldberg (1995) views a resultative construction as transitive if there is a postverbal NP. So (50a/c/d) are two–place resultatives and hence transitive, even though there is a 'fake' object (reflexive) in (50d). (50b) is intransitive since no NP follows the main verb froze. Broccias (2003) is also of the opinion that resultatives with a postverbal NP are transitive, while those without are intransitive.

(50) a. John painted the door green.

b. The river froze solid.

c. Frank ran the pavement thin.

d. She sang herself hoarse.

Rappaport Hovav and Levin (2001) classify English resultatives based on the status of the main verb. That is, (50a) is transitive–based, since *paint* is transitive; (50b) and (50c) are intransitive–based, as *froze* in (50b) and *ran* in (50c) are intransitive.

The first type of classification (e.g. Goldberg 1995, Broccias 2003) views resultative constructions as a whole, so whether there is a postverbal NP matters. The second viewpoint (cf. Rappaport Hovav and Levin 2001), however, focuses more on the main verb, and speciality is highlighted. That is, with a verb that is normally intransitive, an object is unexpected. However, if there is a postverbal NP in this resultative, we may wonder why, and how the resultative works. For example, (50c) is an intransitive–based resultative with a postverbal NP, so its complexity is worth considering. I will adopt Rappaport Hovav and Levin (2001)'s viewpoint in order to see the relation between the main verb and the postverbal NP.

Scholars are in favour of the idea that resultatives are composed of two subevents, one illustrated by the action related to the main verb, the other by the result denoted by the result XP (e.g. Goldberg 1995, Rappaport Hovav and Levin 2001, Broccias 2003). They provide generalizations for mapping the semantics of resultative constructions to a syntactic argument structure.

As mentioned in Section 2.2.2.4, Rappaport Hovav and Levin (2001) propose two types of event structure for English resultatives, namely a simple event structure (e.g. 51a) and a complex one (51b/c). The difference lies in whether there is a causative relation between two subevents: it only exists in the latter, not in the former. Croft (2012) agrees with these two types and provides geometric graphs for the examples stated in the previous section.

(51) a. The river froze solid.

b. John painted the door green.

c. She sang herself hoarse.

Broccias (2003) questions this argument and argues that (51a) also involves a complex event structure with causality between the two subevents (more has been reviewed in Section 2.2.2.6). In my opinion, the single–event structure of (51a) makes sense. A resultative construction essentially represents a result caused by an action. As the graph provided by Croft (2012) shows, there is a result 'becoming solid' led to by the action 'freeze' in (51a). Although only one subevent is involved, the cause–result construal holds true for it.

Along with event structure analysis, the temporal relation between the two subevents in a resultative construction is also an issue under discussion (see Goldberg 1995, Rappaport Hovav and Levin 2001, Broccias 2003, Croft 2012). Divergence lies in whether there is temporal dependence between the two subevents in a resultative with reflexive.

Goldberg (1995) and Croft (2012) suggest that no temporal gap is ever possible between two subevents, whereas Rappaport Hovav and Levin (2001) and Broccias (2003) hold the opposite opinion. First, Goldberg (1995) argues that there is no time interval between the action denoted by the verb and the change of state denoted by the result XP. In other words, the action is interpreted as the direct causation of the result. For instance, in *he ate himself sick*, it is the continuous eating rather than the meal he ate that made him sick. In this way there is temporal dependence in reflexive resultatives. Croft (2012) argues that according to his intuition, he became sick at the end of the eating event without realizing it. So there is temporal dependence between the two subevents involved in resultatives.

Rappaport Hovav and Levin (2001) argue that a bare XP resultative (e.g. *the coat steamed dry*) has a simple event structure with temporal dependence between the two subevents, which means no temporal interval between the two. Hence the sentence mentioned above could be interpreted as 'the coat was dry right after being steamed'. However, the reflexive resultative (e.g. 51c) has a complex event structure, so the two subevents do not need to be temporally dependent. In (51c), the hoarseness occurs some time after the singing is over, for instance the next morning, so there is temporal independence between the two subevents. In addition, Broccias (2003) suggests that visibility is the determinant of temporal dependency. If the result XP refers to a visible state (e.g. *the coat steamed dry*), then there is a dependent temporal relation. If not, as in the sing hoarse example, then there could be a temporal gap between the two subevents. The invisible state of hoarseness could occur after the end of the verb event.

The two viewpoints are of interest for event structure and event integration. The Chinese examples, however, are different from the two opinions caused by distinct intuitions in English. The temporal relation varies in real life in Chinese. For instance, (52a) is construed as 'I listened to his words and as a result understand them' without temporal delay. (52b), on the other hand, is interpreted as 'people drank the sweet drink many times and as a result became tired of it'. The result 'were tired of it' does not happen immediately after the action 'drink' is finished. Therefore, the two subevents are temporally independent. This supports Rappaport Hovav and Levin's (2001) and Broccias's (2003) viewpoint of a temporal relation being involved in resultatives. Specifically, (52b) is interpreted as repeated actions (i.e. people drank the sweet drink many times) rather than a single action, which is different from the English example (e.g. *he ate himself sick*) with temporal independence. This Chinese type also supplements resultatives in general, and issues concerning acceptability will be discussed further in Chapter 5.

(52) a. 我　　听–懂–了　　他的　　话

wo　　*ting-dong-le*　　*tade*　　*hua*

I　　listen–understand–ASP　　his　　words

'I listened to his words and as a result I understood them.'

b. 人们　　喝–腻–了　　甜的

renmen　　*he-ni-le*　　*tiande*

people　　drink–be tired of–ASP　　sweet

'People had drunk (the) sweet (drink) so many times that they were tired of it.'

From all the previous studies on resultatives, one issue to be noted is that subject-oriented resultatives are rare in English. Those instances with such an interpretation are formed as 'fake resultatives' with a reflexive (e.g. 53a). In addition, as the basic form of the English resultative construction is V+NP+AP/PP, I searched for the strings '_{V} _{ART} _{N} (_{A}|{PRP})', '_{V} _{PRON} (_{A}|{PRP})' in the BNC.[12] The first represents the pattern 'verb+article+noun+adjective/ preposition', and the second 'verb+pronoun+adjective/preposition'. Among each of the first 500 random examples (altogether 1,000 sentences), there are 12 resultatives formed with nouns, and one with a pronoun. All 13 resultatives are object–oriented. So subject–oriented resultatives are very infrequent in English. In contrast, 52.8% Chinese resultatives are subject–oriented in the Lancaster Corpus of Mandarin Chinese (LCMC), some with no postverbal NP (see 53b), and some with an object (e.g. 53c). Since there are no real counterparts of examples like (53b/c) in languages like English, the discussion of Chinese is of typological interest. Previous studies on Chinese are also generally based on the object–oriented type (e.g. Li 1990, Sybesma 1992, Shi 2008), whereas more than half of the Chinese resultatives found in the LCMC are subject–oriented. In addition, as mentioned in Chapter 1, Section 1.2, the acceptability of Chinese subject–oriented resultatives varies, which is ignored in scholarship. So the distribution (Chapter 4), the acceptability and the explanation (Chapters 5 and 6) of the subject–oriented type should also be investigated. These aspects will be discussed in this book.

---

12 The nouns can also be formed with other determiners (e.g. *these or some*), but as can be seen from the search results, the numbers will probably be very similar to those with articles. The point is to show that subject–oriented resultatives are very rare in English, and the proportion mentioned here should suffice to support it. So no more searching for various strings is needed.

(53) a. He sang himself hoarse.

b.

他	走–累–了		
ta	*zou-lei-le*		
he	walk–tired–ASP		

'He walked and as a result he was tired.'

c.

我	听–懂–了	他的	话
wo	*ting-dong-le*	*tade*	*hua*
I	listen–understand–ASP	his	words

'I listened to his words and as a result I understood it.'

2.3 The 把 *ba*-construction

As mentioned in Chapter 1, Section 1.1.2, the structure of the 把 *ba*–construction is (54). A 把 *ba*–construction is exemplified by (55a), and (55b) is its counterpart without 把 *ba*. The 把 *ba*–construction has been discussed at great length in the scholarship in terms of syntax (e.g. Thompson 1973, Travis 1984, Tsao 1987, Sybesma 1992, Zou 1993, Gao 1997) and semantics (e.g. Wang 1947, Li 1974, Hopper and Thompson 1980, Sun 1995, Guo 1999, Wang 2003, Xiong 2004, Ye 2004 and Næss 2007).[13]

13 This section is not limited to把 *ba* with resultatives, but about the把 *ba* construction in general.

(54) NP1 ba NP2 V (aspect marker 了 le)

(55) a.

我	把	那	个	苹果	吃	了
wo	*ba*	*na*	*ge*	*pingguo*	*chi*	*le*
I	*ba*	that	CL	apple	eat	ASP

'I ate that apple.'

b.

我	吃	了	那	个	苹果
wo	*chi*	*le*	*na*	*ge*	*pingguo*
I	eat	ASP	that	CL	apple

'I ate that apple.'

2.3.1 Syntactic analysis

Generative grammarians in the scholarship analyze 把 ba in this construction as a preposition (Thompson 1973), a case assigner (Travis 1984), a light verb (Sybesma 1992) or a topic marker (Tsao 1987, Gao 1997).

2.3.1.1 A preposition

Based on the assumption that Chinese is an SVO language, Thompson (1973: 208) views 把 *ba* as a preposition taking an NP from a postverbal position to a preverbal one, where NP movement operates. For instance, the postverbal NP 饭 *fan* 'meal' in (56a) is moved before the main verb and after 把 *ba*, as in (56b).

(56) a.

我	吃-完-了	饭
wo	*chi-wan-le*	*fan*

I	eat–finished–ASP	meal	
'I finished the meal'			
b. 我	把	饭	吃-完-了
wo	*ba*	*fan*	*chi-wan-le*
I	*ba*	meal	eat–finished–ASP
'I finished the meal'			

However, this analysis is problematic as not all transitive sentences with objects can be expressed with 把 *ba*. Recall the well-accepted examples in (55a/b), one with 把 *ba* and the other without; this variation is not possible in the case of (57a/b). (57a) is fine, but if the object 苹果 *pingguo* 'apple' is fronted with 把 *ba* as in (57b), it becomes unacceptable. So the unqualified, simple derivation cannot fully account for the properties of the 把 *ba*-construction.

(57)	a. 我	吃	了	一	个	苹果	
	wo	*chi*	*le*	*yi*	*ge*	*pingguo*	
	I	eat	ASP	one	CL	apple	
	'I ate an apple.'						
	b. *我	把	一	个	苹果	吃	了
	wo	*ba*	*yi*	*ge*	*pingguo*	*chi*	*le*
	I	*ba*	one	CL	apple	eat	ASP
	'I ate an apple.'						

2.3.1.2 A case assigner

Travis (1984) analyzes 把 *ba* as a case assigner. She argues that Mandarin Chinese is an SOV language; the verb assigns its θ-role to the left and case to the right. The 把 *ba*-construction is generated because the verb assigns θ-roles at the deep structure. For example, in (58) 把 *ba* is inserted at the surface structure to assign accusative case to the NP 汽车 *qiche* 'car', since the verb cannot assign case to an NP on the left. The occurrence of 把 *ba* fulfils the Case Filter rule, which requires that each argument is assigned a case (cf. Chomsky 1981: 49).

(58) 他们　把　汽车　修–好–了

tamen　*ba*　*qiche*　*xiu-hao-le*

they　*ba*　car　repair–good–ASP

'They repaired the car.'

Gao (1997) opposes this view, since there are circumstances when 把 *ba* is not present while the NP is still put before the verb, for instance (59c). If 把 *ba* assigns case, then in the non–ba sentence (59c), the fronted NP 饭 *fan* 'meal' cannot receive case, which violates the Case Filter constraint. Nevertheless (59c) is grammatical.[14] So 把 *ba* is not a case assigner.

(59) a. 我　吃–完–了　饭

wo　*chi-wan-le*　*fan*

I　eat–finished–ASP　the meal

'I finished the meal'

14 (51c) might be regarded as an unmarked passive clause based on its interpretation. However, according to Siewierska (1984: 2), the most widely accepted definition of the passive construction is characterized thus: "the subject of the passive clause is a direct object in the corresponding active; the subject of the active sentence could be left unexpressed; the verb is marked passive". Viewed in this way, a passive construction is defined from both semantic and syntactic perspectives, and a passive marker is required. The passive construction is marked with 被 *bei* in Chinese, which is not the case for (59c). Therefore (59c) is a regular active sentence.

b. 我	把	饭	吃-完-了
wo	*ba*	*fan*	*chi-wan-le*
I	*ba*	the meal	eat–finished–ASP

'I finished the meal'

c. 饭	吃-完-了
fan	*chi-wan-le*
the meal	eat–finished–ASP

'(Someone) finished the meal.'

2.3.1.3 A light verb

Sybesma (1992) claims that his proposal is close to Hashimoto's (1971) idea of treating 把 *ba* as the head of a 把 *ba*–sentence. Hashimoto (1971: 66–67; cited by Sybesma 1992: 170) argues that 把 *ba* is a matrix verb which takes two complements: an NP object and a complement sentence. However, as observed by some scholars (e.g. Li 1990, Zou 1993), 把 *ba* cannot be regarded as a main verb, as it cannot take the aspect marker 了 *le* 'ASP' plus an object, whereas the capacity to take these elements is a prototypical characteristic of Chinese verbs. Sybesma (1992) sees 把 *ba* as a light verb CAUS (a causative marker). He argues that 把 *ba* is the head of a 把 *ba*–sentence with VP as its complement. Zou (1993) also shares the idea of viewing 把 *ba* as the head of the 把 *ba*–construction that selects a VP as its complement.

To begin with, Sybesma (1992: 156) introduces a distinction between two notions of subject: one as a semantic notion, referring to an NP bearing the external θ–role of the verb, such as 'agent'; the other as a structural notion, referring to an NP in the usual position of a sentence subject. According to

Sybesma, the latter is a canonical subject. In Mandarin, the sentence–initial element can be an NP bearing an agent role (semantic subject) or an NP/ empty category which is not the agent (structural subject). If the latter, it is not necessarily the topic of a sentence.

For instance, in (60), the NP 这件事 *zhejian shi* 'this case' is a structural subject, as it occupies the sentence initial position but is not an agent. The postverbal NP 张三 *Zhang San* (name) is a semantic subject, since it is an agent and bears the external θ–role of the verb 哭 *ku* 'cry' . 这件事 *zhejian shi* 'this case' cannot be interpreted as a topic, since the subject of 哭 *ku* 'cry' is coindexed with the postverbal NP 张三 *Zhang San* (name). Sybesma argues that the matrix subject in (60), namely 这件事 *zhejian shi* 'this case', is not semantically dependent on the matrix verb 哭 *ku* 'cry', as there is no semantic relation between the two. However, the former should be regarded as the subject since it stays in the subject position and bears the causer–role. In addition, Hoekstra (1990) suggests that, in English, the causer role comes from a higher abstract predicate CAUS. So Sybesma assumes that we have the same in Chinese, with the syntactic structure shown in (61).

(60)	这	件	事	哭-累-了	张三	(Sybesma 1992: 155)
	zhe	*jian*	*shi*	*ku-lei-le*	*Zhang San*	
	this	CL	case	cry–tired–ASP	Zhang San (name)	

'This case got Zhang San tired from crying.'

(61) 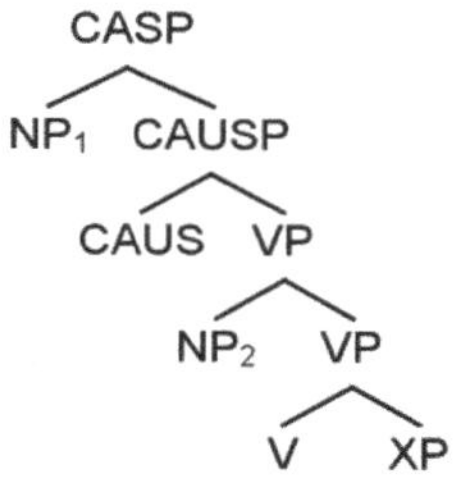

(Sybesma 1992: 155)

The 把 ba–counterpart of (60) is (62), which provides additional evidence for the claim of the intervening CAUS.

(62) 这　件　事　把　张三　哭–累–了

(Sybesma 1992: 155)

zhe	*jian*	*shi*	*ba*	*Zhang San*	*ku-lei-le*
this	CL	case	ba	Zhang San (name)	cry–tired–ASP

'This case got Zhang San tired from crying.'

Sybesma (1992) argues that the head CAUS should be filled phonologically. Two ways are possible: either a complex VP moves to the CAUS head as seen in (60), or a dummy element is inserted, for instance 把 *ba* in (62). He claims that movement or insertion does not change the meaning of the sentence. However, this argument is proposed without any evidence, hence it is questionable. Then based on (61), the syntactic structure of the 把 *ba*–construction in (62) should be (63).

(63) 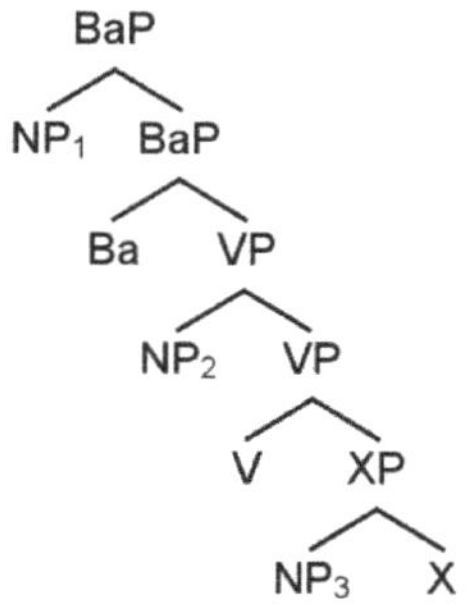

Sybesma (1992: 155)

In (63), NP1 stands in the subject position, which is semantically dependent on 把 *ba*. NP2 is a ba–NP and NP3 is its trace. That is to say, in the 把 *ba*–sentence, the subject of the sentence has no semantic relation with the matrix verb, but with 把 *ba*. The head of CAUS is filled by ba–insertion.

Sybesma's analysis has provided a new approach to the status of 把 *ba*, namely CAUS, which treats 把 *ba* as a light verb. Inspired by Gao's (1997) idea of using adverbs, however, I observe that Sybesma's syntactic construction is problematic when the position of adverbials in the 把 *ba*–sentence is taken into account. The position of adverbials in the 把 *ba*–construction is more flexible than normal. In (64), the adverbial 认真地 *renzhen-de* 'carefully' can occur before or after the light verb 把 *ba*, but always before the main verb 写 *xie* 'write'. In the sentence without 把 *ba*, however, the adverbial can only occur before the verb.

(64) a.

我	认真地	把	作业	写–完–了
wo	*renzhen-de*	*ba*	*zuoye*	*xie-wan-le*
I	carefully	*ba*	homework	write–finished–ASP

'I finished the homework carefully.'

b.

我	把	作业	认真地	写–完–了
wo	*ba*	*zuoye*	*renzhen-de*	*xie-wan-le*
I	*ba*	homework	carefully	write–finished–ASP

'I finished the homework carefully.'

c.

我	认真地	写–完–了	作业
wo	*renzhen-de*	*xie-wan-le*	*zuoye*
I	carefully	write–finished–ASP	homework

'I finished the homework carefully.'

Based on (63), I propose the syntactic structure of (64a) as in (65a), and that of (64b) as in (65b).

(65) a. *wo* $[_{adv.P}$ *renzhen–de* $[_{BaP}$ *ba* $[_{VP}$ *zuoye*$_i$ *xie* $[_{SC}$ t_i *wan–le*]]]].

I carefully *ba* homework write finished–ASP

b. *wo* $[_{BaP}$ *ba* $[_{adv.P}$ *zuoyei* $[_{adv.P}$ *renzhen–de* $[_{VP}$*xie* $[_{SC}$ t_i *wan–le*]]]]].

I *ba* homework carefully write finished–ASP

As suggested by Sybesma, CAUS can be filled either by 把 *ba* insertion or verb movement. The 把 *ba*–sentences in (64a/b) are derived from the former, with the adverbials either before (as in 60a) or after (see 64b) 把 *ba*. The other way of derivation, namely verb movement, if operated, will result in the two counterparts of (65a/b), as in (64c) and (66), respectively. If the structure is correct, the two non–ba–sentences should both be grammatical. However, that is not the case; only (64c) is good. There is only one counterpart for the two 把 *ba*–constructions. Therefore, I consider the syntactic structure proposed by Sybesma to be problematic, with verb movement unlikely to take place.

(66) *我 写–完–了 作业 认真地

wo *xie-wan-le* *zuoye* *renzhen-de*

I write–finished–ASP homework carefully

'I finished the homework carefully.'

2.3.1.4 A topic marker

Tsao (1987) proposes that 把 *ba* marks the following NP as a special topic. Gao (1997) adopts Tsao's (1987) viewpoint and argues that a 把 *ba* NP (the NP following 把 *ba*) is fronted from a postverbal position to a preverbal position with 把 *ba* as a secondary topic marker. Gao (1997) observes that an NP in a preverbal position can be present with 把 *ba* or sentential stress (represented in 67 in bold face). That is, (67) is expressed either with 把 *ba* and no stress on 衣服 *yifu* 'clothes', or without 把 *ba* and stress on 衣服 *yifu* 'clothes'; the two are interpreted the same. So treating 把 *ba* as a topic marker is plausible: the presence of 把 *ba* would serve to stress that the following NP is in focus or for contrast.

(67) 妈， 弟弟 (把) 衣服 穿–反–了 (Gao 1997: 93)

ma, *didi* (*ba*) *yifu* *chuan-fan-le*

mom, younger brother (*ba*) clothes wear–inside out–ASP

'Mom, my younger brother has put on his clothes inside–out.'

Moreover, Gao (1997: 94) suggests that 把 *ba* and the following NP form a constituent which is like a VP adjunct (similar to an adverbial in a non–argument position). Recall the problem with Sybesma's analysis of the position of adverbials. This analysis seems to solve the issue of their different possible positions. Gao (1997: 94) argues that since a 把 *ba*–phrase and an adverbial phrase are both equal NP modifiers, they can switch positions freely, as their functions are the same.

There are, however, several problems with Gao's (1997) analysis. First of all, Gao argues that 把 *ba* and the NP following 把 *ba* form a constituent (i.e. a string) that can be put into the adjunct position of the VP and switch positions with an adverbial. For instance, in (68), if 把 *ba* and the post–ba NP 这–件–外套 *zhe-jian-waitao* 'this CL coat' (this coat) form a constituent, they should be able to pass the constituency tests as in (69a–d).[15] According to Börjars and Burridge (2010: 25), there are four tests to judge whether a string is a constituent, namely substitution (i.e. replace the string with a single word like a pronoun; see 69a), sentence fragment (ask a wh–question and answer it with a string; e.g. 69b and b'), movement (move the string to a different position in the sentence; e.g. 69c) and co–ordination (conjoin the string with other units with and; see 69d). If 把 *ba* and the post–ba NP in (68) form a constituent, it should pass all four tests. Nevertheless, none of the sentences in (69a–d) are acceptable. Therefore, Gao's (1997) argument does not hold true.

(68) a. 她 把 这 件 外套 洗 了

ta ba zhe jian waitao xi le

she *ba* this CL coat wash ASP

'She washed this coat.'

(69) a. *她 它 洗 了

ta ta xi le

she it wash ASP

'She washed it.'

b. 她 洗 了 什么?

ta xi le shenme?

she wash ASP what?

'What did she wash?'

15 According to Croft (2001: 189), constituency tests are 'opportunistic' in the way in which they are typically used. Often, one or more tests are selected that happen to favour the linguist's analysis, and there is no agreement on the inventory of tests to begin with. However, with the problems raised, it does cast doubt on the theory in question.

b'. *把 这 件 外套

ba zhe jian waitao

ba this CL coat

'ba this coat'

c. *把 这 件 外套, 她 洗 了

ba zhe jian waitao, ta xi le

ba this CL coat, she wash ASP

'ba this coat, she washed.'

d. *她 把 这 件 外套 和 把 这 条 裙子 洗 了

ta ba zhe jian waitao he ba zhe tiao qunzi xi le

she ba this CL coat and ba this CL skirt wash ASP

'She washed this coat and this skirt.'

Second, recall the viewpoint of treating 把 *ba* as a case assigner discussed in Section 2.3.1.2, which is objected to by Gao (1997). The grammaticality of (70b) seems to suggest that 把 *ba* is not necessarily a case marker , since it is optional as in (70a/b), whereas a case marker is obligatory (e.g. Chomsky 1981). However, if the 把 *ba*–NP refers to people, 把 *ba* cannot be omitted, as in (71b). As the occurrence of 把 *ba* can be obligatory (e.g. 71b), or optional (e.g. 70b), neither analysis of 把 *ba* can come to a satisfying explanation regarding the distribution of the 把 *ba*–construction in (70) and (71).

(70) a. 我 把 饭 吃–完–了

wo ba fan chi-wan-le

I *ba* meal eat–finished–ASP

'I finished the meal'

	b. 我	饭	吃–完–了
	wo	*fan*	*chi-wan-le*
	I	the meal	eat–finished–ASP
	'I finished the meal.'		

(71)	a. 我	把	她	叫–醒–了
	wo	*ba*	*ta*	*jiao-xing-le*
	I	*ba*	she	call–awake–ASP
	'I called her awake.'			
	b. *我	她	叫–醒–了	
	wo	*ta*	*jiao-xing-le*	
	I	she	call–awake–ASP	
	'I called her awake.'			

2.3.2 Semantic analysis

Semantically, the 把 *ba*–construction has been analyzed as expressing disposal (Wang 1947, Li 1974, Wang 2003), causativity (Guo 1999, Xiong 2004, Ye 2004) and high transitivity (Hopper & Thompson 1980, Sun 1995) in previous scholarship (see Han 2013 for an overview).

2.3.2.1 Disposal

Aoocridng to Wang (1947), 'disposal' means how a person is handled or dealt with, how something is disposed of or how an affair is carried out. that "the disposal form states how a person is handled, manipulated, or dealt with; how something is disposed of; or how an affair is conducted" (Wang 1947: 160, cited by Li 1974: 200). In general, it means physical handling of the P (i.e. the most patient–like argument in a sentence). Many scholars support the idea of 把 *ba* expressing disposal (e.g. Wang 1947, Li 1974, Song 1981, Wang 2003). As is argued by Wang (1947), (72b) is unacceptable, since 我 *wo* 'I' cannot handle 他 *ta* 'he' and love him. In other words, 我 *wo* 'I' did not actually do anything to 他 *ta* 'he', which is why (72b) is not good.

(72) a. 我 爱 他 (Wang 1947: 160)

wo *ai* *ta*

I love he

'I love him.'

b. *我 把 他 爱

wo *ba* *ta* *ai*

I *ba* he love

'I love him.'

However, there are some problems with this analysis. First, what kinds of actions 'disposal' means is unclear. If 'disposal' suggests that an object is dealt with, (73) will be problematic, as 他 *ta* 'he' did not do anything to the song. However, (73) is still acceptable.

(73) 他 认真地 把 歌 唱 完 (CCL 13.1)

ta *renzhende* *ba* *ge* *chang* *wan*

he carefully *ba* song sing finish

'He finished singing the song carefully.'

Another example is (74), which comes from Ye (2004: 26). There is again no physical handling involved, but (74) is acceptable. So the disposal analysis cannot fully account for the 把 *ba*–construction.

(74) 这 部 电影 把 我 看–哭–了 (Ye 2004: 26)

zhe bu dianying ba wo kan-ku-le

this CL movie *ba* I watch–cry–ASP

'This movie made me cry.'

2.3.2.2 Causativity

'Causativity' refers to the situation that an agent causes a patient to reach a result (see Guo 1999, Xiong 2004, Ye 2004). Talmy (1976) argues that compared to an autonomous event, a causative situationis composed of two or more events. A causal relation connects the two events, the causing event and the caused event: the former causes the latter. In line with Talmy's analysis, Ye (2004: 27) states that a 把 *ba*–sentence contains two events that are in a causative relation. There are two participants involved in the causative situation: a causer which motivates the causative situation, and a causee which is affected and undergoes a change of state.

Ye (2004: 27) claims that 把 *ba*–sentences can be divided into two–predicate and one–predicate ones, like (75a) and (75b) respectively. In (75a) there are two events: E1 (*I*) *threw* (*it*) and E_2 (*it*) *was out*, with the former causing the latter. The one–predicate type, according to Ye (2004: 29), is also interpreted as two events: one is the action carried out by the causer, and the other is the state the causee achieves after the action. The second one is implicit. So (75b) is construed as 'that book attracted me, and I was attracted'.

(75) a. 我 把 它 扔 出去 (Ye 2004: 27)

wo ba ta reng chuqu

	I	*ba*	it	throw	out			
	'I threw it out.'							
b.	那	本	书	把	我	吸引	住	了
	na	*ben*	*shu*	*ba*	*wo*	*xiyin*	*zhu*	*le.*
	that	CL	book	*ba*	I	attract	particle	ASP
	'That book attracted me.'							

The causative analysis with the two events involved in the 把 *ba*–construction is problematic considering the one–predicate type. Since 吸引 *xiyin* 'attract' is a telic action in Chinese, it is hard to construe two events in (75b), namely the action of attracting, and the result of achieving the state of being attracted. In other words, it is unacceptable to say 'the book appealed to me but I did not like it' in Chinese. So my view is that there is not necessarily a second event implicated in (75b), which casts doubt on the causative analysis of the 把 *ba*–construction.

2.3.2.3 High transitivity

The third analysis views 把 *ba* as a marker of 'high transitivity', which means that there is a relation of high semantic transitivity between the subject NP1 and the object NP2 (e.g. Chao 1968, Hopper and Thompson 1980, Sun 1995). Hopper and Thompson (1980: 251) propose the term Transitivity as "an activity 'carried–over' or 'transferred' from an agent to a patient". Their definition of semantic transitivity exists in parallel with syntactic transitivity: the former is dissociated from the latter, and the former is primary helping one account for various linguistic phenomena, including passivisation (cf. also Hollmann 2006 for discussion).

They suggest ten parameters of semantic transitivity encoded by languages, namely (a) participants, (b) kinesis, (c) aspect, (d) punctuality, (e) volitionality, (f) affirmation, (g) mode, (h) agency, (i) affectedness of O (O for object) and (j) individuation of O. These parameters determine how an action is transferred from one participant to another, and can be used to rank sentences as high or low in semantic transitivity. Taking parameter (a) as an example, at least two participants are required in a transfer. A sentence with two or more participants is therefore higher in transitivity than one with only one participant (all other things being equal). Theten parameters are divided into two values scaled as high and low in transitivity as in Table 2.1: the more features a clause has in the high column, the more semantically transitive it is.

Table 2.1: Parameters of Transitivity (Hopper and Thompson 1980: 252)

		High	Low
A	Participants	2 or more participants A and O	1 participant
B	Kinesis	Action	non–action
C	Aspect	telic	atelic
D	Punctuality	Punctual	non–punctual
E	Volitionality	volitional	non–volitional
F	Affirmation	affirmative	negative
G	Mode	Realis	irrealis
H	Agency	A high in potency	A low in potency
I	Affectedness of O	O totally affected	O not affected
J	Individuation of O	O highly individuated	O non–individuated

In addition, Hopper and Thompson (1980: 274) suggest that the 把 *ba*–construction is high in transitivity semantically, as “A behaves actively, volitionally, and totally upon a definite or referential O”. These are all parameters of high transitivity. Moreover, the 把 *ba*–clause must be perfective. For instance, with a perfective particle like 了 le as in (76), high transitivity is enhanced semantically in the 把 *ba*–construction, as the aspect marker 了 *le* indicates telicity, which is a parameter signaling high semantic transitivity.

(76)	我	把	那	个	苹果	吃	了
	wo	*ba*	*na*	*ge*	*pingguo*	*chi*	*le*
	I	*ba*	that	CL	apple	eat	ASP

‘I ate that apple.’

Sun (1995) follows Hopper and Thompson’s theory of Transitivity to analyze the 把 *ba*–construction. He makes the point that the constraints on the 把 *ba*–construction – such as monosyllabic verbs not being able to occur in the 把 *ba*–construction without the aspect marker 了 *le*, the NP after 把 *ba* being interpreted as being totally affected, and not being able to have a non–specific meaning are due to the fact that 把 *ba* is a makrer of high semantic transitivity.

To begin with, Sun (1995: 169) argues that the temporal structure in the 把 *ba*–construction has to be bounded, so the aspect marker 了 *le* occurs. For instance, (77a) is good because 了 *le* suggests a change of state (having eaten the soup) occurs. In contrast, (77b) is not acceptable because without 了 *le*, the action of ‘drinking soup’ does not imply an endpoint. This is in line with the aspect parameter of transitivity in semantics proposed by Hopper and Thompson (1980). An action with an endpoint is telic, so high semantic transitivity construed in the 把 *ba*–construction requires the aspect marker 了 *le* to indicate a change of state.

(77) a. 他 把 汤 喝 了 (Sun 1995: 169)

ta ba tang he le

he *ba* soup drink ASP

'He had eaten the soup.'

b. *他 把 汤 喝

ta ba tang he

he *ba* soup drink

'He had eaten the soup.'

Moreover, some of the examples that could not be explained by the disposal analysis may be accounted for in terms of high semantic transitivity. Sun (1995) suggests, for instance, that within the disposal analysis it is not clear why (78a) is not good, whereas (78b) and (78c) are. The post–*ba* NP 头 *tou* 'head' in all three sentences is lifted (disposed), yet one is not acceptable, whilst the other two are. According to him, it is not clear whether the event in (78a), 'lifting one's head' is bounded, which makes (78a) ungrammatical. By contrast, 一 *yi* 'one' in (78b) and 一下 *yi-xia* 'one–CL' in (78c) could indicate the temporal boundedness of the event, since they both spell out a specific quantity. That is, 'in order to lift one's head once, there must be a moment of beginning and a moment of ending it' (Sun 1995: 169).

(78) a. *把 头 抬 (Sun 1995: 161)

ba tou tai

ba head lift

'(Someone) lifted one's head.'

b. 把	头	一	抬
ba	*tou*	*yi*	*tai*
ba	head	one	lift

'(Someone) lifted one's head once (swiftly).'

c. 把	头	抬	了	一下
ba	*tou*	*tai*	*le*	*yi-xia*
ba	head	lift	ASP	one–CL

'(Someone) lifted one's head once.'

Second, Sun (1995: 172) points out that 把 *ba* functions to mark Hopper and Thompson's (1980) notion of object–boundedness. 把 *ba* indicates that a patient in an event is completely affecteded. In (79a), for example, the 把 *ba*–construction implies that he finished the soup and no more soup was left. This suggests the total affectedness on the patient. There is no such implication of finishing the soup in (79b). That is, he ate some soup, but did not finish it.

(79) a. 他	把	汤	喝	了	(Sun 1995: 169)
ta	*ba*	*tang*	*he*	*le*	
he	*ba*	soup	drink	ASP	

'He had the soup eaten.' ('He had eaten the soup.')

b. 他	喝	了	汤
ta	*he*	*le*	*tang*
he	drink	ASP	soup

'He had eaten the soup (but did not finish it)'

According to Sun (1995: 161), the function of 把 *ba* as denoting complete affectedness of the object explains why the post–*ba* NP is analyzed as a patient. It may be the high degree of semantic transitivity that motivates Wang (1947) and others to analyze the 把 *ba*–construction as expressing disposal. I agree with Sun (1995) that disposal may be part of transitivity, since disposal is related to total affectedness. Affectedness is, of course, just one of the parameters of transitivity proposed by Hopper and Thompson (1980). However, as mentioned in Section 2.3.2.1, disposal cannot capture all the contexts of use of the 把 *ba*–construction, whereas high semantic transitivity appears to provide a better explanation.

Third, Sun (1995: 174) argues that, as a marker of high transitivity, 把 *ba* excludes a non–specific reading of the post–ba NP (cf. Lü 1955, Chao 1968). Thompson (1973) too suggests that the NP after 把 *ba* needs to be specific or definite. This endorses the definiteness and referentiality of the parameter Individuation of O. According to Sun (1995), the post–ba NP in (80a) is modified by the numeral classifiers and there is the aspect marker 了 *le*, so (80a) is grammatical. Although the book is not marked with number or other modifiers in (80b), the aspect marker adds a temporally bounded interpretation and a definite reading to the post–ba NP 'book'. However, in (80c), due to the lack of the numeral classifier which could imply a specific reading on the NP it modifies, as well as the aspect marker which indicates the temporal boundedness, the sentence is incompatible with the 把 *ba*–construction. In other words, neither is the event of buying books temporally bounded, nor is the post–*ba* NP definite, which causes the unacceptability of (80c).[16]

---

16 However, Sun does not offer the corresponding counterpart of (80a) without *le* to suggest the impact of the numeral classifier on the post–ba NP, which should be 'he buys six books' without *le*. Yet his argument still hold true for the high transitivity analysis of 把 *ba*, since the example in the previous sentence is ungrammatical.

(80) a. 他 把 六 本 书 买 了 (Sun 1995: 169)

ta *ba* *liu* *ben* *shu* *mai* *le*

he *ba* six CL book buy ASP

'He bought six books.'

b. 他 把 书 买 了

ta *ba* *shu* *mai* *le*

he *ba* book buy ASP

'He bought the book.'

c. *他 把 书 买

ta *ba* *shu* *mai*

he *ba* book buy

'He bought book.'

To summarize, Sun (1995) argues that the 把 *ba*-construction can be explained in terms of high transitivity, including its temporal boundedness, the total affectedness of the post-ba NP, and the definiteness of the post-ba NP. However, he does not mention 把 *ba* + resultatives. It remains to be seen whether the analysis of 把 *ba* as a high-transitivity marker in semantics can explain its behavior in resultatives, which is what I will analyze in this book.

2.4 Combinations of resultative constructions and other constructions

As mentioned in Section 2.1, resultatives can combine with other constructions. In (81a), for instance, we see a resultative patient–subject clause, and in (81b) a resultative with 把 ba. (81c) is an example of the 被 *bei*–construction (passive) and (81d) of the verb–copying construction (which is used for emphasis or description, e.g. Tai 1999). The relations between resultatives and other constructions, the distribution of resultatives in other constructions and possible reasons for it have been examined by Huang (1996), Wang (2001), Song (2004), Ye (2004) and Zhao (2009).

(81) a. 衣服 洗–干净了

yifu *xi-ganjing-le*

clothes wash–clean–ASP

'(Someone) washed the clothes clean.'

b. 他 把 衣服 洗–干净了

ta *ba* *yifu* *xi-ganjing-le*

he *ba* table wash–clean–ASP

'He washed the clothes clean.'

c. 衣服 被 他 洗–干净了

yifu *bei* *ta* *xi-ganjing-le*

clothes *bei* he wash–clean–ASP

'The clothes were washed clean by him.'

d. 我 爬 山 爬-累-了

wo *pa* *shan* *pa-lei-le*

I climb mountain climb–tired–ASP

'I climbed the mountain and as a result I was tired.'

Huang (1996) argues that resultative constructions with the 把 *ba*–construction, the 被 *bei*–construction and the verb–copying construction are in a complementary distribution. That is, if a resultative can occur in the verb–copying construction, it cannot be used in the 把 *ba*/被 *bei*–construction. One would, for instance, only be able to express 'he ate rice and as a result he was full' with the verb–copying construction in (82a), but not with the 把 *ba*–construction in (82b) or the 被 *bei*–construction in (82c).

(82) a. 他 吃 米饭 吃-饱-了

ta *chi* *mifan* *chi-bao-le*

he eat rice eat–full–ASP

'He ate rice and as a result he was full.'

b. *他 把 米饭 吃-饱-了

ta *ba* *mifan* *chifull-le*

he *ba* rice eat–full–ASP

'He ate rice and as a result he was full.

c *米饭 被 他 吃-饱-了

mifan *bei* *ta* *chi-bao-le*

rice *bei* he eat–full–ASP

'He ate rice and as a result he was full.'

Wang (2001) disagrees with this idea, and provides some counterexamples, as in (83). These resultatives are equally acceptable when combined with the verb–copying construction in (83a), the 把 *ba*–construction in (83b) and the 被 *bei*–construction in (83c).

(83) a. 他们 打 官司 打–赢–了 (Wang 2001: 8)
tamen da guansi da-ying-le
they fight case fight–win–ASP
'They fought the case and as a result they won'

b. 他们 把 官司 打–赢–了
tamen ba guansi da-ying-le
they *ba* case fight–win–ASP
'They fought the case and as a result they won'

c. 官司 被 他们 打–赢–了
guansi bei tamen da-ying-le
case *bei* they fight–win–ASP
'The case was fought and as result won by them.'

Nevertheless, Song (2004) points out that although Wang (2001) presents some sentences opposing Huang's idea, there are still some examples which cast doubt on Wang's argument. Wang (2001) generally suggests a type of resultative that is acceptable when combined with both the verb–copying construction and the 把 *ba*–construction. Consider (84) and (85): in (84a) and (85a), we have two resultatives expressed with a verb–copying construction.[17] When combining a resultative and 把 *ba*, as predicted by Wang (2001), they

17 One may wonder whether (84a) and (85a) are resultatives. Both are formed as verb + result XP and express the result of the action, construed with an interpretation of an evaluation of the result, with the result XP predicated of the object.

should be acceptable (e.g. 84a). This is, however, not true of (85a), as (85b) shows. I observe that the resultative is good with the verb–copying construction as in (85a), but unacceptable with 把 *ba* as in (85b). Besides, Wang only provides instances without explanations for the acceptability of resultatives + various constructions.

(84)	a. 他	炒	菜	炒–咸–了	(Wang 2001: 10)
	ta	*chao*	*cai*	*chao-xian-le*	
	he	fry	dish	fry–salty–ASP	

‘He fried a dish and as a result the dish was salty.’

b.	他	把	菜	炒–咸–了
	ta	*ba*	*cai*	*chao-xian-le*
	he	*ba*	dish	fry–salty–ASP

‘He fried a dish and as a result the dish was salty.’

(85)	a. 他	买	菜	买–贵–了
	ta	*mai*	*cai*	*mai-gui-le*
	he	buy	vegetable	buy–expensive–ASP

‘He bought the vegetable but found out it was expensive.’

b.	*他	把	菜	买–贵–了
	ta	*ba*	*cai*	*mai-gui-le*
	he	*ba*	vegetable	buy–expensive–ASP

‘He bought the vegetable but found out it was expensive.’

Song (2004) analyzes resultatives in terms of motion events (cf. Talmy 2000), which are discussed in Section 2.2.2.3. He further proposes several principles for the combination of resultatives and other constructions. He argues that the most prominent concept should occur in the most prominent syntactic position and that there are several hierarchies to obey, as in (86):

(86) a. The frame–event is more prominent than the co–event. (Song 2004: 15)

b. Prominence hierarchy: subject in 被 *bei* > object in 把 *ba* > object in verb–copying > the element after the resultative in a self–contained event.

According to Song (2003: 37), a frame–event is a theme that the attention is focused on, and a co–event is the background, so the former is more prominent than the latter. The subject in 被 *bei* is the most prominent.[18] Based on this, Song further explains why the verb–copying sentence in (87a) is acceptable whereas the 把 *ba*–construction in (87b) is not.

(87) a. 他　吃　苹果　吃–饱–了

ta　*chi*　*pingguo*　*chi-bao-le*

he　eat　apple　eat–full–ASP

'He ate apples and as a result he was full.'

b. *他　把　苹果　吃–饱–了

ta　*ba*　*pingguo*　*chifull-le*

he　*ba*　apple　eat–full–ASP

'He ate apples and as a result he was full.'

c. [*ta* (he) MOVE INTO *bao*(full)] $_{\text{frame–event}}$ + [*ta chi pingguo* (he eat apple)] $_{\text{co–event}}$

18 Regarding the question as to why the subject in 被 *bei* is the most prominent, since it is not closely related to this thesis, it will not be elaborated here. More can be found in Song (2003: 47–50).

The event structure of 吃–饱 *chi-bao* 'eat–full' is illustrated in (87c). 饱 *bao* 'full' in (87a) refers to the subject. As explained in Section 2.2.2.3, it is a nonagentive event. 苹果 *pingguo* 'apple' as a concept in the co–event is thus low in prominence compared to one in the frame–event. So it can only appear in the object position in the verb–copying sentence, not in the object position of the 把 *ba*–construction. The latter requires a concept of higher prominence.

However, I found counter examples which cannot be explained by Song's hierarchy in (86b). As a self–contained event in (88), 问题 *wenti* 'question' is a concept in a co–event similar to苹果 *pingguo* 'apple' in (87), so it is lower in prominence than the concept in the frame–event. But 问题 *wenti* 'question' can appear in both the object position in the verb–copying sentence as in (88b), and the object position in the 把 *ba*–construction as in (88c). Therefore, Song's analysis cannot hold true for resultatives like (88a).

(88) a.

他	想–明白–了	这	个	问题
ta	*xiang-mingbai-le*	*zhe*	*ge*	*wenti*
he	think–understand–ASP	this	CL	question

'He thought about this question and as a result he understood it.'

b.

他	想	这	个	问题	想–明白–了
ta	*xiang*	*zhe*	*ge*	*wenti*	*xiang-mingbai-le*
he	think	this	CL	question	think–understand–ASP

'He thought about this question and as a result he understood it.'

c.

他	把	这	个	问题	想–明白–了
ta	*ba*	*zhe*	*ge*	*wenti*	*xiang-mingbai-le*
he	*ba*	this	CL	question	think–understand–ASP

'He thought about this question and as a result he understood it.'

Apart from the discussion on the distribution of the resultative in other constructions which are problematic, there are two more analyses on the combinations of resultatives and the 把 *ba*–construction (Ye 2004, Zhao 2009), both of which are mentioned in Section 2.3.2. I will first discuss their analyses in detail, and then problematise their arguments.

First, as stated in Section 2.3.2.2, Ye (2004: 37) suggests that the 把 *ba*–construction is composed of two subevents, the causing (E_1) and caused (E_2) event. She describes the argument relation in the 把 *ba*–sentence. According to her, two semantic levels are involved, namely a transitive relation (a lower one) and a causative relation (a higher one). The transitive relation is the intrinsic characteristics of the main verb (i.e. whether it could take a patient), whereas the causative relation is formed in different situations (e.g. the把 *ba*–sentence). The transitive arguments in the lower level are upgraded to be the arguments in the causative relation, which are the causer and causee. Three components are involved in the causative situation, namely A (the causer), B (the causee), and VP (causative situation with E_1 and E_2). Among the three, B connects the causing and caused event.

For instance, in (89) 他 *ta* 'he' is the agent, and 衣服 *yifu* 'clothes' the patient in the causing event (he) washed (the clothes), whereas 衣服 *yifu* 'clothes' is the agent in the caused event (the clothes) were clean. However, in my opinion, it is more appropriate to analyze 衣服 *yifu* 'clothes' as theme in the caused event. Then Ye (2004) claims that the two subevents compose a causative relation (VP), hence a new argument relation is formed in the 把 ba–sentence, with 他 *ta* 'he' the causer (A) and 衣服 *yifu* 'clothes' the causee (B). A is always from E1 and B is always the agent or patient (the subject) upgraded from E_2.

(89) 他 把 衣服 洗–干净–了 (Ye 2004: 27)

ta ba yifu xi-ganjing-le

he *ba* clothes wash–clean–ASP

'He washed the clothes and as a result the clothes were clean.'

Regarding *ba* + subject–oriented resultatives, for instance (90a), B (causee) is not the subject yet the object in E_2[19]. This violates the previous analysis that B is always the subject of E_2. Ye (2004: 37) further states that words like 懂 *dong* 'understand', 会 *hui* 'can' are all predicates which denoting cognition. She claims that according to Halliday (1985), the physical process is unidirectional, but the cognitive process is bidirectional. Therefore the subject (thinker) and the object of the cognitive process could be the more agent–like argument. The occurrence of the cognitive predicates such as 懂 *dong* 'understand', 会 *hui* 'can' and 明白 *mingbai* understand' in the 把 *ba*–sentence may be caused by the bidirectional property of the predicates. Nevertheless, Ye did not elaborate this argument, which makes the view obscure. Moreover, 把 *ba* + V–懂 *dong* 'understand' in (90b) is not fully acceptable. All these make Ye's (2004) analysis questionable.

(90) a. 我 把 游泳 学–会–了

wo ba youyong xue-hui-le

I *ba* swim learn–can–ASP

'I learned to swim and as a result I could swim.'

19 Ye (2004) did not mention what E_2denotes, but I assume it is *can swim* in line with her argument.

b. ?观众　　把　　剧情　　看–懂–了

guanzhong ba juqing kan-dong-le

audience *ba* plot watch–understand–ASP

'The audience watched (the play) and as a result understood the plot.

Second, as illustrated in Section 2.2.2.1, Zhao (2009b) analyzes Chinese resultatives in line with Construction grammar (cf. Goldberg 1995) and proposes the problematic 'loose argument realization'. She also analyzes the combination of 把 *ba* + resultative. Following Shen (2002) who argues that the 把 *ba*–construction expresses subjective disposal,[20] Zhao (2009b) claims that this account offers a unified explanation for the 把 *ba*–structure. However, she does not mention how this works for all types of the 把 *ba*–construction, which is potentially confusing.

In addition, it is not the case that all 把 *ba* + resultatives are equally acceptable. (91) is well accepted before and after being combined with 把 *ba*, but not (92). Both (91a) and (92a) are subject–oriented resultatives with equal acceptability. The former is acceptable if combined with 把 ba, as in (91b); the latter is not, as in (92b).

(91) a. 她　学–会–了　这　出　戏 (Zhao 2009: 130)

ta xue-hui-le zhe chu xi

she learn–can–ASP this CL drama

'She learned this drama and as a result she could play it.'

---

20 According to Zhao (2009), the notion of subjectivity is proposed by Lyons (1977), which means "a characteristic of language that speakers tend to express their stands, attitudes, feelings towards what they say by leaving traces of their selfhood in utterances" (Lyons 1977: 739, cited from Zhao 2009: 129).

b. 她 把 这 出 戏 学–会–了

ta ba zhe chu xi xue-hui-le

she *ba* this CL drama learn–can–ASP

'She learned this drama and as a result she could play it.'

(92) a. 他 喝–腻–了 这 种 茶

ta he-ni-le zhe zhong cha

he drink–be tired of–ASP this kind tea

'He had drunk this kind of tea so many times that he was tired of it.'

b. *他 把 这 种 茶 喝–腻–了

ta ba zhe zhong cha he-ni-le

he *ba* this kind tea drink–be tired of–ASP

'He had drunk this kind of tea so many times that he was tired of it.'

In general, there are ongoing discussions on the resultative construction, the 把 *ba*–construction and the combination of the two within Chinese scholarship. However, gaps still exist. First, there are problems with the analyses of subject–oriented resultatives (e.g. Song 2004, Zhao 2009). Second, even though the high semantic transitivity analysis of the 把 *ba*–construction seems to hold true for the construction on its own (e.g. Sun 1995), ba+resultative is not discussed in this regard. Third, in terms of the combination of the two, scholars either offer no explanation for the acceptability of this combination (e.g. Huang 1996, Wang 2001) or provide problematic analyses (e.g. Song 2004, Ye 2004, Zhao 2009,). Furthermore, different degrees of acceptability in 把 *ba*+subject–oriented resultative constructions have not been made. All the issues listed above will be tackled in this book.

2.5 Corpus studies on Chinese resultatives

As stated in Chapter 1, there is a need for a corpus study of Chinese resultatives. They have rarely been discussed from a corpus–based point of view in the literature. To the best of my knowledge, there are only two papers that take this approach. First, Yang and Wang (2009) searched for 98 monosyllabic verbs that could be used in resultatives (cf. Lü 1999) in the corpus built by the Center for Chinese Linguistics PKU (CCL) and obtained 15,000 sentences, which was the basis for a database of 3,000 randomized examples. Although the database they built is large in size, the research carried out is limited as it has only investigated one aspect: the temporal relation of two subevents in a resultative. They look at temporal relations in English and Chinese resultatives from the perspective of event structure within the framework of Construction grammar (Goldberg 1995). As stated in Section 2.2.3, Goldberg (1995) argues that there is no temporal relation between the two subevents of a resultative construction. The results of Yang and Wang's (2009) study suggest that there is no interval between the two subevents in Chinese. Recall what has been stated in Section 2.2.3: there are examples of Chinese resultatives construed as having an independent temporal relation between the two subevents, for instance (93), where it could be only after drinking the sweet drink several times that people became tired of it. This casts some doubt on Yang and Wang's analysis.

(93)	人们	喝–腻–了	甜的
	renmen	*he-ni-le*	*tiande*
	people	drink–be tired of–ASP	sweet

'People had drunk (the) sweet (drink) so many times that they were tired of it.'

Second, Luo et al. (2010) compare English and Chines resultatives with an adjectival result phrase. The research was conducted based on the BNC and the CCL with respect to the properties of adjectives used in resultatives in the two languages. According to Luo et al. (2010: 270), 67% adjectives that occur in English resultatives are monosyllabic, and 91% Chinese adjectives used in resultatives are formed with one syllable. Comparatively, the monosyllabic adjectives are less frequently used as non–resultatives in Chinese (15/740). So resultatives have a monosyllabic–adjective preference. However, this argument is only evident in Chinese. The frequency of monosyllabic adjectives used as non–resultatives in English is not provided, so it cannot be argued that English has the preference for monosyllabic adjectives used in resultatives. It might be that monosyllabic adjectives are more frequent in all contexts. Although the numbers do suggest a monosyllabic–preference in Chinese, whether the findings for English point to something is unclear. Therefore the comparisons between English and Chinese in this regard are suspicious.

Moreover, the authors claim that the expected results tend to occur in English resultatives. That is, the adjectives found to occur with particular adjectives in English are generally not that suprising, for instance *clean/ dry* for WIPE. Nevertheless, both expected and non–ideal results can occur in Chinese resultatives (e.g. 'clean/ dry/ dirty/ wet' for 'WIPE'). However, the types of 'expected' and 'non–ideal' results are not defined by Luo et al. (2010), which makes the comparisons between English and Chinese unclear. Moreover, no frequencies of resultatives of these types in either language are mentioned. The analysis is, in other words, in need of refinement. In sum, the paper presents some usages of English and Chinese resultatives in those corpora. Nevertheless, the evidence provided by the authors is insufficient for the claims they make.

In general, previous studies on Chinese resultatives based on corpus data have been restricted to comparisons between English and Chinese. The characteristics of Chinese resultatives deserve to be investigated in their own right from a corpus–based perspective. The results of such an investigation will be presented in detail in Chapter 4 (for instance Chinese resultatives can be classified as prototypical/marginal, agent/patient/location oriented and so forth).

It is clear from the preceding paragraphs that little corpus–based research has been done. There is, however, a clear need for it. A lot of the literature is, for instance, concerned with sentences that do not seem particularly acceptable, despite claims to the contrary. As mentioned in Chapter 1, Section 1.1.1, Li (1990, 1995) discusses Chinese V–V compounds under the framework of GB theory concerning the ambiguity of (94), which is an example made up by generative linguists and widely discussed in the Chinese scholarship on resultatives (e.g. Gao 1997, Shen 2004, Shi 2008). Nevertheless, (94) is not natural for native speakers. A study of authentic language seems to be called for, which is why this book undertakes a corpus analysis of Chinese resultatives, whilst also including a relatively large–scale acceptability judgement component using the so–called magnitude estimation approach (see e.g. Bard et al. 1996, Cowart 1997; for more details see Chapter 3, Section 3.3.3).

(94) 淘淘 追－累－了 悠悠 (Li 1995: 257)

Taotao *zhui-lei-le* *Youyou*

Taotao (name) chase–tired–ASP Youyou (name)

a. Taotao chased Youyou and as a result Youyou was tired.

b. Taotao chased Youyou and as a result Taotao was tired.

c. Youyou chased Taotao and as a result Youyou was tired.

2.6 Concluding remarks

It should be clear from the literature review in Sections 2.1–2.5 that considerable attention, from generative and cognitive linguists, has been paid to the resultative construction in Chinese and other languages, to the 把 *ba*–construction in Chinese and, to some extent, also to the combination of the two. There are still a number of gaps, though. They include, for instance, the relative neglect of subject–oriented resultatives in Chinese, the different degrees of acceptability of 把 *ba* in resultatives and the function of 把 *ba*. Finally, there is a clear need to investigate these matters from the point of view of authentic language. The rest of this book aims to fill those gaps, taking a corpus–based and also acceptability judgement–based approach using magnitude estimation (e.g. Bard et al. 1996).

Chapter 3 Methodology

3.1 Introduction

This study will draw on two different methodologies in line with a usage–based model, namely, a corpus–based approach, and an acceptability judgement approach. The corpus–based approach will be discussed in Section 3.2, the acceptability judgement one in Section 3.3. Section 3.4 is the conclusion.

3.2 Corpus-based approach

As discussed in Chapter 1, there is a need for a study of Chinese resultatives in authentic use. Recall Questions 1–3 as follows: What qualifies as a Chinese resultative construction? What do Chinese resultatives look like in actual usage? How can Chinese resultatives be viewed from a typological perspective? In order to answer these questions, studies based on linguists' intuitions and a limited number of examples are not sufficient. A corpus approach can help to answer these questions. Corpus linguistics is a methodology involving large collections of electronically transcribed texts used with computer tools to investigate language (McEnery et al. 2006: 7). So, this method can collect abundant data and show actual usage of resultatives in Mandarin.

According to Song and Wang (2013: 42) and Zhang (2017), corpus studies of Chinese have focused on various areas, such as language teaching, translation, grammar, semantics, lexicography and lexicology. Zhang (2017) conducted a review of corpus studies in China from 1992 to 2015. According to him, among 3,128 articles published in core Chinese journals, 581 (18.57%) are on language teaching, 524 (16.75%) on theoretical research (e.g. corpus building) and 512 (16.37%) on semantics. The remaining articles deal with translation (16.05%), lexicology (15.57%) and grammar (10.93%). So, the grammatical research is quite limited. One further issue to be noted is that Song and Wang (2013) and Zhang (2017) do not differentiate between theoretical linguistics and applied linguistics. Although there are several studies on grammar, this part mainly includes research on English grammar, Chinese grammar and grammar of Chinese people learning English. Actually, few studies are based on Chinese grammar, so this is what I will investigate in Chapter 4.

In addition, Song and Wang (2013: 42) and Zhang (2017) only mention some articles in each field, and they do not distinguish specific languages in these aspects. Based on my search, the analyses discuss English, Chinese and contrastive studies of Chinese and other languages (e.g. English). So studies of Chinese language are quite rare; what little there is will be included in my considerations in this book.

Moreover, based on Song and Wang's (2013) analysis, most corpora are developed by researchers specifically for language teaching and translation studies. Song and Wang (2013: 45), Zhang (2017:40) argue that one of the limitations of Chinese corpora is their lack of part of speech (POS) tagging. As tagging of Chinese is highly demanding, technology not being advanced enough for machine operation, much of the work needs to be done manually. This intensive laborious work results in corpora without POS tagging.

To the best of my knowledge, there are several corpora for Chinese language studies, for instance the corpus built by the Center for Chinese Linguistics PKU (CCL) (e.g. Zhan et al. 2003),[1] the Lancaster Corpus of Mandarin Chinese (LCMC; McEnery and Xiao 2004),[2] the corpus of Contemporary Chinese built by the National Language Committee (NLCC; Jin, et al. 2005),[3] Texts of Recent Chinese corpus 2009/2014 built by the Beijing Foreign Studies University (ToRCH),[4] and the corpus built by Beijing Language and Culture University Corpus Center (BCC; Xun et al. 2016).[5] These corpora will be briefly introduced as follows.

The CCL is a big corpus built by the Center for Chinese Linguistics PKU, covering over 63 million words of Contemporary Chinese (both written and spoken language from 1919 until now) and 22 million words of Ancient Chinese (Chinese used before 1919). It contains nine genres and no POS tagging. The LCMC includes one million words in 15 genres. It focuses on

1 The CCL website: http://ccl.pku.edu.cn:8080/ccl_corpus/index.jsp?dir=xiandai

2 The LCMC project website: https://cqpweb.lancs.ac.uk/lcmc/

3 The NLCC Project website: http://corpus.zhonghuayuwen.org/index.aspx

4 The ToRCH Project website: http://corpus.bfsu.edu.cn/corpora

5 The BCC project website: http://bcc.blcu.edu.cn/

written language with POS tagging. The NLCC is composed of nearly 20 million words with POS tagging, five genres in written and oral Chinese. The ToRCH (2009) is built with one million words from 15 genres and no POS tagging. The texts in this corpus were mostly published in 2009. Later on there is a ToRCH (2014) version, with the texts published in 2014. The BCC is a new corpus comprising 15 billion words in written and oral language, four genres and with POS tagging.

These corpora have their advantages and disadvantages. The NLCC and the BCC are large in size, but only have five and four genres respectively, which are far fewer than the LCMC and the ToRCH with 15 genres, and the CCL with nine genres. So the former ones are not well balanced. In addition, the BCC was still under construction and development when I conducted my corpus analysis, which made it unsuitable for my research. The ToRCH series is well–balanced, but they only contain texts from 2009 and 2014, which makes their content limited for my corpus study. Besides, its lack of POS–tagging makes it hard for the searching. Therefore in this book, I will employ the PKU–CCL, the LCMC and the Online Database on Verb–Resultative Constructions in Contemporary Chinese (ODVRC, see Zhan et al. 2015). These two corpora and the database will be discussed in detail below.

As mentioned earlier, the CCL is a large comprehensive Chinese corpus covering over 63 million words of Contemporary Chinese. However, the drawback of the CCL is its lack of POS tagging. This makes it difficult to extract resultative constructions: after a certain result XP is searched, the instances used as adjectives have to be selected manually. Taking into account the size of the corpus, it would be very time–consuming if not impossible to retrieve and analyze all the resultatives used in the CCL. Therefore, the CCL is mainly used to provide additional examples.

The LCMC is a corpus intended to be a Chinese counterpart of the Freiburg–Brown corpus (Frown) of American English and the Freiburg–LOB (Lancaster–Oslo/Bergen; FLOB) corpus of British English. Both beginning in 1991,[6] the Frown and FLOB contain 500 texts of around 2,000 words each, which are distributed across 15 text registers. With one million words each, the Frown and FLOB were built as representatives of American and British English in the early 1990s, respectively.

As a match of the Frown and FLOB corpora, the LCMC can be regarded as fairly representative of Mandarin Chinese from around 1991. It contains one million words from 15 genres in written language with POS tagging (see Table 3.1). The LCMC is chosen for the corpus study of Chinese resultatives because it is as balanced a corpus as FLOB and Frown. In addition, its size and complete POS tagging make it possible to obtain all resultatives.

Table 3.1: Text types of the LCMC (McEnery and Xiao 2004: 1176)

Code	Text category	Samples	Proportion
A	Press reportage	44	8.8%
B	Press editorials	27	5.4%
C	Press reviews	17	3.4%
D	Religion	17	3.4%
E	Skills/trades/hobbies	38	7.6%
F	Popular lore	44	8.8%

6 For more information, see: http://www.helsinki.fi/varieng/CoRD/corpora/FROWN/index.html

Table 3.1 (Continued)

Code	Text category	Samples	Proportion
G	Biographies/essays	77	15.4%
H	Miscellaneous	30	6%
J	Science	80	16%
K	General fiction	29	5.8%
L	Mystery/detective	24	4.8%
M	Fiction	6	1.2%
N	Science fiction	29	5.8%
P	Martial arts fiction	29	5.8%
R	Romantic fiction Humour	9	1.8%
Total		500	100%

The LCMC has some limitations, though. First, it does not contain spoken data, which means the corpus analysis of Chinese resultatives will only reflect written usage. Second, its size of one million words means that it may occasionally not provide sufficient data. So, the CCL is adopted to supplement the LCMC, although the former does not have POS tagging. Due to the insufficiency of the LCMC, I refer to the CCL for more instances.

The ODVRC is adopted as a basis for the quantitative study of Chinese resultatives.[7] According to the introduction to the database, it was built based on the dictionary of Chinese verb–resultative construction (Sunaoka 2013) and the A/B levels of HSK (Hanyu Shuiping Kaoshi; Chinese Proficiency Test) vocabulary. That is, all the words listed in these sources that can be used

7 The ODVRC project website: http://ccl.pku.edu.cn/vc/default.asp

in a resultative construction are included in the database, except for some dubious instances in the dictionary and some low–frequency items in the HSK vocabulary. It contains 25,190 verb–complement patterns, which are combinations of 2,707 predicates/verbs and 579 adjectives or directionals that can occur after verbs (they are called complements in Chinese scholarship). For each combination, there is an explanation and three or four examples. According to Zhan et al. (2015: 2), this database is assumed to reflect the collocations of verbs and complements in Chinese, as well as the characteristics of Chinese verb–complement combinations in general.

The database's name refers to 'verb–resultative constructions', but a more precise name for this database would be 'predicate–complement constructions', because apart from resultatives, the ODVRC also contains collocations of predicates and complements, such as (1). As mentioned in Chapter 1, Section 1.1.1, although (1) looks like predicate + AP, it does not fit the definition of a resultative construction, so it will not be included in my research.

(1)	我们的	生活	简单–极–了	(ODVRC)
	womende	*shenghuo*	*jiandan-ji-le*	
	our	life	simple–extreme–ASP	
	'Our life was extremely simple.'			

I aim to search the LCMC for all items used as result XPs in the ODVRC. After obtaining all the instances of resultatives from the LCMC, the number of resultatives is calculated and compared in terms of type and token frequency. In order to see whether there are significant differences of distribution among various types, chi–square tests are also run. Further discussion of corpus data and analysis can be found in Chapter 4.

3.3 Acceptability judgement approach

Regarding what determines the acceptability of resultatives with and without 把 *ba*, corpus data are not sufficient here because although there are examples in the CCL and the LCMC, not enough data can be found in these corpora in terms of subject-oriented resultatives. So acceptability judgement is the best methodology as it can distinguish and illustrate the fine-grained nature of this phenomenon. As (2) makes clear, there seem to be some differences in acceptability of 把 *ba* + subject-oriented resultatives in (2) (all equally acceptable without 把 *ba*). In order to tackle these issues, acceptability judgements of Chinese resultatives (including with and without 把 *ba*) are required.

(2) a. 他 把 这 个 问题 想–明白–了

ta ba zhe ge wenti xiang-mingbai-le

he *ba* this CL question think–understand–ASP

'He thought about this question and as a result he understood it.'

b. ?冬冬 把 他的 话 听–懂–了

Dongdong ba tade hua ting-dong-le

Dongdong *ba* his words listen–understand–ASP

(name)

'Dongdong listened to his words and as a result Dongdong understood them.'

c. *人们 把 甜的 喝-腻-了

renmen *ba* *tiande* *he-ni-le*

people *ba* sweet drink–be tired of–ASP

'People had drunk (the) sweet (drink) so many times that they were tired of it.'

3.3.1 Grammaticality verus acceptability

According to Bard et al. (1996: 33), a distinction should be made between grammaticality and acceptability. The traditional way of judging sentences also tests acceptability, but judgements are often taken as evidence of grammaticality. Bard et al. (1996: 33) define *grammaticality* as "compatibility with the grammar of a particular language, or well-formedness under the assumptions about linguistic competence used to build the grammar". They point out that views received from speakers do not give direct access to their linguistic competence. Instead, a particular kind of linguistic behaviour (or performance) is observed, which may not match grammar linguists' hypotheses. Therefore, a three-way distinction has to be made among grammaticality, which refers to a feature of a linguistic stimulus, *acceptability*, defined as a feature of a stimulus realized by a speaker, and an *acceptability judgement*, which means the speaker's reply to the linguist's enquiries. For instance, (3a) is fully acceptable and grammatical, (3b) is ungrammatical and unacceptable, whereas (3c) is grammatical and acceptable but may be judged differently with respect to an acceptability judgement.

(3) a. John gave Mary a book.

b. *John Mary a book gave.

c. ?John gave to Mary a book.

Bard et al. (1996) also propose a distinction between relative grammaticality and relative acceptability: the former refers to a natural characteristic of grammar, whereas the latter is what is sensed by the informant. Taking the examples in (3), (3a) will be judged as fully acceptable, (3b) as unacceptable, (3c) as marginally acceptable.

Cowart (1997) argues that, for a sentence, there is no such thing as absolutely acceptable or unacceptable, though there might be absolutely grammatical or ungrammatical. Acceptability should be considered as a continuum (e.g. Bard et al. 1996, Featherston 2005). No matter how acceptable or unacceptable a sentence is, it is possible that there will be some other sentences that are even better or worse. Therefore, Cowart (1997) suggests that the goal of forming acceptability judgements is to access the relative acceptability of sentences. Acceptability judgements vary along a continuum, on which no discrete levels are established.

One thing to be noted is that, traditionally, generative linguists regard grammaticality and acceptability as distinct (with grammaticality being binary but acceptability scalar; cf. Chomsky 1995), whereas functional linguists typically do not (e.g. Li and Thompson 1981). Instead they view grammaticality as related to the system but acceptability to the speaker's assessment. Thereby, they may view both grammaticality and acceptability as scalar. In this book I will not consider grammaticality as defined in a binary manner, but rather focus on acceptability as a scalar phenomenon, and use that term not necessarily in opposition to grammaticality.

3.3.2 Traditional ways of making acceptability judgements

A further issue of concern is how to make acceptability judgements. Whether a sentence is grammatical is judged by linguists' or their close associates' intuitions (i.e. the so–called 'ask Sally' or 'hi Sally' method,[8] Bard et al. 1996). To test intuition, several types of scales are adopted for acceptability judgements. To begin with, syntacticians use a binary model, namely whether a sentence is grammatical or not (Featherston 2005). Second, terms such as good, bad, very bad are used and coded with symbols such as 0, ?,* (Bard et al. 1996). This technique is referred to as an n–point scale. That is, some scales for judgements are illustrated by means of ** (very bad), * (just bad), ? (questionable) and '0' (OK). For example, sentences in (4) may be judged with the symbols.

(4) a. John gave Mary a book.

b. *John Mary a book gave.

c. ?John gave to Mary a book.

---

8 The 'ask Sally' or 'hi Sally' method refers to a way of sentence judgement such that a linguist asks a colleague, say Sally, "Hi Sally! Do you think this sentence is grammatical or not?" Then, based on the answer given by Sally, and his/her own introspective judgement, the linguist makes a judgement of the sentence.

Another example is the Likert scale (e.g. Gordon and Hendrick 1997). Subjects are supposed to rate sentences on a numerical scale, for instance, from 0 (very bad) to 5 (very good). Sentence (4a), for instance, could be rated as 5, (4b) as 0 and (4c) as 2.

However, there are two problems with the aforementioned judgement methods. To begin with, whether linguists or general native speakers shall be asked about linguistic acceptability judgements is an issue to be considered. According to Cowart (1997), the binary model is unstable. Sometimes there may be extreme disagreements among linguists, or informants may disagree among themselves if a stimulus is given in a different context. Viewed in this way, a method for more people to be tested is necessary so that the acceptability judgements can be more reliable. The n–point scale like Likert scale can involve more subjects.

Second, how should acceptability judgements be made? A binary model cannot distinguish the different degrees in acceptability. In addition, Bard et al. (1996: 35) argue that a symbol (or numerical) scale is not precise enough to reflect differences in sentence acceptability among various subjects. For example, suppose there are three sentences, Sa and the corresponding sentences Sb and Sc. Subjects may make acceptability judgements on a 5–point numerical scale. Suppose that Sa is marked 3. Sb is less acceptable, but not totally unacceptable, so it is judged as 2. Then, what shall the subjects do if the acceptability of Sc is between 2 and 3?

It is impossible to distinguish the three sentences on this five–point scale. The discrete nature of a Likert scale as such does not do justice to the relativity of acceptability judgements. More distinctions may exist but people are forced to make a choice that they do not really acknowledge (e.g. turning Sb into 1 and then having Sc as 2, but what about another sentence Sd that is between Sb and Sc?) Subjects are restricted by the scales set by linguists, therefore not able to make judgements and provide enough information about sentence acceptability. To sum up, the binarly model used by linguists fails to involve more subjects and illustrate various degrees in acceptability. Regarding Likert scale, although it can be applied to more informants, the acceptability judgements obtained by this method are not fine–grained enough.

3.3.3 Magnitude estimation

Facing the forementioned problems, Bard et al. (1996) propose that an approach developed in psychophysics for judgements of loudness or brightness could be used for acceptability judgements in linguistics, namely magnitude estimation (ME).

According to Stevens (1956; cited by Bard et al. 1996: 40), ME provides scales for the measurement of physical continua in psychophysics, such as estimations of brightness. For instance, a subject associates a number with a physical stimulus (e.g. light). Once the initial stimulus, or modulus, is presented, the subject assigns a number to the following stimulus which can reflect the relationship between that stimulus and the modulus. That is, if a stimulus appears five times as bright as the modulus, it is given a number five times the number assigned to the modulus.

Based on this, Bard et al. (1996) apply ME to linguistic acceptability judgements. Generally, informants give their evaluations of each stimulus (a test sentence) by assigning it a number. The number given to the first sentence may be as small or as large as the subjects like (but not negative). Then, the subjects give all following items scores, with numbers in proportion to the other stimuli. That is, if one sentence is judged to be three times as good as another one, the former should get a number triple the latter one. A different strategy to get similar results is asking subjects to draw a line to represent the first sentence. The actual length does not really matter. Then, the subject represents all following sentences with more lines, with the length always in proportion to the ones drawn for other sentences. For example, if a subject draws a line of about 5 cm for the first sentence. Then, s/he may judge the second one to be twice as good as the first one, so s/he should draw a line of 10 cm for the second sentence.

Bard et al. (1996) carried out more studies to ensure the utility of ME to elicit acceptability judgements, which included validation studies and reliability studies. According to them, if a method for accessing human judgements is reliable, it works not only among but across informants. Validation studies demonstrate reliability within subjects, while reliability studies aim to test across subjects. Bard et al. (1996: 63) argue that the results suggest that ME can be applied to linguistic acceptability judgements: its validity "comes from intrasubject consistency" and its reliability from intersubject consistency.[9] The two tests verify that ME is of use to linguistic acceptability judgments.

ME addresses the problems with former ways of acceptability judgements, namely the type of informant (i.e. just linguists vs. a wider group of native

9 See Bard et al. (1996) for more information about the two tests.

speakers) and the judgement method (binary, n–point scale, ME). The two can be combined in different ways, which may lead to problems. For example, if the Likert scale is used by only a few people, the number of subjects will not be enough to get reliable judgements. Or even if using binary judgements for a large group, yes–or–no judgements will still not be valid for linguistic research.

In contrast, ME, if applied in line with the way in which it is also used in psychophysics, involves more participants and provides a more reliable way of obtaining judgements without restrictions on informants. To be specific, first, it guarantees that acceptability judgements are obtained from a large group of native speakers by adopting ME via questionnaire surveys.

Second, as a type of ratio scale, ME allows the elicitation of grammaticality judgements with a minimum of restrictions of scale on the informants. Subjects can express their intuitions and choose a scale of numbers to make judgements with complete freedom (e.g. Bard et al. 1996, Featherston 2005). Subtle differences of acceptability can be revealed by using ME, which means hidden phenomena ignored by previous studies may be detected. Furthermore, the validity of this method can be crossed–checked with standard introspective judgements of linguists, which further enhances the reliability of acceptability judgements.

However, as suggested by Cowart (1997: 74), a key disadvantage of this method is that it requires a modest degree of mathematical knowledge on the part of the informants, if a method for assigning numerical scores is adopted. Some subjects may not feel comfortable with numbers, so they may not use ME properly. This can be avoided by using the line–drawing method. But measuring lines by hand may be prone to error and time–consuming. Therefore, if one wants to stick to a numerical method, it is advisable to be careful with the selection of subjects and choose informants with a certain level of mathematical background, for example college students.

One point to be noted is that, recently, the effectiveness of different measures of acceptability judgements (including the binary model, Likert scale and ME paradigm) has been investigated and compared (e.g. Weskott & Fanselow 2008, 2011; Sprouse 2011). The results suggest that the Likert scale can be as gradated and informative as ME. ME may not be the only way to reveal gradience and provide substantial information regarding acceptability. In my opinion, although similar results may be arrived at by adopting one way or another (i.e. n–point scale or ME), it is worth trying to use ME in my study, as it is the first attempt to apply such a paradigm to Chinese. ME is robust enough to yield statistically significant results (Sorace & Keller 2005: 1501).

3.3.4 Questionnaire survey

To get my data, I designed questionnaires, which will now be briefly discussed. Data were collected by inviting a number of participants (university students) in person to do questionnaire surveys (more information about how the surveys were conducted will be introduced below and more in Chapter 5, Section 5.3.2, and Chapter 6, Section 6.1.2). The questionnaire was designed as follows. I first looked for examples in the CCL and the LCMC with the help of the patterns listed in the ODVRC. Second, based on these examples, I selected a number of parameters possibly relevant for the acceptability of 把 *ba* in resultatives, such as subject– versus object–oriented resultatives, and with versus without 把 *ba*.

Test sentences were revised based on these parameters. For instance, (5a) is an example extracted from the CCL, which contains the parameter 'subject–oriented' and 'without 把 *ba*'. It is used as a test sentence in my questionnaire survey. The counterpart of (5a) with the parameter 'with 把 ba' is (5b), which is also an item tested in the survey.

(5)	a. 他	想–明白–了	这	个	问题	(CCL 7.1)
	ta	*xiang-mingbai-le*	*zhe*	*ge*	*wenti*	
	he	think–understand–ASP	this	CL	question	

'He thought about this question and as a result he understood it.'

b. 他	把	这	个	问题	想–明白–了
ta	*ba*	*zhe*	*ge*	*wenti*	*xiang-mingbai-le*
he	*ba*	this	CL	question	think–understand–ASP

'He thought about this question and as a result he understood it.'

In order to avoid the purpose of the survey being figured out by the subjects, equal numbers of fillers and test sentences are needed. The fillers are designed with a similar format, length and NPs as the test sentences (e.g. some with 把 *ba*, some without 把 *ba*). Sentences with different degrees of acceptability are distributed evenly among the fillers (cf. Keller and Sorace 2003). In addition, subjects might be happy to make judgements from the beginning. But their attention span may be limited, so the judgements of later sentences could be affected. Therefore, a version with a reversed order of sentences was devised. More about the test sentences will be illustrated in relevant chapters (Chapters 5 and 6). The whole questionnaire surveys can be found in Appendix A and B. The surveys were given ethical approval by

Lancaster University.

Except for the sentences, each survey contains the following parts in Chinese: a participant information sheet and a consent form. On the information sheet there is a brief introduction to the whole project and the survey, for instance the aim of the research, the reason for inviting participants, the confidentiality of the survey, contact information for my supervisors and me. The consent form stresses the fact that subjects do not need to participate in the survey. If they agree to take part in it they should sign their name and put the date on a consent form.

The title of the main questionnaire is *Chinese Grammar experiment*. The next part of the questionnaire requests demographic information, including name, date of birth, gender, whether a dialect speaker. Then, there are short instructions about magnitude estimation, with the wording as follows:

(6) Assign a number to the first test sentence. No requirement on how large or small the number is (as long as it is not negative). Then assign all following items scores as well, though every time in proportion to the other sentences. (Hollmann 2013)

There is then a drill for the informants to practise. In the drill there is a set of three sentences with different degrees of acceptability. The items in the drill differ from the sentences in the final survey. After the subjects practise and become familiar with the way of making judgements, it comes to the test part with sentences (e.g. 5a/b).

The whole process is as follows. Subjects were shown the information sheet and consent form for the survey. Then, they were asked whether they agreed to participate. If yes, they signed a consent form and gave demographic information. If they did not want to reveal personal information, this step could be skipped. Then the task for the participants was to practise magnitude estimation. After they were confident with this method, they began to judge the test sentences. It took approximately ten minutes to finish the whole survey, which was monitored by the researchers. After finishing the survey, questionnaires were collected by the experimenters.

As mentioned in Chapter 1, Section 1.1.1, I did a pilot study by conducting a questionnaire survey on four native speakers at Lancaster University before the survey was applied to more informants. This survey investigated the acceptability of subject–/ object–oriented resultatives, with and without 把 ba, with test sentences and fillers included. The process was carried out as mentioned above. The informants read the informant sheet, and completed a consent form and a demographic sheet. Then they practised with ME, and finally judged the sentences. The results suggest that the subjects were able to use ME properly. Gradiece in the acceptability of 把 *ba*+subject–oriented resultatives was also illustrated.

There are two surveys for my research questions, namely the acceptability of Chinese subject–oriented resultatives (survey 1) and the acceptability of Chinese subject/object–oriented resultatives (survey 2). The two surveys were carried out under different circumstances. Survey 1 was mainly carried out by a professor during a lecture in China, and survey 2 was monitored by me in libraries and classrooms in Chinese colleges and Lancaster University. Those who did not sign a consent form yet still completed the questionnaire in Survey 1 were excluded. More about how the questionnaires were administered is described in Chapters 5 (survey 1) and 6 (survey 2), respectively.

For the analysis, the statistical method I adopt is to compare the mean scores of sentences rated by subjects by examining the means of p–values obtained through a t–test and ANOVA, the latter comparing scores among more than two groups. To be specific, data are calculated and analyzed in terms of mean, median and t–test between two groups in Excel, as well as ANOVA and post hoc tests (multiple comparisons) among groups of more than two in SPSS. After the standard deviation (z–score) is calculated in SPSS, further case selections are made in order to guarantee the validity of the data. In line with routine statistical analysis (Koestenberger et al. 2009), if a z–score is >3 or <–3, it is viewed as an extreme outlier. Since it cannot reflect the general trend, and will affect the result, it is excluded from the data for further analysis. Therefore, the data I present in the analyses are those which satisfy the condition –3<= *z-score*<=3. More will be explained in Chapters 5 and 6.

3.4 Concluding remarks

The methodology of this book makes a contribution to the scholarship on the Chinese language. It is the first attempt to apply magnitude estimation to sentence acceptability judgements in Chinese. The validity of this technique is hypothesized, which sheds light on the trend of integrating experiments with grammar research, and casts doubt on the traditional way of sentence judgements in terms of grammaticality based on linguists' intuition.

In addition, the combination of corpora and questionnaire surveys is a methodological contribution. There are advantages and disadvantages if research is solely based on one method. A corpus study on one topic (e.g. resultatives) could reflect the linguistic phenomenon in use. However, it is generally descriptive, and if there are no examples found in the corpus, it does not necessarily mean a sentence is unacceptable. On the other hand, the way of sentences being judged by linguists does not always hold true. The adoption of magnitude estimation brings new possibilities to research on grammar in Chinese linguistics. By obtaining certain examples from one or more corpora, and then carrying out questionnaire surveys based on these examples with designed parameters, a linguistic phenomenon can be studied more comprehensively, not only its description in use, but also with explanations and further predictions. Moreover, magnitude estimation can detect delicate but significant differences among sentences, which brings to light interesting phenomena missed by previous studies.

Chapter 4 A corpus study of Chinese resultatives

4.1 Introduction

4.1.1 Motivation for the corpus analysis of Chinese resultatives

As stated in Chapters 1 and 2, due to the unsolved issues in the literature, a corpus study of Chinese resultative constructions is necessary. My aim in this chapter is to conduct a corpus study of Chinese resultatives from a descriptive perspective.

As mentioned in Chapter 1, Section 1.1.1, in the Chinese literature on resultatives, (1) has been widely discussed regarding its ambiguous interpretations, first by generative linguists (e.g. Cheng and Huang 1994, Li 1995, Gao 1997), then by some cognitive linguists (cf. Shen 2004, Shi 2008, Zhao 2009). Whilst the debate may be theoretically interesting, I did not find any data in the corpus on 追－累 *zhui-lei* 'chase–tired'. Furthermore, my native speaker informants, including myself, do not find (1) natural. Thus a study of authentic resultatives seems to be in order.

(1)	淘淘	追–累–了	悠悠	(Li 1995: 257)
	Taotao	*zhui-lei-le*	*Youyou*	
	Taotao (name)	chase–tired–ASP	Youyou (name)	

a. Taotao chased Youyou and as a result Youyou was tired.

b. Taotao chased Youyou and as a result Taotao was tired.

c. Youyou chased Taotao and as a result Youyou was tired.

The second reason for analyzing corpus data is that, in the literature discussed in Chapter 2, Section 2.5, Chinese resultatives have been rarely discussed based on corpora, with only two papers found (Yang and Wang 2009, Luo et al. 2010). In comparison to earlier work, what I will do is to present a study of Chinese resultatives that looks at the data from a wider range of perspectives, and that starts from authentic Chinese data, rather than English adjectives.

The third motivation for this chapter, as mentioned in Chapert 1, Secion 1.1.1, is the inadequacy of the Online Database on Verb–Resultative Constructions in Contemporary Chinese (ODVRC). Although the ODVRC lists various patterns of result XPs, it is not a corpus and cannot show the whole picture of Chinese resultatives in use. In addition, as argued in Chapter1, Section 1.1.1, many of the patterns are arguably not resultatives, which requires a clearer definition and some tests to judge whether a sentence is a resultative construction. The tests to be discussed in Section 4.2.2 provide a method to identify Chinese resultatives.

4.1.2 Structure of the chapter

The remainder of this chapter consists of four parts. In Section 4.2, the methodology is discussed, including data collection from the Lancaster Corpus of Mandarin Chinese (LCMC), and the ODVRC–database. I discuss why certain patterns in the ODVRC do not count as resultatives and introduce two tests that can be used to identity genuine Chinese resultatives. Then, various criteria used in the analysis of the corpus data are explained. Section 4.3 deals with the results of my corpus analysis of the LCMC. I also examine how different criteria are linked with each other in terms of their distribution. Section 4.4 is a discussion. I consider how my findings differ from what has been discussed in the literature. Section 4.5 concludes this chapter.

4.2 Methodology

4.2.1 Corpus

As introduced in Chapter 3, Section 3.2, two corpora and a database will be used for the corpus study of Chinese resultatives, namely the LCMC (McEnery and Xiao 2004), the Center for Chinese Linguistics PKU (CCL) and the ODVRC (Zhan et al. 2015). The LCMC is adopted as the source to search for result XPs. Nevertheless, recalling the discussion of the LCMC in Chapter 3, its size at one million words may limit the research.

The CCL is a large comprehensive Chinese corpus with 63 million words of Contemporary Chinese. However, due to its lack of Parts of Speech (POS) tagging, it will be difficult to search for the required result XPs. Given the insufficiency of the LCMC, I refer to the CCL for more instances.

The ODVRC is employed as the basis for research. With 25,190 verb–complement items composed of 2,707 predicates/verbs and 579 adjectives or directionals, this database provides aboundant resultative instances (e.g. 2). However, as discussed in Chapter 3, other than result XPs, the ODVRC also include patterns which express directionals, potential and degree, and prepositions (Zhan et al. 2015). These complements are excluded from my research as they do not qualify as resultatives.

(2) 大 火 烧–坏–了 屋顶 (ODVRC)

da *huo* *shao-huai-le* *wuding*

big fire burn–break–ASP roof

'The big fire burned the roof and as a result the roof was broken.'

To be specific, among the 579 complements, 23 are directionals (e.g. 3), which are beyond the scope of this book for the reasons stated in Chapter 1, Section 1.1. That is, a directional focuses on the direction of the action denoted by the verb rather than the change of state of an NP.

(3) 他 拿–出 一 包 树种 (ODVRC)

ta *na-chu* *yi* *bao* *shuzhong*

he take–out one pack tree seads

'He took out a pack of tree seeds.'

46 complements in the ODVRC express the degree of a state, either

with a particle 得 *de* as in (4), or with the pattern 极–了 *ji–le* 'extreme–ASP' (extremely; see 5). Examples like these are formed with a preceding AP rather than a verb, so they do not express the result of an action. Four complements suggest potential or possibility of an action, which are formed as 得了 *de liao* 'can; possible', 不了 *bu liao* 'cannot; impossible' or start with the negative form 不 *bu* 'not' .[1] For instance, in (6) 不了 *bu liao* 'cannot' expresses the impossibility of the action 'meet' rather than a result. Five are prepositions (like 在 *zai* 'at; in' in 7) that denote the location of the NP. None of the complements mentioned above will be taken into account for my further study, since they are not resultatives, though they are listed in the ODVRC.

(4)	现在	我们	比	过去	好–得–多 (ODVRC)[2]
	xianzai	*women*	*bi*	*guoqu*	*hao-de-duo*
	now	we	compare	past	good–ASP–more

'Now we are much better than before.'

(5)	我们的	生活	简单–极–了	(ODVRC)
	womende	*shenghuo*	*jiandan-ji-le*	
	our	life	simple–extreme–ASP	

'Our life was extremely simple.'

(6)	我	今天	见–不了	他	了	(ODVRC)
	wo	*jintian*	*jian-bu liao*	*ta*	*le*	
	I	today	see–not liao	he	ASP	

'I cannot see him today.'

---

1 了 *liao/le* is a polyphone. Here used as the former, a particle meaning 'able'.

2 得 *de* is a particle indicating comparisons, which is used before an adjective.

(7) 电话	锁	在	一	个	木盒	里 (ODVRC)
dianhua	*suo*	*zai*	*yi*	*ge*	*mu he*	*li*
telephone	lock	at	one	CL	wooden case	in

'The telephone was locked in a wooden case.'

A resultative construction is structured as verb + result XP in Mandarin, where the result XP is a verb or an adjective which can indicate the state of an NP. Therefore, I searched for all the words suggested as being result XPs by the ODVRC in the LCMC, and picked out combinations of verb + result XP (verb/adjective) to form a database for further analysis. Nevertheless, apart from the complements presented above which I excluded from my data (discussed further in Section 4.3.1), there are some patterns that may be interpreted as resultatives, but they differ from examples such as (2). Therefore, some tests will be proposed to identify Chinese resultatives.

4.2.2 Two tests for the identification of Chinese resultatives

4.2.2.1 到 *dao* 'arrive; get': a resultative or not?

In the ODVRC 到 *dao* is analyzed as a result XP. It may occur after a verb as a preposition, for instance (8a), which is excluded from my search. It may also be used as in (8b). This is categorized as a 'preposition complement' in the ODVRC, similar to directionals like 来 *lai* 'come' and 去 *qu* 'go' , which I do not take into account either. More similar examples are like 跑–到 *pao-dao* 'run–to' (a place), 读–到 *du-dao* 'read–to' (a certain page).

(8) a. 他 数 到 五 (CCL 4.1)

ta *shu* *dao* *wu*

he count to five

'He counted to five'

b. 他 走–到 宿舍 (CCL 1.1)

ta *zou-dao* *sushe*

he walk–to dorm

'He walked to the dorm.'

买–到 *mai-dao* 'buy–get' in (9) is formed as verb + result XP; however, whether it should be interpreted as a resultative is worth discussing. If we construe (9a) as 'he bought the train ticket', 到 *dao* 'get' seems to play little role in the semantics, since there is no apparent difference between (9a) and (9b), both expressing 'he bought the ticket', though (9b) emphasizes the result of getting the ticket.

(9) a. 他 买–到–了 火车 票 (CCL 94.1)

ta *mai-dao-le* *huoche* *piao*

he buy–get–ASP train ticket

'He bought the train ticket.'

b. 他 买–了 火车 票

ta *mai-le* *huoche* *piao*

he buy–ASP train ticket

'He bought the train ticket.'

Nevertheless, if a negative form 没 *mei* 'not' is added, there will be an overt difference between买–到 *mai-dao* 'buy–get' in (10a) and买 *mai* 'buy' in (10b). (10a) is construed as 'he went to buy the ticket, but was unable to get one', whereas in (10b) he did not buy the ticket (without starting the action of buying). Since 到 *dao* 'get' in (10a) adds a piece of information to the action 买 *mai* 'buy' (suggesting the result of the action 'buy'), and indicates a change of state of the NP (the subject 他 *ta* 'he' getting the ticket), 买–到 *mai-dao* 'buy–get' could be viewed as a resultative. This implies that there is a semantic difference between 买–到 *mai-dao* 'buy–get' in (10a) and 买 *mai* 'buy', and the difference is highlighted when negated. So questions arise as to the function of 到 *dao* 'get' and whether 买–到 *mai-dao* 'buy–get' is a resultative.

(10) a. 他 没 买–到 火车 票

ta *mei* *mai-dao* *huoche* *piao*

he not buy–get train ticket

'He did not get the train ticket.'

b. 他 没 买 火车 票

ta *mei* *mai* *huoche* *piao*

he not buy train ticket

'He did not buy the train ticket.'

4.2.2.2 Two tests for identifying Chinese resultatives

Concerning the uncertainty of patterns like 买–到 *mai–dao* 'buy–get', we can take a close look at the definitions of resultatives in the scholarship. As mentioned in Chapter 2, Seciton 2.2.3, English resultative constructions are discussed in terms of event structure in semantics (e.g. Rappaport Hovav and Levin 2001, Broccias 2003, Croft 2012). Rappaport Hovav and Levin (2001) and Croft (2012) argue that the bare XP resultative (e.g. 11) has a simple event structure with temporal dependence. That is, the process denoted by the verb and the state presented by the result XP occur simultaneously (Rappaport Hovav and Levin 2001: 775). In (11), the process of freezing and that of becoming solid occur at the same time, so there is only one subevent in the bare XP resultative.

(11) The pond froze solid. (Rappaport Hovav and Levin 2001: 781)

Croft (2012) is in favour of a simple–event analysis of (11). As stated in Chapter 2, Section 2.2.2.7, he illustrates a graphic representation of (11), as in (12).

(12) The pond froze solid.

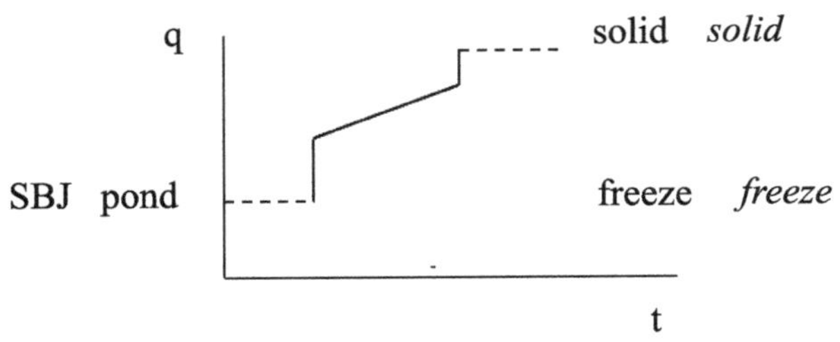

(Croft 2012: 329)

As proposed by Rappaport Hovav and Levin (2001) and Croft (2012), answering the question as to whether there are one or two subevents involved is not necessary for defining a resultative. There could be a single event, for instance, the bare resultative in English, which is analyzed with a simple event structure. As mentioned in Section 4.1 and above, a resultative construction (V + result XP) should be defined with the presence of a result XP denoting the result of a change of state or location of a referent of an NP, which is caused by the action denoted by the verb. Recall the example of 买–到 *mai-dao* 'buy–get' in Section 4.2.2.1, which may be construed as a single event of buying the ticket. However, when a negative form is added, the presence of 到 *dao* 'get' indicates a change of state of the NP (the subject 他 ta 'he' getting the ticket; recall the differences between没买–到 *mei mai-dao* 'not buy–get' and没买 *mei mai* 'not buy'). This suggests that 买–到 *mai-dao* 'buy–get' is different from 买 *mai* 'buy'. The result is caused by the action 'buy'. Consequently, 买–到 *mai-dao* 'buy–get' should be classified as a resultative in Mandarin.

However, V–到 *dao* 'get' is not as prototypical (prototype will be discussed further later in this section) as resultatives like 烧–坏 *shao-huai* 'burn–broken' mentioned in Section 4.2.1, since the former does not indicate a change of state of the NP as much as the latter does. V–到 *dao* 'get' may be viewed as a type of resultative undergoing a process of grammaticalization from verb to perfective (Chen 2008, Shi 2011). The original meaning of到 *dao* is 'to arrive' (e.g. 我到了 *wo dao le* 'I arrived'). Now it is widely used after verbs, such as 抓–到 *zhua-dao* 'grab–get' (catch), 寻找–到 *xunzhao-dao* 'look for–get' (find) and 学–到 *xue-dao* 'study–get' (learn), but not all of them can be viewed as resultatives. For instance, in (13a), we can see the change of state denoted by 到 *dao* 'get'. But in (13b) 到 *dao* 'get' is used in a similar way to a preposition, which suggests orientation of the action 'attract', not the result. Therefore (13b) is not a resultative. To sum up, we shall take semantics into account regarding various patterns with the form V + result XP. Some tests may be formulated to see whether a sentence is a resultative, rather than make judgements according to their form, or how many subevents are construed in a sentence.

(13) a. 他 寻找–到 一 个 拍摄 点 (LCMC E32)

ta xunzhao-dao yi ge paishe dian

he look for–get one CL shooting point

'He looked for (many places) and as a result found a place for shooting.'

b. 许多 语言学家 被 吸引–到 这 一 领域

xuduo yuyanxuejia bei xiyin-dao zhe yi lingyu

many linguists bei (passive) attract–to this one field

中 来 (LCMC J67)

zhong lai

middle come

'Many linguists were attracted into this field.'

With respect to plausible tests that can be employed to identify whether a sentence is a resultative or not, one to distinguish between implicative and non–implicative causatives (Hollmann 2003) can be revised and adopted. Among causative constructions, if a verb necessarily causes a lower clause event, it is implicative (e.g. make in 14a); if a verb may but need not lead to a lower clause event (e.g. *ask, order* in 14b), then it is nonimplicative. Tests are instantiated in (14).

(14) a. *I made him do it, but he didn't do it → X MAKE Y INF is implicative

b. I ordered him to do it, but he didn't do it →X ORDER Y to–INF is non–implicative

Derived from the tests in (14), similar ones can tentatively be used to identify resultative constructions. With respect to sentence (15), if there is a difference in acceptability between (16a) and (16b) such that (16a) is acceptable but (16b) is not, it means an action denoted by the verb is carried out and could (but does not necessarily) lead to a result (expressed by the result XP) referring to a change of state of an NP (subject or object in 16a). 'Subject (or object) not result–XP' in (16a) suggests the result could be caused by the action, and the result XP could be predicated of the subject/object denoting its change of state, coinciding with the definition of a resultative construction I propose. Hence (15) is a resultative. If (16a) and (16b) are unacceptable, it means the result XP may play no role in denoting a result led to by the action in (16b), since it cannot be predicated of the subject/object (as in 16b) to suggest a change of state. Consequently, (15) may not be a resultative. This is Test 1 (T1).

(15) subject V–result XP (object)

(16) a. subject V (object) but subject (or object) not result–XP.

b. *subject V–result XP (object) but subject (or object) not result–XP

If (15) cannot pass T1, it can be considered by adding the negative form 没 *mei* 'not' as in (17) to see whether there is a semantic difference between (17a) and (17b). If yes, as mentioned in Section 4.2.2.1, the semantic difference between with and without the result XP is brought to the fore by negating, which indicates the function of the result XP, namely denoting a change of state of an NP. This is in line with the definition of resultatives. Therefore (15) is a resultative, though the fact of being unable to pass T1 does make it different from those passing T1. Otherwise, if there is no semantic difference between (17a/b), (15) will not be considered a resultative due to the fact that the 'result XP' is unable to express a change of state caused by the action, since even negation cannot make the difference prominent. This is Test 2 (T2).

(17) a. subject 没 mei ‘not’ V (object)

b. subject 没 mei ‘not’ V–result XP (object)

We shall use some examples to support the validity of the tests. For the Chinese resultatives in (18a) and (19a), we can see in terms of T1 that both (18b) and (19b) are acceptable, whereas (18c) and (19c) are not, so (18a) and (19a) are resultatives.

(18) a.

她	哭–累–了 (CCL 13.1)
ta	*ku-lei-le*
she	cry–tired–ASP

‘She cried and as a result she was tired.’

b.

她	哭	了，	但	她	不	累
ta	*ku*	*le,*	*dan*	*ta*	*bu*	*lei*
she	cry	ASP,	but	she	not	tired

‘She cried but she was not tired.’

c.

*她	哭–累–了，	但	她	不	累
ta	*ku-lei-le*	*dan*	*ta*	*bu*	*lei*
she	cry–tired–ASP,	but	she	not	tired

‘She cried, tired, but she was not tired.’

(19) a.

她	擦–干–了	头发 (CCL 89.1)
ta	*ca-gan-le*	*toufa*
she	wipe–dry–ASP	hair

‘She wiped her hair dry.’

b. 她 擦-了 头发， 但 头发 没 干
ta ca -le toufa, dan toufa mei gan
she wipe–ASP hair, but hair not dry
'She wiped her hair but her hair was not dry.'

c. *她 擦-干-了 头发， 但 头发 没 干
ta ca -le toufa, dan toufa mei gan
she wipe–dry–ASP hair, but hair not dry
'She wiped her hair dry but her hair was not dry.'

Then, recall the pattern买-到 *mai-dao* 'buy–get' (see 20). In terms of T1, as in (21), both (21a) and (21b) are unacceptable as 到 *dao* 'get' cannot be predicated of the NP independently without a change in meaning, so we shall adopt T2, as in (22). As discussed in Section 4.2.2.1, (22a) and (22b) are construed differently semantically, the former suggesting he started the action of buying the ticket, the latter implying he wanted to buy a ticket but did not manage to get one. By adding the negative form没 *mei* 'not' as in (22), the function of 到 *dao* 'get' to denote a change of state of an NP can be perceived. Therefore (20) is a resultative construction.

(20) 他 买-到-了 火车 票 (CCL 94.1)
ta mai-dao-le huoche piao
he buy–get–ASP train ticket
'He bought the train ticket.'

(21) a. *他 买-了 火车 票， 但 他 没 到 票
ta mai-le huoche piao, dan ta mei dao piao

he buy–ASP train ticket, but he not get ticket

'He bought the train ticket but he did not get the ticket.'

b. *他 买–到–了 火车 票， 但 他 没 到 票

ta mai-dao-le huoche piao, dan ta mei dao piao

he buy–get–ASP train ticket, but he not get ticket

'He bought the train ticket but he did not get the ticket.'

(22) a. 他 没 买 火车 票

ta mei mai huoche piao

he not buy train ticket

'He did not buy the train ticket.'

b. 他 没 买–到 火车 票

ta mei mai-get huoche piao

he not buy–get train ticket

'He did not get the train ticket.'

A further issue is that there is an aspectual difference between 买 *mai* 'buy' and 买–到 *mai-dao* 'buy–get', as in (23). The adverb 正在 *zhengzai* 'in the process of', which indicates the progressive aspect, can only be used with the former (see 23a), not the latter (as in 23b).

(23) a. 一 位 老 大妈 正在 买 萝卜 (CCL 8.1)

yi wei lao dama zhengzai mai luobo

one CL old aunt in the progress of buy turnip

'An old aunt was buying turnips.'

b. *一 位 老 大妈 正在 买–到 萝卜

yi wei lao dama zhengzai mai-dao luobo

one CL old aunt in the progress of buy–get turnip

'An old aunt was buying and getting turnips.'

Vendler (1967) proposes four categories of verbs, namely state (situations that do not change over time, e.g. love), activity (situations changing over time, which are durative without a natural endpoint, e.g. sing), achievement (processes with an instantaneous change of state and, e.g. reach [the summit]) and accomplishment (processes that have a natural endpoint, read [a book]). Although the classification is arguable and not clear–cut, according to Croft (2012: 35), the four types hold true in a general sense. For instance, there is an apparent difference between love and sing, in that the former is static, while the latter describes an activity. Moreover, following Dahl (1986), Croft (2012: 37) also argues that a predicate does not belong to a single type. It can be construed in different aspectual types in various contexts.

In my opinion, if perceived carefully, 买 *mai* 'buy' in Chinese can be viewed as belonging to both accomplishment and activity types. That is, it can describe the process of buying something with the result of getting it (accomplishment), or just the action without necessarily a result (i.e. activity). In (23a), the aktionsart (i.e. kinds of actions, cf. Comrie 1976: 6–7) — also called lexical aspect (Olsen 1997, quoted in Tantucci 2015: 60) — of 'buy' is an activity, so it allows the aspectual marking 正在 *zhengzai* 'in the process of' to, express the progressive aspect. 买–到 *mai-dao* 'buy–get' in (23b), on the other hand, is instantaneous with a result achieved, so it cannot be modified by the progressive marking. This difference in aspect also provides evidence for distinguishing 买 *mai* 'buy' and 买–到 *mai-dao* 'buy–get'.

Another point to be noted is compositionality (Bybee 2010, Traugott & Trousdale 2013). It refers to the extent to which the link between form and meaning is transparent (Traugott & Trousdale 2013: 19). That is, how much the meaning of the whole form/construction is predictable from that of the component part (Bybee 2010: 45). From a constructional perspective, compositionality is viewed in terms of a match or mismatch between aspects of form and aspects of meaning. For example, the expression 'kick the bucket' means not only 'to kick' an item, but also 'to die'. There is a mismatch between the form and meaning of the construction. So the degree of compositionality of this construction is lower or less transparent than 'kick the ball'.

With respect to V–到 *dao* 'get' , as mentioned earlier, it is undergoing a process of grammaticalization, which result in a decrease in compositionality (Traugott & Trousdale 2013: 121). However, these words are not fully grammaticalized as 了 *le* 'ASP' in Chinese. When combined with verbs to form examples like 买/听–到 *mai/ting-dao* 'buy/listen–get' (buy/ hear), the compositionality of the construction is low. Then within the framework of construction grammar, the meaning is provided by a resultative construction such that a change of state of an NP ('I got the ticket') is caused by an action denoted by the verb (buy). In addition, Test 2 in (22) highlights the function of 到 *dao* 'get' express a result. Therefore V–到 *dao* 'get' is interpreted as a resultative in (20).

So, these two tests are used to judge whether a pattern suggested as a result XP in the ODVRC fits the definition of a resultative construction proposed in this book. More examples and further application of the tests will be illustrated in Section 4.3.1.2. One way to view the status of these resultatives is via the adoption of prototype theory (Rosch 1973, 1978; cf. Croft and Cruse 2004, Hollmann 2003). The main argument is that, within a category, not all members have the same status; some are more central than others. For instance, according to Rosch (1973), in the category [BIRD], robins are viewed as more central than penguins, and therefore the former are more prototypical than the latter. Prototype theory has been widely applied in various ways in cognitive linguistics, for instance frame semantics (Fillmore 1982), construction grammar (Goldberg 1995), and can shed light on the status of various Chinese resultatives.

Therefore, we may label patterns which pass T1 and can be predicated of an NP independently to suggest a change of state of an NP as prototypical resultatives, and those which only pass T2 and cannot be predicated of an NP on their own as marginal resultatives. More about prototypical and marginal resultatives in use will be stated in Sections 4.3 and 4.4. In general, prototypical resultatives are in high type and token frequency, whereas marginal resultatives are in low type frequency and high token frequency.

4.2.3 Criteria for corpus analysis: classifications of resultatives

After extraction from the LCMC, the sentences were analyzed in terms of type and token frequency, therefore the classification of resultatives is also taken as a methodology.

As discussed in Chapter 2, Section 2.2.2, resultative constructions are classified from various perspectives in the literature. To begin with, Washio (1997) proposes strong/weak/spurious resultatives. Formed as S–V–O–AP in English, in the strong type, the AP adds a piece of information to the verb which is not predictable from the meaning of the verb, for instance (24a/b). In the weak type, the AP and the verb are related semantically, but the former does not repeat the latter in meaning (e.g. 25a/b).

(24) a. The joggers ran the pavement thin. (Washio 1997: 7)

b. They pounded the metal flat.

(25) a. The river froze solid. (Washio 1997: 10)

b. She wiped the table clean.

With respect to spurious resultatives, Washio (1997) argues that the AP specifies the result caused by the manner of the action, which is interchangable with the corresponding adverb without a change in meaning, for example (26a/b).

(26) a. He tied his shoelaces loose/loosely. (Washio 1997: 17)

b. He cut the meat thick/thickly.

Rappaport Hovav and Levin (2001) propose two types of resultatives in English, subject–oriented and object–oriented, the two differing in whether the result XP is predicated of the subject (27a) or object (27b/c). Moreover, they classify English resultatives into transitive–based (as in 27a/b) and intransitive–based (e.g. 27c).

(26) a. The wise men followed the star out of Bethlehem.

(Rappaport Hovav and Levin 2001:770)

b. The police shot the robber to death.

c. The joggers ran the pavement thin. (Washio 1997: 7)

From the examples above, we can see that there are differences as well as overlaps among the classifications. For example, (27c) belongs to the strong type, but is also object–oriented and intransitive–based. These categories will be adopted as criteria for the corpus analysis.

4.3 A corpus study of Chinese resultatives: results

4.3.1 Preliminaries

As mentioned in Section 4.2.1, there are 579 complements listed in the ODVRC. However, except for patterns labelled as directionals, complements expressing potential and degree, and prepositions, some other items are worth discussing, some of which will not be searched for in the LCMC, though they all share the same form as verb + result XP.

4.3.1.1 Patterns in the ODVRC to be excluded

4.3.1.1.1 Completives

A few patterns suggested as resultatives in the ODVRC are formed as V + adjective/verb, such as 完 *wan* 'finish' (see 28), 罢 *ba* 'finish' and 好 *hao* 'good'. V–完 *wan* 'finish' is regarded as a resultative, since完 *wan* 'finish' can denote the state of the NP caused by an action. For instance, (28a) can be interpreted as 'they ate the meal and as a result the meal was finished', with 完 *wan* 'finish' indicating the state of the object 饭 *fan* 'meal'. However, in (28b) we can see that 完 *wan* 'finish' simply suggests completion of the action 说 *shuo* 'speak' without a resultative reading.

(28) a. 他们 吃–完–了 饭 (LCMC K05 9)

tamnen *chi-wan-le* *fan*

they eat–finish–ASP meal

'They finished eating the meal.'

b. 说–完 爷俩 退出 书房 (LCMC N13 40)

shuo-wan *yelia* *tuichu* *shufang*

speak–finish the father and the son exit study

'After finishing speaking the father and the son exited the study.'

In the literature, there is a difference between completives and resultatives (cf. Bybee et al. 1994, Chen 2008, Tantucci 2015). Bybee et al. (1994: 104) argue that resultative constructions denote 'a state that was brought about by some action in the past', can be used with still and only with telic verbs. For instance, *is closed in the door is closed* is a resultative construction from Bybee's viewpoint. On the other hand, completives means *to do something thoroughly and to completion*, such as *to shoot someone dead or to eat up* (Bybee et al. 1994: 54, cited by Tantucci 2015: 65). For instance, the Chinese particle 了 *liao/le*, a completive phrasal marker, originates from a verb meaning *to complete/ finish*. We shall not adopt the definition of resultatives suggested by Bybee et al. (1994), since it ignores the presence of the result XP. However, we can see the differences between completives and resultatives, and thus distinguish the two.

Xiao (2002: 217) also differentiates between completion and the result state of a situation. He argues that since a result is achieved when an action is completed, a completive is implied by a resultative, which makes the two similar. However, the two differ in their focus. Completives focus on completion and may imply result states, whereas resultatives emphasize the result of an event and imply completion.

According to Chen (2008: 96), completives such as 完 *wan* 'finish' (in 29a) and 好 *hao* 'good' (29c) in Mandarin suggest the conclusion of an action without a result, whereas resultatives such as 到 *dao* 'get' and 见 *jian* 'see' indicate not only the completion of an action, but also a result caused by an action. For instance, in (28a), repeated below as in (29a), though 完 *wan* 'finish' may be predicated of the object 饭 *fan* 'meal', it does not refer to its state (it does not really mean the meal was finished) but rather denotes completion of the action 吃 *chi* 'eat'. A similar pattern V–罢 *ba* 'finish' in (29b) is in the same situation as (28b). There is no object following, and then another clause follows the previous sentence. So V–罢 *ba* 'finish' is also viewed as a completive. In (29c), 好 *hao* 'good' indicates the completion of the action 'buy', since it cannot refer to either 他 *ta* 'he' or 票 *piao* 'ticket'; none of the NPs became good as a result of the action 'buy'.

(29) a. 他们　　吃–完–了　　饭 (LCMC K05 9)

tamnen　　*chi-wan-le*　　*fan*

they　　eat–finish–ASP　　meal

'They finished eating the meal'.

b. 说–罢　　站　　起来 (LCMC G28 3)

shuo-ba　　*zhan*　　*qilai*

speak–finish　　stand　　up

'(Someone) finished speaking, then stood up.'

c. 她 买–好–了 火车 票 (LCMC F12 1)

ta *mai-hao-le* *huoche* *piao*

he buy–good–ASP train ticket

'She bought the train ticket.'

A pattern V–成 *cheng* 'become; successful; complete' is worth considering. When meaning 'become' as in (30), it is not a resultative, since 成 *cheng* 'become' does not refer to the a change of state of the NP 小麦 *xiaomai* 'wheat'. In (30) the NP is processed into different material. Therefore, V–成 *cheng* with the meaning 'become' will not be viewed as a resultative.

(30) 小麦 加工 成 面粉 时 (LCMC J35 3)

xiaomai *jiagong* *cheng* *mianfen* *shi*

wheat process become flour when

'When the wheat is processed and becomes flour (when the wheat is processed into flour)'

Nevertheless, if in the meaning 'successful, complete' as in (31) and (32), 成 *cheng* is similar to 完 *wan* 'finish' and 好 *hao* 'good', since they all express the completion of an action (Shi 2011: 134). In (31) and (32), 成 *cheng* 'successful; complete' and 完 *wan* 'finish' or 好 *hao* 'good' are interchangeable without many differences in meaning, though 成 *cheng* 'successful; complete' and 好 *hao* 'good' may suggest the action is completed in a satisfactory way, whereas 完 *wan* 'finish' merely denotes completion of the action. Therefore, V–成 *cheng* will not be considered a resultative.

(31) 初 稿 写–成 后 (LCMC G25 3)

chu *gao* *xie-cheng* *hou*

first　　draft　　write-complete　　after

'After the first draft was completed'

(32) 总算　　画-成-了　　(LCMC P24 3)

zongsuan　　*hua-cheng-le*

finally　　paint-complete-ASP

'Finally completed painting.'

To sum up, completives and resultatives should be discriminated, and the patterns discussed above are excluded from my data.

4.3.1.1.2 Patterns in the ODVRC failing the two tests

As mentioned in Section 4.2.1, some complements starting with the negative form 不 *bu* 'not' are complements expressing the possibility of an action. Nevertheless, some are classified as resultatives in the ODVRC, such as 不错 *bu cuo* 'not bad' (see 33), 不止 bu zhi 'not stop'. In (33) 不错 *bu cuo* 'not bad' modifies the action 'perform' rather than illustrating a result. Patterns like this do not express a change of state of an NP, hence they are not resultatives.

(33) 中国　　女　　队　　发挥-不错　　(ODVRC)

zhongguo　　*nv*　　*dui*　　*fahui-bu cuo*

Chinese　　female　　team　　perform-not bad

'Chinese female team performed well.'

Some adjectives can be used with verbs, but the combinations of verb + AP do not have resultative interpretations. For instance, in the ODVRC, 迟钝 *chidun* 'obtuse' can only be used with 变 *bian* 'become' (e.g. 34). However, there is no resultative reading in (34), since 变 *bian* 'become' simply suggests a change of state of the NP 舌头 *shetou* 'tongue' without referring to an action (although 变 *bian* ‘become’ is a verb, it does not denote a specific action which can cause a change of state). Items used with 变 *bian* ‘become’ include 缓 *huan* ‘slow’, 厉害 *lihai* ‘cruel’ and so forth, the number of which is counted as 68. And there are no instances of the 68 patterns used as resultatives in the LCMC.

(34) 舌头 变–迟钝–了
shetou *bian-chidun-le*
tongue become–obtuse–ASP
‘Tongue became obtuse.’

入 *ru* ‘enter; in’ is suggested to be a result XP in the ODVRC. 入 *ru* ‘enter; in’ is a verb, but usually follows other verbs, as in 跑–入 *pao-ru* ‘run–in’ (run into a place), 放–入 *fang-ru* ‘put–enter’ (put in), and rarely occurs independently (only in 入了党 *ru le dang* ‘enter ASP party’; join in the party). According to the ODVRC, the patterns with 入 ru ‘enter; in’ are either directional complements (e.g. 刺–入 *ci-ru* ‘pierce–in’, 买–入 *mai-ru* ‘buy–in’ ‘buy’) or resultatives, such as 放–入 *fang-ru* ‘put–enter’ (put in), 掺–入 *chan-ru* ‘mix–in’ (mix). It is not clear on what basis the former are classified as directionals, whereas the latter are resultatives, since 入 ru ‘enter’ may suggest the direction of a movement or the direction of an action (e.g. 放–入 *fang-ru* ‘put–in’) but does not necessarily indicate the direction in 买–入 *mai-ru* ‘buy–in’ (buy). Now we will look at the examples found in the LCMC with the two tests.

In (35), since 入 *ru* ‘enter; in’ cannot be predicated of the NP 大厦 *dasha* ‘building’, it will fail T1. Regarding T2, there is no difference between (36a) and (36b), both suggesting ‘he did not buy the embassy building first.’

Therefore 买–入 *mai-ru* 'buy–in' (buy) is not a resultative.

(35) 他 首先 买–入 使馆 大厦 (LCMC G52 5)

ta shouxian mai-ru shiguan dasha

he first buy–in embassy building

'He bought the embassy building first.'

(36) a. 他 首先 没 买 使馆 大厦

ta shouxian mei mai shiguan dasha

he first not buy embassy building

'He did not buy the embassy building first.'

b. 他 首先 没 买–入 使馆 大厦

ta shouxian mei mai-ru shiguan dasha

he first not buy–in embassy building

'He did not buy the embassy building first.'

There are two situations with the pattern 放–入 *fang-ru* 'put–in'. Firstly, as in (37), since there is a postposition 内 nei 'inside' demonstrating the location, 入 *ru* 'enter; in' should be viewed as a directional which indicates the orientation of the action 放 *fang* 'put'. Secondly, in (38a) the location is sentence–initial. Then a similar sentence as in (39a) is found in the LCMC, which is without 入 *ru* 'in' but interpreted the same as (38a). Or if construed carefully, (38a) may suggest the direction of the action, while (39a) may not. In addition, since 入 *ru* 'in' cannot be used as a verb, (38a) will fail T1. Then if the negative form 没 *mei* 'not' is added, there is no difference between (38b) and (39b). Hence 放–入*fang-ru* 'put–in' cannot be verified as a resultative. The tests are applied to other examples with 入ru 'in' and lead to similar results, which exclude V–入 *ru* 'in' from resultatives as a whole.

(37) 将 配料 放–入 碗 内 (LCMC E11 82)
jiang peiliao fang-ru wan nei
with ingredient put–in bowl inside
'Put the ingredients into the bowl.'

(38) a. 炒锅 内 放–入 植物 油 (LCMC E11 90)
chao guo nei fang-ru zhiwu you
frying pan inside put–in vegetable oil
'Put the vegetable oil into the frying pan.'

b. 炒锅 内 没 放–入 植物 油
chao guo nei mei fang-ru zhiwu you
frying pan inside not put–in vegetable oil
'The vegetable oil is not put into the frying pan.'

(39) a. 锅 内 放 植物 油 (LCMC E11 193)
guo nei fang zhiwu you
pan inside put vegetable oil
'Put the vegetable oil into the pan.'

b. 锅 内 没 放 植物 油
guo nei mei fang zhiwu you
pan inside not put vegetable oil
'The vegetable oil is not put into the pan.'

In sum, none of the patterns mentioned above is in line with the definition of resultatives in this book, thereby they are excluded from further analysis.

4.3.1.2 Patterns in the ODVRC failing one of the tests

As discussed in Section 4.2.2, uncertain items can be verified by two tests. It is not uncommon that for the same result XP, combinations with various verbs can lead to different results. To begin with, considering the pattern 住 *zhu* 'hold' as in (40), we can see that in terms of T1, both (41a) and (41b) are unacceptable, since 住 *zhu* 'hold' cannot be used as a predicate of the NP 我们 *women* 'us' with the same meaning (this may suggest patterns like 住 *zhu* 'hold' and 到 *dao* 'get' are undergoing a process of grammaticalization but are not as fully grammaticalized as the past–tense marker 了 le 'ASP'). Then we come to T2, as in (42). From my point of view, both (42a) and (42b) are construed as 'this piece of news did not attract us' without any apparent difference. As a result, 吸引–住 *xiyin-zhu* 'attract–hold' may not be viewed as a resultative.

(40) 这 个 新闻 吸引–住–了 我们 (LCMC K26 3)
zhe ge xinwen xiyin-zhu-le women
this CL news attract–hold–ASP us
'This piece of news attracted us.'

(41) a. *这 个 新闻 吸引–了 我们，但 我们 没 住
zhe ge xinwe xiyin-le women, dan women mei zhu
this CL news attract–ASP us, but we not hold
'This piece of news attracted us, but we were not held.'

b. *这 个 新闻 吸引–住–了 我们，但 我们

zhe ge xinwen xiyin-zhu-le women, dan women

this CL News attract–hold–ASP us, but we

没 住

mei zhu

not hold

'This piece of news attracted us, but we were not held.'

(42) a. 这 个 新闻 没 吸引 我们

zhe ge xinwen mei xiyin women

this CL news not attract us

'This piece of news did not attract us.'

b. 这 个 新闻 没 吸引–住 我们

zhe ge xinwen mei xiyin-zhu women

this CL news not attract–hold us

'This piece of news did not attract us.'

Nevertheless, the pattern 扶–住 *zhu* 'hold; stop' in (43) will be regarded differently. Both (44a) and (44b) are unacceptable in T1 (住 *zhu* 'hold' cannot be used as a predicate of the NP 姑娘 *guniang* 'the girl'). Then considering T2, as in (45), the difference between (45a) and (45b) is similar to that for 买–到 *mai-dao* 'buy–get'. (45a) is construed as 'the chop did not help the girl by propping her', whereas (45b) is interpreted as 'the chap propped (or tried to prop) the girl, but was unable to prop her up'. Therefore, 扶–住 *fu-zhu* 'prop–hold' is used as a resultative. So with the same result XP, sentences will be judged differently according to semantics.

(43) 小伙子 扶–住 姑娘 (LCMC R09 3)

xiaohuozi *fu-zhu* *guniang*

chap prop–hold girl

'The chap propped up the girl.'

(44) a. *小伙子 扶–了 姑娘, 但 姑娘 没 住

xiaohuozi *fu-le* *guniang,* *dan* *guniang* *mei* *hold*

chap prop–ASP girl, but girl not hold

'The chap propped up the girl, but the girl was not held.'

b. *小伙子 扶–住–了 姑娘, 但 姑娘 没 住

xiaohuozi *fu-zhu-le* *guniang,* *dan* *guniang* *mei* *hold*

chap prop–hold–ASP girl, but girl not hold

'The chap propped up the girl, but the girl was not held.'

(45) a. 小伙子 没 扶 姑娘

xiaohuozi *mei* *fu* *guniang*

chap not prop girl

'The chap did not prop the girl.'

b. 小伙子 没 扶–住 姑娘

xiaohuozi *mei* *fu-zhu* *guniang*

chap not prop–hold girl

'The chap did not prop up the girl.'

Second, 见 *jian* 'see' is suggested by the ODVRC as a result XP. 见 *jian* 'see' can be used as a predicate of an NP, as in (46a). However, it also appears in disyllabic words, such as 参见 *can-jian* 'refer to', 遇见 *yu-jian* 'come across'. For a resultative construction V–result XP, the verb should be able to be predicated of an NP, whereas a result XP may or may not be. If a verb cannot be used separately with an NP but has to be combined with another word to express a meaning, then we can see that the pattern V–result XP is used as a word or verb, rather than a resultative construction. Consequently, the patterns 参见 *can-jian* 'refer to', 遇见 *yu-jian* 'come across' are judged to be disyllabic verbs rather than combinations of lexical items as (46c) is unacceptable. 参 *can*, 遇 *yu* has to be combined with 见 *jian* 'see' to express a meaning. In (46), 遇 *yu* 'meet' as a morpheme cannot be used as a verb, nor can it be followed by the aspect marker 了 *le* (see 46c). Shi (2011: 30) also suggests that patterns like 遇见*yu-jian* ' come across' are verbs.

(46) a.

我	见	过	他
wo	*jian*	*guo*	*ta*
I	see	ASP	he

'I have seen him.'

b.

我	遇见	一	个	同学 (LCMC B19 1)
wo	*yujian*	*yi*	*ge*	*tongxue*
I	came across	one	CL	classmate

'I came across a classmate'

c.

*我	遇/遇 了	一	个	同学
wo	*yu/yu le*	*yi*	*ge*	*tongxue*
I	meet/meet ASP	one	CL	classmate

'I met a classmate'

However, there are some patterns of V–见 *jian* 'see' that may be viewed as between resultatives and complex verbs, since the first part V can be used as a predicate on its own, and the following 见 *jian* 'see' emphasizes the result, though one may construe the combination of V–见 *jian* 'see' as a verb. For instance, 看 *kan* 'look' can be used as a verb as in (47a), which makes it possible to form a resultative with V–见 *jian* 'see' like (47b). Then we can adopt the tests below.

(47) a. 你 看

ni *kan*

you look

'Look!'

b. 我 看–见–了 花 (LCMC G39 3)

wo *kan-jian-le* *hua*

I look–see–ASP flower

'I saw flowers'.

Similar to 买–到 *mai-dao* 'buy–get' mentioned before, in terms of T1, (48a) and (48b) are unacceptable. Nevertheless, when tested as in (49), both (49a) and (49b) are acceptable, though with differences in semantics: the former meaning 'I did not look at flowers', whereas the latter is 'I did not see flowers'. So 见 *jian* 'meet; see' expresses the result caused by the action 看 *kan* 'look'. The semantic differences between (49a) and (49b) validate the status of 看–见 *kan-jian* 'see' as a resultative. Similar tests can be applied to 听–见 *ting-jian* 'listen–see' (hear), 望–见 *wang-jian* 'watch–see' (see), 瞧–见 *qiao-jian* 'look–see' (see), all of which are resultatives.

(48) a. *我 看–了 花， 但 我 没 见 花

wo kan-le hua, dan wo mei jian hua

I look–ASP flower, but I not see flower

'I looked at flowers, but I did not see flowers.'

b. *我 看–见–了 花， 但 我 没 见 花

wo kan-jian-le hua, dan wo mei jian hua

I look–see–ASP flower, but I not see flower

'I saw flowers, but I did not see flowers.'

(49) a. 我 没 看 花

wo mei kan hua

I not look flower

'I did not look at flowers.'

b. 我 没 看–见 花

wo mei kan-jian hua

I not look–see flower

'I did not see flowers.'

Third, V–掉 *diao* 'drop; disappear' is listed in the ODVRC as a result XP, and the examples found in the LCMC should be analyzed in detail. 掉 *diao* 'drop; disappear' cannot be predicated of an NP. For example, in (50), 故障掉–了 *guzhang diao-le* 'trouble disappear–ASP' (the trouble disappeared) is unacceptable, hence the application of T1 to (50a) will fail. Then regarding T2, as in (50b/c), there is no difference between with and without 掉 *diao* 'disappear', therefore, (50) is not judged as a resultative. Similarly, 抛–掉 *pao-diao*'throw–disappear' (throw away)，脱–掉 *tuo-diao*'strip–drop' (take away), 否定–掉 *fouding-diao* 'deny–disappear' (deny) are excluded from resultatives.

(50) a. 我们 很快 就 把 故障 排除–掉 (LCMC C06 36)
women henkuai jiu ba guzhang paichu-diao
we quickly then *ba* trouble eliminate–disappear
'Then we quickly eliminated the trouble.'

b. 我们 没 很快 把 故障 排除
women mei henkuai ba guzhang paichu
we not quickly *ba* trouble eliminate
'We did not quickly eliminate the trouble.'

c. 我们 没 很快 把 故障 排除–掉
women mei henkuai ba guzhang paichu-diao
we not quickly *ba* trouble eliminate–disappear
'We did not quickly eliminate the trouble.'

However, there are some cases where 掉 *diao* 'drop; disappear' can have a different construal. For instance, in (51), since 掉 *diao* 'drop; disappear' cannot be used on its own with the NP 面膜 *mainmo* 'mask', it will fail T1. In T2, as in (52), we can see there is a difference between (52a) and (52b). So (51) is classified as a resultative construction. The other patterns like 刮–掉 *gua-diao*'scrape–drop', 咬–掉 *yao-diao* 'bite–drop' (bite off), 吃–掉 *chi-diao*'eat–disappear' (eat up) are all attested to be resultatives for the same reason.

(51) 面膜 用 冷 水 洗–掉 (LCMC E07 11)
mianmo yong leng shui xi-diao
mask use cold water wash–disappear

'The mask was washed off with cold water.'

(52) a. 面膜 没 用 冷 水 洗

mianmo mei yong leng shui xi

mask not use cold water wash

'The mask was not washed with cold water.'

b. 面膜 没 用 冷 水 洗–掉

mianmo mei yong leng shui xi-diao

mask not use cold water wash–disappear

'The mask was not washed off with cold water.'

Fourth, according to the ODVRC, two patterns are resultatives, namely 走 *zou* 'walk; leave' and 开 *kai* 'open; separate'. These two act as main verbs in the meaning of 'walk' and 'open', respectively (both are polysemy, but this is irrelevant here), as in (53a) and (54a). However, when used after a verb as in (53b) and (54b), they cannot be predicated of the NP on their own. If tested by T1, both will fail. However, in terms of T2, similar to the previous examples, there are semantic differences between without and with the result XP when the negative form 没 *mei* 'not' is added (see 53c vs. 53d; 54c vs. 54d). Examples like (53b) and (54b) are construed as having causative meaning.

(53) a. 他 走 过来 (LCMC F29 190)

ta zou guolai

he walk over come

'He came over.'

b. 村干部 拉–走 猪子 (LCMC F26 3)

cunganbu la-zou zhuzi

village cadre pull–leave pig

'The village cadre pulled the pig and caused the pig to leave.' (The village cadre pulled the pig away.)

c. 村干部 没 拉 猪子

cunganbu *mei* *la* *zhuzi*

village cadre not pull pig

'The village cadre did not pull the pig.'

d. 村干部 没 拉–走 猪子

cunganbu *mei* *la-zou* *zhuzi*

village cadre not pull–leave pig

'The village cadre did not pull the pig so as to cause the pig to leave.' (The village cadre did not pull the pig away.)

(54) a. 那 女人 开 了 门 (CCL 6.1)

na *nvren* *kai* *le* *men*

that woman open ASP door

'That woman opened the door.'

b. 要 挑–开 电源 (LCMC F35 2)

yao *tiao-kai* *dianyuan*

will raise–separate electric source

'Will raise the electric source (wire) so as to separate it.'

c. 不 要 挑 电源

bu *yao* *tiao* *dianyuan*

not will raise electric source

'Do not raise the electric source (wire).'

d. 不 要 挑–开 电源

bu yao tiao-kai dianyuan

not will raise–separate electric source

'Do not raise the electric source (wire) so as to separate it.'

In terms of another pattern, V–满 *man* 'full', as in (55a), the subject refers to a location, which means there is no agent in the sentence. V–满 *man* 'full' is regarded as a resultative since it can be interpreted as 'an action is carried out and as a result it makes something (e.g. a place) full'. There is a difference between without and with满 *man* 'full' in (55b) and (55c): the former suggests people stood on the step, whereas the latter indicates people stood on the step, causing it to be full of people. We could perceive the result 'full' as caused by the action 'stand'. Or if tested by T1 as in (55b) and (55c), we can see (55b) is acceptable, but (55c) is not. Viewed in this way, V–满 *man* 'full' should be regarded as a resultative. One point to be noted is that although V–满 *man* 'full' can pass T1, it differs from the prototypical resultatives, since the former indicates a change of state of a location, whereas the latter designates that of an argument (e.g. agent or patient).

(55) a. 台阶 上 站–满–了 观望 的 人(LCMC A29 1)

taijie shang zhan-man-le guanwang de ren

step on stand–full–ASP watch POSS people

'People who were watching stood on the step and as a result it was full of people.'

b. 台阶 上 站–了 观望 的 人, 但

taijie shang zhan-le guanwang de ren, dan

step on stand–ASP watch POSS people, but
台阶 没 满
taijie mei man
step not full
"People who were watching stood on the step but it was not full of people.'

c. *台阶 上 站–满–了 观望 的 人， 但
taijie shang zhan-man-le guanwang de ren, dan
step on stand–full–ASP watch POSS people, but
台阶 没 满
taijie mei man
step not full
'People who were watching stood on the step and as a result it was full of people, but it was not full'.

Taking into account what has been mentioned in Section 4.2.1 and before, altogether 194 patterns will be excluded from my data, since they are not resultatives I shall discuss in this book. I searched for the remaining 385 result XPs in the LCMC, firstly querying the result XP, for instance 饱 *bao* 'full', and then clicking 'sort' by choosing '1 left' with 'v' tag to get all the sentences of the verb + 饱 *bao* 'full'. Afterwards I selected resultative constructions manually. Among the 385 result XPs suggested by the ODVRC, 138 patterns used as resultatives were found in the LCMC, whereas 247 could not be found with such a usage in the LCMC. So my data are collected based on 138 result XPs. One point to be noted is why so many result XPs cannot be found in the

LCMC. I assume it is caused by the size of the corpus. One million words may not be enough to include all result XPs. Nevertheless, with the 138 patterns there are 1,332 examples of resultatives extracted from the LCMC, which is sufficient to reflect the usage of Chinese resultatives from a descriptive viewpoint.

4.3.2 Classification of Chinese resultatives and more dimensions

Based on the classification introduced in Section 4.2.3, according to Rappaport Hovav and Levin (2001), Chinese resultatives can be divided into subject–oriented (see 56; a change of state refers to the subject 他 *ta* 'he') and object–oriented, as in (57), with the result XP 干 *gan* 'dry' predicated of the object 头发 *toufa* 'hair'. Meanwhile, Chinese resultative constructions can be intransitive–based, as in (56), which is subject–oriented, and transitive–based like (57), object–oriented. Subject–oriented resultatives in Chinese can also be transitive–based, as in (58).

(56) 他 走–累–了 (CCL 2.1)

ta *zou-lei-le*

he walk–tired–ASP

'He walked and as a result he was tired.'

(57) 她 擦–干–了 头发 (CCL 89.1)

ta *ca-gan-le* *toufa*

she wipe–dry–ASP hair

'She wiped her hair dry.'

(58) 我 听–懂–了 他的 话 (CCL 14.1)

wo *ting-dong-le* *tade* *hua*

I listen–understand–ASP his words

'I listened to his words and as a result I understood them.'

Based on Washio's (1997) classification, Chinese resultative constructions can be divided into weak (see 59), strong (e.g. 60–62) and spurious, as in (63). In (59), the result XP 净 *jing* 'clean' is implied in the meaning of the main verb 洗 *xi* 'wash', so it belongs to the weak type. Regarding the strong type, for instance (60), the result XP 累 *lei* 'tired' cannot be predicted from the meaning of the verb 走 *zou* 'walk', similarly for (61) and (62): 湿 *shi* 'wet' and 懂 *dong* 'understand' are not predictable from 哭 *ku* 'cry' and 听 *ting* 'listen', respectively. In (63), as the result XP 紧 *jin* 'tight' denotes the manner of the action 系 *ji* 'tie', it is classified as a spurious resultative.

(59) 雨 洗–净–了 小桥 (LCMC N18)

yu *xi-jing-le* *xiaoqiao*

rain wash–clean–ASP little bridge

'Rain washed the little bridge clean.'

(60) 他 走–累–了 (CCL 2.1)

ta *zou-lei-le*

he walk–tired–ASP

'He walked and as a result he was tired.'

(61) 妹妹 哭–湿–了 手绢 (CCL 1.1)

meimei *ku-shi-le* *shoujuan*

younger sister cry–wet–ASP handkerchief

'The younger sister cried and as a result the handkerchief was wet.' (The younger sister cried the handkerchief wet)

(62) 我 听–懂–了 他的 话 (CCL 14.1)

wo *ting-dong-le* *tade* *hua*

I listen–understand–ASP his words

'I listened to his words and as a result I understood them.'

(63) 我 系–紧 鞋带 (CCL 48.1)

wo *ji-jin* *xiedai*

I tie–tight shoelace

'I tied the shoelaces tight/ tightly.'

From the examples we can see there are overlaps among the classifications. The resultatives can be transitive–based, as in (59), (62) and (63), and intransitive–based, as in (60) and (61). That is to say, a weak one like (59) is transitive–based, and strong ones can be intransitive–based, like (60) and (61), and transitive–based as in (62). The subject–oriented type like (60) and (62) are strong resultatives, and the object–oriented type can be both weak, like (59), and strong, as in (61).

The spurious type as in (63) is worth discussing. According to Washio (1997), they are considered to be spurious in that they share the same form as genuine resultatives, like S–V–O–AP in English. This holds true in Mandarin, both being formed as S–V–AP–O. Therefore in the literature, many discussions on Chinese resultatives are based on this form, which include spurious resultatives. If we take into account the definition of resultatives and make sophisticated assessments of these sentences, we can see why they are called spurious. This can be instantiated by V–紧 *jin* 'tight' in (64). Washio (1997) suggests that the AP in a spurious resultative modifies the manner of the action, though seemingly the AP is related to the postverbal NP. In (64a) 紧 *jin* 'tight' can refer to the manner of the action 'bite', or the object 'lip'. Therefore 紧 *jin* 'tight' in (64a) will be viewed as a word with an adverbial function, which makes (64a) a spurious resultative. Though a resulting state of becoming tight can be construed in (64a), it is natural since in an activity like biting one's lip, the manner of the action can lead to such a result.

(64) a. 她 咬–紧 下唇 (LCMC N21 1)

ta yao-jin xiachun

she bite–tight underlip

'She bit her underlip tight/tightly.'

b. 她 咬 下唇，但 下唇 不 紧

ta yao xiachun, dan xiachun bu jin

she bite underlip, but underlip not tight

'She bit her underlip, but the underlip was not tight.'

c. *她 咬–紧 下唇，但 下唇 不 紧

ta yao-jin xiachun, dan xiachun bu jin

she bite–tight underlip, but underlip not tight

'She bit her underlip tight/tightly, but the underlip was not tight.'

With respect to the application of the two tests to the spurious type, (64a), being able to pass T1 as in (64b/c) above suggests that 咬–紧 *yao-jin* 'bite–tight' possesses some features of resultatives. Nevertheless, its semantics concerns whether it modifies the verb or the NP, which makes it different from the resultatives in (59–62).

This is also the case with V–准 *zhun* 'accurate' in (65), V–清 *qing* 'clear' in (66) and V–错 *cuo* 'wrong' in (67). 准 *zhun* literally means the result of an action lives up to one's expectations. With regard to (65), in the activity of choosing a position, the action will lead to a result of finding one. 准 *zhun* 'accurate' modifies the action 'choose' , and the change of state is caused by the manner of the action. Therefore, (65) is labelled as spurious. As regards V–清 *qing* 'clear', it could be predicated of the subject in (66), but also the manner of the action 'see', which matters. That is, the way the subject 'sees' leads to the result that 'I' was not clear. With respect to错 *cuo* 'wrong' in (67), the manner of the action 'cut' still leads to a wrong result. Though 错 *cuo* 'wrong' could be predicated of the subject, it is directly related to the action, which is carried out by the subject 你 *ni* 'you'. Therefore 错 *cuo* 'wrong' could refer to the subject, but in an indirect way. Clearly, it is a spurious type. In sum, I shall include sentences like the patterns mentioned above in my data, but analyze them separately from the other resultatives.

(65) 选–准 钓位 后 (LCMC E02 1)

xuan-zhun *diaowei* *hou*

choose–accurate fishing position after

'After choosing a right fishing position'

(66) 我 当时 没 看–清 (LCMC L09 6)

wo *dangshi* *mei* *kan-qing*

I at that time no see–clear

'I did not see clearly at that time.'

(67) 你 这 一 刀 砍–错–了 (LCMC N04 20)

ni zhe yi dao kan-cuo-le

you this one knife cut–wrong–ASP

'You made a wrong cut.'

The categories proposed in the literature are thus subject/object–oriented resultatives, transitive/intransitive–based resultatives (Rappaport Hovav and Levin 2001), and weak/strong/spurious (Washio 1997). However, further differences in the resultatives extracted from the LCMC were found within subject/object–oriented types. It is not always the case that the subject in a subject–oriented resultative is the agent. Instead, it could be the patient (as in 68), or the location (e.g. 69), which is discussed with respect to the pattern V–满 *man* 'full' and a patient in a passive construction with a passive marker 被 *bei* (see 70). Therefore, a further distinction is made according to the semantic role of the argument, namely agent/patient/location–oriented resultatives.

(68) 衣服 洗–净 后 (LCMC E06 7)

yifu xi-jing hou

clothes wash–clean after

'After the clothes were washed clean'

(69) 库房, 摆–满–了 产品 (LCMC A07 3)

kufang, bai-man-le chanpin

warehouse, put–full–ASP product

'The products were put in the warehouse and as a result it was full of products.'

(70) 几 幢 楼 被 炮火 熏–黑 (LCMC A05 2)

ji zhuang lou bei paohuo xun-hei

several CL building bei (passive) gunfire smoke–black

'Several buildings were smoked by the gunfire and as a result they were black.'

In terms of the usage of Chinese resultatives, there are ones with/without 把 *ba*, and with/without 终于 *zhongyu* 'finally'. As mentioned in Chapter 1, Section 1.1.1, the reason for considering 把 *ba* is that 'wipe–clean' in (71a) is a commonly discussed example in the scholarship (e.g. Goldberg 1995, Washio 1997, Rappaport Hovav and Levin 2001, Croft 2012), though its literal translation into Chinese does not sound natural to native speakers (see 71b). (71b) would be more acceptable if combined with 把 *ba* (as in 71c). However, various resultatives are not equally acceptable when used with 把 *ba*. For instance, as mini–pairs between with and without 把 *ba* of Chinese resultatives, (71c) is more acceptable than (71b), whereas (72a) and (72b) are equally acceptable. Appreantly, the insertion of 把 *ba* into resultatives is an issue worth noticing. Therefore, 把 *ba* is adopted as a criterion for the corpus analysis of Chinese resultatives, and the acceptability of 把 *ba* + resultatives will be discussed in Chapters 5–6.

(71) a. She wiped the table clean. (Washio 1997:10)

b. ?她 擦–干净了 桌子

ta ca-ganjing-le zhuozi

she wipe–clean–ASP table

'She wiped the table clean.'

c. 她 把 桌子 擦–干净了

ta *ba* *zhuozi* *ca-ganjing-le*

she *ba* table wipe–clean–ASP

'She wiped the table clean.'

(72) a. 他 擦–干–了 头发 (CCL89.1)

ta *ca-gan-le* *toufa*

he wipe–dry–ASP hair

'He wiped her hair dry.'

b. 他 把 头发 擦–干了

ta *ba* *toufa* *ca-gan-le*

he *ba* hair wipe–dry–ASP

'He wiped his hair dry.'

The reason for 终于 *zhongyu* 'finally' is similar to that for 把 *ba*. As mentioned above, some Chinese resultatives are acceptable, but they do not have equal acceptability if combined with 把 *ba*. Nevertheless, if a pattern is not well accepted with 把 *ba* (see 73b), adding the adverb 终于 *zhongyu* 'finally' (as in 73c) will make it more acceptable. Consequently, 终于 *zhongyu* 'finally' is also regarded as a domain for further analysis. More about 把 ba and 终于 *zhongyu* 'finally'will be discussed in Chapter 5.

(73) a. 我 听–懂–了 他的 话 (CCL 36.1)

wo *ting-dong-le* *tade* *hua*

I listen–understand–ASP his words

'I listened to his words and as a result I understood them.'

b. ?我	把	他的	话	听－懂－了
wo	*ba*	*tade*	*hua*	*ting-dong-le*
I	*ba*	his	words	listen–understand–ASP

'I listened to his words and as a result I understood them.'

c. 我	终于	把	他的	话	听－懂－了
wo	*zhongyu*	*ba*	*tade*	*hua*	*ting-dong-le*
I	finally	*ba*	his	words	listen–understand–ASP

'I listened to his words and finally as a result I understood them.'

4.3.3 A general corpus analysis of Chinese resultatives

Taking into account the six domains mentioned in Section 4.3.2, namely subject/object–oriented, weak/strong/spurious, transitive/intransitive–based, agent/ patient/location–oriented, with/without 把 *ba*, and with/without 终于 *zhongyu* 'finally', I conducted a basic quantitative analysis of the first 500 examples after randomizing (in Excel) all the items found in the LCMC. The spurious type is ambiguous as the result XP could refer to either an NP or the manner of the action, which means it could be labelled as subject–, object– or verb–oriented. Therefore, I separate spurious resultatives from other types. A general analysis with the token frequency of each type and its proportion is presented in Table 4.1. The frequency of spurious resultatives in terms of diverse features is displayed in Table 4.2.

Table 4.1: Frequency of Chinese resultatives

	Type	Sub-type	Token frequency	Proportion (out of 500)
Resultatives 467	Subject/object-oriented	subject-oriented	264	52.8%
		object-oriented	203	40.6%
	Weak/strong	weak	146	29.2%
		strong	321	64.2%
	Transitive/ intransitive-based	transitive-based	448	89.6%
		intransitive-based	19	3.8%
	Without/ with *ba*	without *ba*	429	85.8%
		with *ba*	38	7.6%
	Without/with *zhongyu* 'finally'	without *zhongyu* 'finally'	463	92.6%
		with *zhongyu* 'finally'	4	0.8%
	Agent/ patient/ location-oriented	agent-oriented	158	31.6%
		patient-oriented	285	57.0%
		location-oriented	24	4.8%
Spurious Resultatives 33	Spurious		33	6.6%

Table 4.2: Frequency of Chinese spurious resultatives

	Type	Sub-type	Token frequency	Proportion (out of 33)
Spurious Resultatives 33	Transitive/ intransitive-based	transitive-based	33	100%
		intransitive-based	0	0
	Without/ with *ba*	without *ba*	32	97.0%
		with *ba*	1	3.0%
	Without/with *zhongyu* 'finally'	without *zhongyu* 'finally'	33	100%
		with *zhongyu*'finally'	0	0

From Table 4.1 we can observe that, generally subject–oriented resultatives play a large part in the 500 examples (52.8%), which contain marginal resultatives (including location–oriented ones), patient–front sentences and passive constructions, as mentioned in Section 4.3.2. More resultatives fall into the strong type (64.2%) and take transitive verbs (89.6%). Only a few are with 把 *ba* (7.6%) and with 终于 *zhongyu* 'finally' (0.8%). The number of patient–oriented sentences is overwhelmingly higher (57.0%) than that of agent–oriented (31.6%) and location–oriented (4.8%). Spurious resultatives, as demonstrated in Table 4.2, are all transitive–based, one with 把 *ba* and none with 终于 *zhongyu* 'finally'.

Regarding the frequency of marginal resultatives in Table 4.3, there are many more subject–oriented sentences (64.2%) than object–oriented ones (35.8%), more weak than strong (57.2% vs. 42.8%). Unlike the general situation in Table 4.1, the number of agent–oriented resultatives of the marginal type (48.4%) exceeds that of the patient–oriented (40.5%) and location–oriented (11.1%) types. Reasons will be suggested in Section 4.4.1.

Table 4.3: Frequency of Chinese marginal resultatives

	Type	Sub–type	Token frequency	Proportion (out of 215)
Marginal Resultatives 215	Subject/object–Oriented	subject–oriented	138	64.2%
		object–oriented	77	35.8%
	Weak/strong	weak	123	57.2%
		strong	92	42.8%
	Transitive/ intransitive–based	transitive–based	212	98.6%
		intransitive–based	3	1.4%

Table 4.3（Continued）

	Type	Sub-type	Token frequency	Proportion (out of 215)
Marginal Resultatives 215	Without/ with *ba*	without *ba*	204	94.9%
		with *ba*	11	5.1%
	Without/with *zhongyu* 'finally'	without *zhongyu* 'finally'	214	99.5%
		with *zhongyu* 'finally'	1	0.5%
	Agent/ patient/ location-oriented	agent-oriented	104	48.4%
		patient-oriented	87	40.5%
		location-oriented	24	11.1%

In terms of prototypical resultatives, as illustrated in Table 4.4, the examples are distributed evenly in terms of subject/object-oriented types (50% each). This is significantly different from the distribution of subject/ object-oriented resultatives in the marginal patterns ($p<.05$; see Table 4.5). The distributions of strong/weak and agent/ patient-oriented criteria between marginal and prototypical resultatives also differ significantly ($p<.05$ in Table 4.5). To be specific, in striking contrast to the distribution of marginal sentences of the strong/weak type, there are more prototypical resultatives of the strong type (90.9%) than the weak one (9.1%). This is also the case with respect to semantic-role orientation ($p<.05$): there are fewer agent-oriented sentences (21.4%) than patient-oriented (78.6%) ones. In addition, more intransitive verbs are found in prototypical resultatives than in marginal (16 vs. 3) ones. Based on these, the most frequently used types of prototypical resultatives are subject- and object-oriented, strong, transitive-based and patient-oriented. This will be discussed further in Section 4.4.2.

Table 4.4: Frequency of Chinese prototypical resultatives

	Type	Sub-type	Token frequency	Proportion (out of 252)
Prototypical Resultatives 252	Subject/object-oriented	subject-oriented	126	50.0%
		object-oriented	126	50.0%
	Weak/strong	weak	23	9.1%
		strong	229	90.9%
	Transitive/ intransitive-based	transitive-based	236	93.7%
		intransitive-based	16	6.3%
	Without/ with *ba*	without *ba*	225	89.3%
		with *ba*	27	10.7%
	Without/with *zhongyu* 'finally'	without *zhongyu* 'finally'	249	98.8%
		with *zhongyu*'finally'	3	1.2%
	Agent/ Patient/ Location-oriented	agent-oriented	54	21.4%
		patient-oriented	198	78.6%
		location-oriented	0	0

Table 4.5: Distributions of types between marginal and prototypical resultatives with significant differences (p<.05)

Type	subject/object-oriented	weak/strong	agent/patient-oriented
p-value (chi-square test)	0.0028	<.0001	<.0001

Relations among various criteria are presented in the tables below. From Table 4.1 we can see that there are overlaps among various features of Chinese resultatives. In terms of subject-/object-oriented in Table 4.6, although there are more subject-oriented resultatives than object-oriented, more subject-oriented items fall into the weak type than object–oriented (72.6% vs. 27.4%), whereas the distribution of subject– and object–oriented types with a strong feature is approximately the same (49.2% vs. 50.8%). More subject–oriented sentences take intransitive verbs than do object–oriented (15 vs. 4; this will be discussed further in Section 4.4.2). More object–oriented than subject–oriented resultatives are combined with 把 *ba* (36 vs. 2). With respect to semantic–role orientation, as stated in Section 4.3.2, though most agent–oriented resultatives are subject–oriented (98.7%), not all subject–oriented ones are agent–oriented. There can be patient–/location–oriented. This is also the case with the object–oriented type. Most object–oriented resultatives are patient–oriented (198), though some are location–oriented (3) and subject–oriented (2).

Table 4.6: Distribution of subject–/object–oriented resultatives in other features

Type	Subtype	Total 467 (100%)	Subject–oriented 264 (56.5%)	Object–oriented 203 (44.5%)
Weak/strong	Weak	146 (100%)	106 (72.6%)	40 (27.4%)
	Strong	321 (100%)	158 (49.2%)	163 (50.8%)
Transitive/ intransitive–based	transitive–based	448 (100%)	249 (55.6%)	199 (44.4%)
	intransitive–based	19 (100%)	15 (78.9%)	4 (21.1%)
Without/ with *ba*	without *ba*	429 (100%)	262 (61.1%)	167 (30.9%)
	with *ba*	38 (100%)	2 (5.3%)	36 (94.7%)
Without/with *zhongyu* 'finally'	without *zhongyu* 'finally'	463 (100%)	261 (56.4%)	202 (43.6%)
	with *zhongyu* 'finally'	4 (100%)	3 (75%)	1 (25%)
Agent/ Patient/ Location–oriented	agent–oriented	158 (100%)	156 (98.7%)	2 (1.3%)
	patient–oriented	285 (100%)	87 (30.5%)	198 (69.5%)
	location–oriented	24 (100%)	21 (87.5%)	3 (22.5%)

With regard to the weak/strong classification in Table 4.7, except for the relation between subject–/object–oriented mentioned above, we can see that although strong resultatives have a much higher token frequency than do weak ones, there are striking differences between strong and weak resultatives in terms of intransitive–based verbs (19 vs. 0; this will be discussed further in Section 4.4.2) and with 把 *ba* (30 vs. 8). In terms of semantic role, more weak instances than strong ones are agent–oriented (59.5% vs. 40.5%). This is in contrast to the patient–oriented type: there are notably more strong (81.8%) than weak (18.2%) ones. That is, more agent–oriented sentences are weak resultatives, and more patient–oriented ones are strong. Besides, all location–oriented resultatives belong to the strong type.

Table 4.7: Distribution of weak/strong resultatives in other features

Type	Subtype	Total 467 (100%)	Weak 146 (31.3%)	Strong 321 (68.7%)
Subject/object –oriented	subject–oriented	264 (100%)	106 (40.2%)	158 (59.8%)
	object–oriented	203 (100%)	40 (19.7%)	163 (80.3%)
Transitive/ intransitive–based	transitive–based	448 (100%)	146 (32.6%)	302 (67.4%)
	intransitive–based	19 (100%)	0 (0)	19 (100%)
Without/ with *ba*	without *ba*	429 (100%)	138 (32.2%)	291 (67.8%)
	with *ba*	38 (100%)	8 (21.1%)	30 (78.9%)
Without/with *zhongyu* 'finally'	without *zhongyu* 'finally'	463 (100%)	145 (31.3%)	318 (68.7%)
	with *zhongyu* 'finally'	4 (100%)	1 (25.0%)	3 (75.0%)
Agent/ Patient/ Location–oriented	agent–oriented	158 (100%)	94 (59.5%)	64 (40.5%)
	patient–oriented	285 (100%)	52 (18.2%)	233 (81.8%)
	location–oriented	24 (100%)	0 (0)	24 (100%)

Considering the transitive–/intransitive–based distinction in Table 4.8, apart from the relations between subject/object–oriented, weak/strong mentioned above, all examples with 把 *ba* are formed with transitive verbs. This is also the case for the feature 终于 *zhongyu* 'finally'. Regarding the distribution of verb types in the semantic–role orientation criterion, there are more transitive–verb based than intransitive–verb ones in all the three types.

Table 4.8: Distribution of transitive/intransitive–based resultatives in other features

Type	Subtype	Total 467 (100%)	Transitive based 448 (95.9%)	Intransitive–based 19 (4.1%)
Subject/object –oriented	subject–oriented	264 (100%)	249 (94.3%)	15 (5.7%)
	object–oriented	203 (100%)	199 (98.0%)	4 (2.0%)
Weak/strong	weak	146 (100%)	146 (100%)	0 (0)
	strong	321 (100%)	302 (94.1%)	19 (5.9%)
Without/ with *ba*	without *ba*	429 (100%)	410 (95.6%)	19 (4.4%)
	with *ba*	38 (100%)	38 (100%)	0 (0)
Without/with *zhongyu* 'finally'	without *zhongyu* 'finally'	463 (100%)	444 (95.9%)	19 (4.1%)
	with *zhongyu* 'finally'	4 (100%)	4 (100%)	0 (0)
Agent/ Patient/ Location–oriented	agent–oriented	158 (100%)	146 (92.4%)	12 (7.6%)
	patient–oriented	285 (100%)	279 (97.9%)	6 (2.1%)
	location–oriented	24 (100%)	23 (95.8%)	1 (4.2%)

Regarding semantic–role orientation (Table 4.9), since the relations between this domain and some other features have been stated, one point worth noticing is that there are many more patient–oriented sentences with 把 *ba* than agent–oriented sentences (36 vs. 2). No location–oriented sentences take 把 *ba* or 终于 *zhongyu* 'finally'. In addition, more resultatives are patient-oriented (279) than agent- (146) and location-oriented (23) in the transitive-based type, compared to more agent-oriented (12) than patient- oriented (6) and location-oriented (1) in the intransitive-based sentences.

Table 4.9: Distribution of agent/patient/location-oriented resultatives in other features

Type	Subtype	Total 467 (100%)	Agent-Oriented 158 (33.8%)	Patient-oriented 285 (61.0%)	Location-Oriented 24 (5.2%)
Subject/object-oriented	subject-oriented	264 (100%)	156 (59.1%)	87 (33.0%)	21 (7.9%)
	object-oriented	203 (100%)	2 (1.0%)	198 (97.5%)	3 (1.5%)
Weak/strong	weak	146 (100%)	94 (64.4%)	52 (35.6%)	0 (0)
	strong	321 (100%)	64 (19.9%)	233 (72.6%)	24 (7.5%)
Transitive/ intransitive-based	transitive-based	448 (100%)	146 (32.6%)	279 (62.3%)	23 (5.1%)
	intransitive-based	19 (100%)	12 (63.2%)	6 (31.8%)	1 (5.0%)
Without/ with *ba*	without *ba*	429 (100%)	156 (36.4%)	249 (58.0%)	24 (5.6%)
	with *ba*	38 (100%)	2 (5.3%)	36 (94.7%)	0 (0)
Without/with *zhongyu* 'finally'	without *zhongyu* 'finally'	463 (100%)	156 (33.7%)	283 (61.1%)	24 (5.2%)
	with *zhongyu* 'finally'	4 (100%)	2 (50.0%)	2 (50.0%)	0 (0)

Then, in terms of the parameters 把 *ba* and 终于 *zhongyu* 'finally', as their relation and other features have been indicated before, a conclusion to be drawn is that among the 38 resultatives with 把 *ba*, most are object-oriented (36), strong (30) and patient-oriented (36), all are transitive-based, and one is with 终于 *zhongyu* 'finally'. Regarding 终于 *zhongyu* 'finally', although only four sentences are found in the LCMC, three are subject-oriented and strong, all are transitive–based, two are agent–oriented and two patient–oriented. More issues regarding the two domains will be elaborated in Chapters 5 and 6 alomng with the acceptability of 把 *ba* + subject–/ object–oriented resultatives.

4.4 A corpus study of Chinese resultatives: discussion

4.4.1 Chinese resultatives: a typological point of view

From the results presented in Section 4.3.3, we can offer empirical evidence for or against the analyses of resultatives in the scholarship. To begin with, Rappaport Hovav and Levin (2001: 792) argue that most transitive verbs describing events involve the transmission of force, which can only be found in object–oriented resultative constructions with subcategorized NP. As a result, few subject–oriented result XPs can be used with transitive verbs, only some like (74a).[3] More subject–oriented resultatives are like (74b/c), which are intransitive–based (all taken from Rappaport Hovav and Levin 2001:770).

(74) a. The wise men followed the star out of Bethlehem.

b. John danced mazurkas across the room.

c. John swam laps to exhaustion.

3 (74a) refers to a change of location of the subject 'the wise men', which is not in line with the resultatives in my thesis. However, it is a rare instance of English subject–oriented resultatives.

This could offer an explanation for the phenomenon mentioned in Section 4.3.3 that intransitive verbs are found more in subject–oriented sentences (as in 75a) than object–oriented ones (see 75b; 15 vs. 4), since intransitive verbs do not take objects. However, this is also challenged by the examples found in the LCMC. From Table 4.6 regarding the relation between subject–/object–oriented and transitive–/ intransitive–based, we can see there are many more subject–oriented result XPs used with transitive verbs than intransitive ones (249 vs. 15). Among subject–oriented and transitive–based sentences, there are many patient–oriented (including passive constructions and patient–subject sentences mentioned in Section 4.3.2) and location–oriented items, which do not resemble the examples provided by Rappaport Hovav and Levin (2001), as in (74a). If we merely consider agent–oriented resultatives, there are still 144 sentences with transitive verbs, among which 44 are prototypical (as in 76a) and 100 marginal (e.g. 76b). So we can see it is not the case that subject–oriented result XPs cannot be largely formed by transitive verbs.

(75) a. 二姐 跌–死 (LCMC G67)

erjie *die-si*

second sister fall–die

'The second sister fell down and as a result died.'

b. 她 几乎 笑–弯–了 腰 (LCMC P03)

ta *jihu* *xiao-wan-le* *yao*

she almost laugh–bend–ASP waist

'She laughed and as a result she almost bent her waist.' (She laughed [so heavily] that she almost bent over)'

(76) a. 她 终于 学–会–了 游泳 (LCMC P10 7)

ta *zhongyu* *xue-hui-le* *youyong*

she finally learn–can–ASP swim

'She learned to swim and finally as a result she could swim.'

b. 我 看–见–了 花 (LCMC G39 3)

wo *kan-jian-le* *hua*

I look–see–ASP flower

'I saw flowers'.

As such, subject–oriented resultatives in Chinese are in contrast with that in English. The former form a large proportion (52.8%) and can be classified in terms of various criteria, such as weak/strong, transitive/intransitive, agent–/ patient–/ location–oriented, whereas the latter is limited to a few examples as in (74a–c). This will be discussed further in Section 4.4.2.3.2.

Washio (1997: 8) suggests that intransitive–based resultatives can only be strong, as in (77). According to him, since intransitive verbs like *run* cannot entail any semantics of a postverbal NP, the change of state of the NP (becoming thin in 77) caused by the action *run* cannot be predicted from the verb, which makes (77) a strong resultative. This could explain the phenomenon mentioned in Section 4.3.3 that all 19 intransitive–based resultatives are strong in Chinese.

(77) The joggers ran the pavement thin. (Washio 1997: 8)

In addition, Washio (1997: 8) argues that languages can be divided into two types, those (like English) that permit both strong and weak resultatives, and those only allowing weak resultatives, like Japanese, French and Italian. Viewed in this way, Chinese is categorized as the former type, since both weak and strong resultatives are found in Chinese.

4.4.2 Chinese marginal and prototypical resultatives

4.4.2.1 Type and token frequency

Recall the differences between prototypical and marginal resultatives mentioned in Section 4.2.3; in terms of frequency, we can see from Table 4.10 that although marginal resultatives have a high token frequency (43.0%), they have low type frequency. In the 500 examples with 91 patterns of result XPs, only seven are found in the marginal examples (7.7%). This is in contrast to prototypical resultatives in terms of number, 252 sentences (50.4%) with 80 patterns of result XPs (87.9%). This confirms the idea of classifying Chinese resultatives into prototypical and marginal types.

It also suggests that Chinese resultatives are highly productive. According to Bybee (1985) (cf. Clausner and Croft 1997, Barðdal 2006), within the usage–based model, a linguistic item with the highest type frequency represents a highly entrenched schema and suggests full productivity.[4] Since prototypical resultatives have a high type frequency, they may be highly entrenched at the schematic level and form new resultative constructions. Most instances of the marginal type, however, have a high token frequency, which means that

4 Bybee (1985), Clausner and Croft (1997) discuss productivity in the linguistic scholarship. For instance, the past–tense formation with the suffix *–ed* has the highest type frequency, which means a highly entrenched schema and full productivity. The irregular form with a vowel change (e.g. begin–began) in the stem has low type frequency, but instances have very high token frequency. This suggests that instances, not the schema, are entrenched, resulting in low productivity. See more about productivity also in Barðdal (2006).

examples rather than the schema are entrenched, therefore low in productivity. Finally, the number of spurious resultatives has both low type and token frequency. As mentioned above, they share the same form as prototypical ones but in 'spurious interpretations'. Their rarity in type and token further confirms the necessity of distinguishing them from the other two. The histograms in Figure 4.1 and 4.2 display the frequencies of the the three types intuitively.

Table 4.10: Chinese resultatives: type and token frequency

	Type frequency (result XP)	Proportion (out of 91)	Token frequency (examples)	Proportion (out of 500)
Prototypical Resultatives	80	87.9%	252	50.4%
Marginal Resultatives	7	7.7%	215	43.0%
Spurious Resultatives	4	4.4%	33	6.6%
Total	91	100%	500	100%

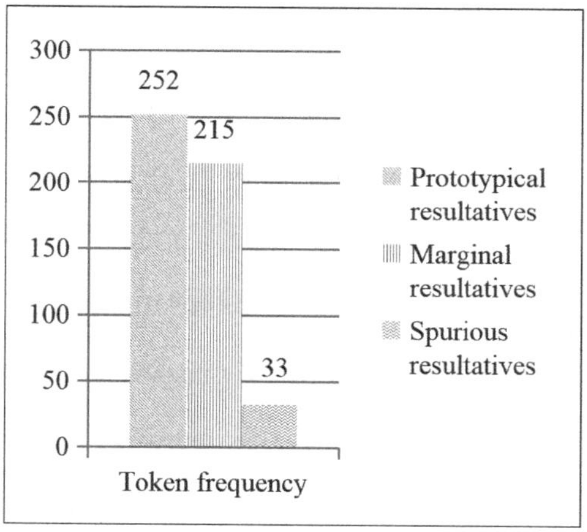

Figure 4.1: Token frequency of resultatives

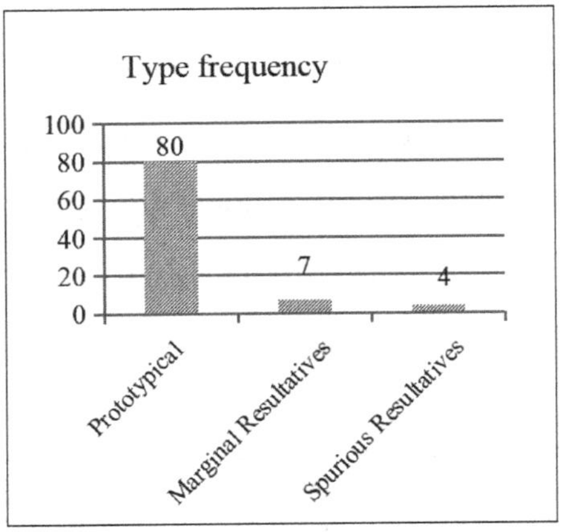

Figure 4.2: Type frequency of resultatives

4.4.2.2 Marginal resultatives

As described in Section 4.3.3, among the marginal resultatives there are more subject–oriented sentences than object–oriented ones, and more weak than strong. Recall the two tests discussed in Sections 4.2.2 and 4.3.2; instances taking patterns like 到 *dao* 'get' and 住 *zhu* 'hold' cannot pass Test 1, since these items cannot be predicated of an NP on their own, and verbs entail most result XPs semantically. That is, many verbs can designate a result meaning independently, for instance 买 *mai* 'buy', and the occurrence of a result XP (e.g. 到 *dao* 'get') may just emphasize the change of state of an NP. However, Test 2 does suggest the function of these patterns as resultatives. So weak resultatives are more numerous than strong ones in the marginal type, as the verb implies the meaning of the result XP. Moreover, in marginal resultatives, since most verbs imply the result, the verbs should be transitive. This explains why fewer intransitive verbs are the marginal type than the prototypical type.

From Table 4.11 we can see the token frequency of each item of marginal resultative, among which many form subject–oriented resultatives, such as 见 *jian* 'see' (as in 78a), 到 *dao* 'get' (see 78b) and 满 *man* 'full' (e.g. 78c). These patterns are more frequent in subject–oriented sentences than in object–oriented ones. Their number also leads to more agent–oriented marginal resultatives than patient–oriented ones, since examples used with 见 *jian* 'see' (as in 78a), 到 *dao* 'get' (see 78b) are also agent–oriented: the result XP is predicated of the subject/agent.

Table 4.11: Frequency of result XPs in marginal resultatives

Result XP (marginal resultative)	Token frequency
见 *jian* 'see'	71
到 *dao* 'get'	30
住 *zhu* 'hold; stop'	60
掉 *diao* 'drop; disappear'	7
走 *zou* 'leave'	14
开 *kai* 'open; separate'	9
满 *man* 'full'	24
Total	215

(78) a. 我　看–见–了　花　(LCMC G39 3)

wo　*kan-jian-le*　*hua*

I　look–see–ASP　flower

'I saw flowers'.

b. 他　申请–到　公司　赞助　(LCMC K20)

ta　*shenqing- dao*　*gongsi*　*zanzhu*

he　apply–get　company　grant

'He applied for a grant from the company and as a result got it.'

c. 台阶 上 站–满–了 观望 的 人(LCMC A29 1)

taijie shang zhan-man-le guanwang de ren

step on stand–full–ASP watch POSS people

'People who were watching stood on the step, and as a result it was full of people.'

4.4.2.3 Prototypical resultatives

4.4.2.3.1 A general analysis

As mentioned in Section 4.3.3, subject–oriented resultatives and object–oriented ones have the same proportions (50% each) in the 252 prototypical sentences. This is due to the passive construction and patient–subject sentences (see Section 4.3.2), which further motivates the agent–/patient–/location–oriented classification. Actually 54 are both subject–oriented and agent–oriented, which will be discussed in Section 4.4.2.3.2. Then we can understand why more are subject–oriented than object–oriented, but fewer are agent–oriented than patient–oriented. Seeing that many of the subject–oriented resultatives are patient–oriented, this mismatch is unsurprising.

Strong resultatives play a large part in the prototypical type. Based on the discussion in Section 4.4.2.1, prototypical resultatives in Chinese are highly productive. The result XP does not need to be implied by a verb: as long as the former is caused by the latter and leads to a change of state of an NP, they can form a resultative construction. In contrast, the weak type requires that the verb imply the meaning of the result XP. Consequently, weak resultatives are limited to a few examples with the verb entailing the result XP, such as 擦–净 *ca-jing* 'wipe–clean' (the most discussed pattern in the literature, e.g. Washio 1997, Croft 2012); see (79).

(79) 将 断 叶 上 的 浆水 彻底 擦–净(LCMC E05)

jiang duan ye shang de jiangshui chedi ca-jing

take broken leaf on POSS seriflux thoroughly wipe–clean

'Wipe the seriflux on the broken leaf clean thoroughly.'

With respect to the verb types and result XPs used in resultative constructions, there are 129 verbs and 80 result XPs used in prototypical examples, with seven verbs and 10 result XPs with high token frequencies as displayed in Table 4.12. Generally, we can see that the seven verbs are all typically used as transitive, with five action verbs, like洗 *xi* 'wash', 吃 *chi* 'eat'. Although吃 *chi* 'eat' can form the subject–oriented type (e.g. 吃–饱 *chi-bao* 'eat–full'), the other four action verbs are used in the object–oriented type, for instance洗–净 *xi-jing* 'wash–clean', 打–伤 *da-shang* 'beat–hurt'. There are two verbs related to mental processes, 学 *xue* 'learn' and 看 *kan* 'see', both related to subject/agent–oriented resultatives. So we may see subject–oriented resultatives are more frequent with mental verbs, whereas object–oriented ones more frequently describe actions.

In terms of result XPs, among the top 10 items, eight describe a state (e.g. 干 *gan* 'dry', 平 *ping* 'flat' 7), and two a mental trait, namely 会 *hui* 'can' and 清楚 *qingchu* 'clear'.

Table 4.12: Frequency of verbs and result XPs in prototypical resultatives

Verb/ Token frequency	Result XP/ Token frequency
学 *xue* 'learn' 14	死 *si* 'dead' 18
洗 *xi* 'wash' 10	会 *hui* 'can' 13

Table 4.12 (Continued)

Verb/ Token frequency	Result XP/ Token frequency
吃 *chi* 'eat' 7	干 *gan* 'dry' 12
打 *da* 'hit' 7	净 *jing*'clean' 11
看 *kan* 'see' 6	定 *ding* 'fixed' 10
烧 *shao* 'burn' 5	清楚 *qingchu* 'clear' 9
碰 *peng* 'touch; knock' 5	倒 *dao* 'fall' 7
	平 *ping* 'flat' 7
	大 *da* 'big' 7
	饱 *bao* 'full' 6

4.4.2.3.2 Chinese subject/agent–oriented resultatives

As pointed out in Section 4.4.1, Chinese subject–oriented resultatives are worth noticing. In terms of structure, we may contrast (80a) with (80b). A Chinese resultative (80a) is formed with a verb and a result XP, whereas its counterpart in English requires a reflexive (see 80b). So a distinguishing feature of Chinese subject–oriented resultatives is that they do not require a postverbal NP, no matter whether the main verb is normally transitive (80a) or intransitive (81). However, in English as suggested by Rappaport Hovav and Levin (2001), subject–oriented resultatives should take intransitive verbs like (80d) (with only one exception in 80e). Otherwise, if there is a transitive verb with an object following (either an object as in 80c or a fake object,[5] e.g. reflexive in 80b), it will be object–oriented. This feature leads to the diversity of Chinese subject–oriented resultatives.

5 Cf. Washio 1997, Rappaport Hovav and Levin 2001.

(80) a. 他 吃-饱-了 之后 (LCMC N13)

ta *chi-bao-le* *zhihou*

he eat–full–ASP after

'After he ate and as a result was full.'

b. He ate himself full.

c. Why paint your house purple? (Gordon & Lakoff 1971; cited in Goldberg 1995: 22)

d. John danced mazurkas across the room. (Rappaport Hovav and Levin 2001: 770).

e. The wise men followed the star out of Bethlehem. (Rappaport Hovav and Levin 2001:770)

(81) 他 走-累-了 (CCL 2.1)

ta *zou-lei-le*

he walk–tired–ASP

'He walked and as a result he was tired.'

In semantics, as illustrated in Section 4.3.2, there are patient–/location–oriented resultatives in the Chinese subject–oriented type. Apart from those, among the 158 subject– and agent–oriented sentences, 104 are marginal and 54 prototypical. Since much has been discussed in terms of the marginal type, we come to the 54 prototypical subject– and agent–oriented resultatives.

Although the postverbal NP is a crucial factor, it is not obligatory. A subject–oriented resultative can take a postverbal NP, as in (83). Therefore, the 54 sentences differ in two aspects. First, whether there is a postverbal NP. Second, if yes, where the NP is (i.e. postverbal like 83 or before the agent as in 84). There are 30 (55.6%) agent–oriented resultatives without a postverbal NP, like 吃–饱 *chi-bao* 'eat–full' (see 82), 跌–死 *die-si* 'fall–die', 19 (35.2%) with a postverbal NP (e.g. 83), and five (9.2%) that are object–fronted (e.g.84), including two with 把 *ba*. Recall that there are 44 transitive–based sentences (and hence 10 intransitive–based ones) in the prototypical subject– and agent–oriented resultatives, the mismatch between the 10 intransitive–based and 30 without a postverbal NP suggests that even if a verb is transitive (as in 82), it does not necessarily take a postverbal NP. We may see prototypically agent–oriented resultatives take no postverbal NP, as the change of state refers to the agent, which makes a patient (postverbal NP) unnecessary.

(82) a. 他 还 没 吃–饱 (LCMC G76 6)

ta *hai* *mei* *chi-bao*

he still not eat–full

'He ate but was not full as a result.'

(83) 她 终于 学–会–了 游泳 (LCMC P10 7)

ta *zhongyu* *xue-hui-le* *youyong*

she finally learn–can–ASP swim

'She learned to swim and finally as a result she could swim.'

(84) 出 入 开关 我 都 想 办法 弄–清楚 (LCMC N19 5)

chu ru kaiguan wo dou xiang banfa nong-qingchu

in out switch I all think way do–clear

'I shall think of a way to find the access switches so that I will be clear with them.'

If a postverbal NP is mentioned, it will be put before the agent (as in 84), or be fronted by using the 把 *ba*–construction (see 85a). However, some agent–oriented verb–result XPs are able to take a patient, but only limited to certain patterns, like 学/背–会 *xue/bei-hui* 'learn/recite–can' (13 sentences; e.g. 83), 看–懂 *kan-dong* 'see–understand' (see 85b), 听/过–惯 *ting/guo-guan* 'listen/live–be used to' (e.g. 85c), 吃–够 *chi-gou* 'eat–enough' (see 85d) and 打–赢 *da-ying* 'beat–win' (as in 85e). Basically, we can see that the patterns are related to mental verbs (e.g. 学/背–会 *xue/bei-hui* 'learn/recite–can', 看–懂 *kan-dong* 'see–understand') or repeated actions (like 听/过–惯 *ting/guo-guan* 'listen/live–be used to', 吃–够 *chi-gou* 'eat–enough'), although there is one exception 打–赢 *da-ying* 'fight–win'. The reasons for this phenomenon will be discussed in Chapter 5, Section 5.5.1.

(85) a. 读者 如 一开始 就 能 把 它 记–熟(LCMC E28)
duzhe ru yikaishi jiu neng ba ta ji-shu
reader if at the beginning then can ba it memorize–familiar
'If the reader can memorize it and as a result be familiar with it (words).'

b. 我 就是 无法 看–懂 水 是 由
wo jiushi wufa kan-dong shui shi you
I just cannot see–understand water is by
什么 组成 (LCMCG27)
shenme zucheng
what compose
'I just cannot see so as to understand what water is composed of.'

c.

老浦	过–惯–了	公子少爷	的	生活(LCMCK08)
Laopu	*guo-guan-le*	*gongzishaoye*	*de*	*shenghuo*
Laopu (name)	live–be used to	childe	POSS	life

'Laopu (name) lived a childe's life and as a result he was used to this kind of life.'

d.

中国	早	已	吃–够–了	闭关锁国	的
zhongguo	*zao*	*yi*	*chi-gou-le*	*biguansuoguo*	*de*
China	early	already	eat–enough–ASP	seclusion	POSS
苦头	(LCMC E08)				
kutou					
hardship					

'China had already tasted the hardship of seclusion and as a result had had enough of it.'

e.

他们	如何	打–赢	未来的	战争 (LCMC A34)
tamen	*ruhe*	*da-ying*	*weilaide*	*Zhanzheng*
they	how	fight–win	future	war

'How could they fight so as to win the future war?'

4.5 Concluding remarks

In this chapter I have discussed various Chinese resultatives in order to include or exclude certain patterns in/from my analysis. A description of resultatives on the basis of the corpus LCMC has been given with regard to frequency (type and token), verb frequency, examples with 把 *ba* and with 终于 *zhongyu* 'finally'. Consequently, I postulate a distinction between marginal resultatives and prototypical resultatives. In addition, based on the 'subject–/ object–oriented' classification made by Rappaport Hovav and Levin (2001), and taking into account the properties of Chinese resultatives, one more dimension of agent–/patient–/location–oriented resultatives is suggested.

Regarding my findings, first, a large proportion of subject–oriented resultatives are formed with transitive verbs, though not all are agent–oriented. This is in contrast to what is argued by Rappaport Hovav and Levin (2001) that few subject–oriented resultatives are transitive–based. Second, Chinese is in the same type as English, both of which permit strong and weak resultatives. They are different from languages only allowing weak resultatives (e.g. French and Japanese). Third, within the usage–based framework (Bybee 1985, Croft and Cruse 2004), prototypical resultative constructions have a higher type frequency, hence are more productive than the marginal resultatives. Finally, the postverbal NP is a significant factor in subject/agent–oriented resultatives, which makes Chinese resultatives distinct from those in languages like English.

This could form a data foundation for my further discussion on the acceptability of 把 *ba* + subject–/object –oriented resultatives in Chapters 5–6.

Chapter 5 把 *ba* + subject/agent-oriented resultatives: acceptability judgements

5.1 Introduction

5.1.1 Chinese subject-oriented resultative constructions

As discussed in Chapter 4, there are prototypical and marginal resultatives in the subject–oriented type in Chinese, exemplified in (1a) and (2a) respectively. Both subject–oriented, the two differ in whether the result XP can be predicated of the NP independently and pass the tests. In (2a) the meaning of 住 *zhu* 'stop' is highly abstract and cannot be used independently with 他 *ta* 'he' as in (2b).[1] However, our tests used to classify resultatives (see Chapter 4, Section 4.2.2) verify the status of (2a) as a resultative construction. So (2a) is a marginal resultative. In contrast, 迷糊 *mihu* 'dazed' is a predicate that can be used independently, as in (1b), which makes (1a) prototypical.

1 Though 他到–了 *ta dao-le* 'he arrived–ASP' (he arrived) is acceptable, 到 *dao* 'arrive' is used as a verb with meaning 'arrive' rather than 'get'.

(1) a. 我 睡-迷糊-了 (CCL 12.1)

wo *shui-mihu-le*

I sleep-dazed-ASP

'I slept (so much) and as a result I was dazed.'

b. 我 迷糊-了 (CCL 2.1)

wo *mihu-le*

I dazed-ASP

'I was dazed.'

(2) a. 他 叫-住-了 我 (CCL 48.1)

ta *jiao-zhu-le* *wo*

he call-stay-ASP me

'He called me.'

b. *他 住-了 我

ta *zhu-le* *wo*

he stay-ASP me

'He called me.'

Based on the classification made in Chapter 4, Section 4.3.2 in terms of the semantic role of the argument, there are agent/patient/location-oriented resultatives in Chinese. The agent-oriented type (e.g. 1a) in the prototypical subject-oriented resultatives corresponds to the subject-oriented ones suggested by Rappaport Hovav and Levin (2001), like (3). In both of them, the result XP is predicated of the subject which is also an agent. This chapter will mainly focus on this type.

(3) The wise men followed the star out of Bethlehem. (Rappaport Hovav and Levin 2001:770)

5.1.2 把 *ba* + subject/agent-oriented resultatives in Chinese

I discussed the 把 *ba*–construction in Chapter 2, Section 2.3. The 把 *ba*–construction is formed as NP1 + ba+ NP2 + V (+ 了 *le* [ASP]). A crucial feature is that a post–ba NP (e.g. 鸡蛋 *jidan* 'egg' in 4a) is always required in the 把 *ba*–construction, although the verb can be transitive (see 4a) or intransitive (see 4b).

(4) a. 她 把 鸡蛋 卖–了 (CCL 108.1)

ta ba jidan mai-le

she *ba* egg sell–ASP

'She sold the eggs.'

b. 她们 把 腰 都 笑–弯–了 (CCL 31.1)

tamen ba yao dou xiao-wan-le

they *ba* waist even laugh–bend–ASP

'They laughed and as a result they even bent her waist.' (They laughed so heavily that they even bent over)'

Meanwhile, as illustrated in Chapter 4, Section 4.4.2.3.2, the postverbal NP in subject/ agent–oriented resultatives is to be noted. Subject/agent–oriented resultatives usually take no postverbal NP in that the change of state is related to an agent, therefore the patient (a postverbal NP) does not need to occur. In the Lancaster Corpus of Mandarin Chinese (LCMC), there is no postverbal

NP in more than half (55.6%) of the agent–oriented resultatives (e.g. 5a). So the combination of 把 *ba* + subject/agent–oriented resultatives is not common, since the 把 *ba*–construction needs a postverbal NP, but the subject/agent–oriented resultative constructions take no patient. However, there are some patterns found in the LCMC which take a postverbal NP in different positions: 35.2% with a postverbal NP (e.g. 5b), and 9.2% with the object fronted, as in (5c). These sentences with a patient thus provide opportunities for the combination with 把 *ba*.

(5) a.

他	还	没	吃–饱	(LCMC G76 6)
ta	*hai*	*mei*	*chi-bao*	
he	still	no	eat–full	

'He ate but was not as a result to be full.'

b.

她	终于	学–会–了	游泳	(LCMC P10 7)
ta	*zhongyu*	*xue-hui-le*	*youyong*	
she	finally	learn–can–ASP	swim	

'She learned to swim and finally as a result she could swim.'

c.

出	入	开关	我	都	想	办法	弄–清楚	(LCMC N19 5)
chu	*ru*	*kaiguan*	*wo*	*dou*	*xiang*	*banfa*	*nong-qingchu*	
in	out	switch	I	all	think	way	do–clear	

'I shall think a way to find the access switches so that I will be clear with them.'

So one thing to be considered is that most subject/agent–oriented resultatives cannot take postverbal NP as in (6b, 7b), but why some can (e.g. 5b, 6c) (Question 4). I argue in Section 5.5.1 that this is related to the status of the vrerb and the result XP as well as the semantics of the resultative construction.

(6) a. 他 走–累–了 (CCL2.1)

ta *zou-lei-le*

he walk–tired–ASP

'He walked and as a result he was tired.'

b. *他 走–累–了 山路

ta *zou-lei-le* *shanlu*

he walk–tired–ASP mountain road

'He walked on the mountain road and as a result he was tired.'

c. 山里人 走–惯–了 山路 (CCL18.1)

shanliren *zou- guan -le* *shanlu*

mountain in people walk–be used to–ASP mountain road

'People in the mountain walked on the mountain road (for so many times) and as a result they were used to it.'

(7) a. 她 做 题 做 到 深夜。 做–累–了， 她...(CCL1.1)

ta *zuo* *ti* *zuo* *dao* *shenye.* *zuo-lei-le,* *ta...*

she do drill do until midnight. do–tired–ASP, she ⋯

'She did the drills until midnight. She did it and a result she was tired ⋯ '

b. *她 做–累–了 题目

ta *zuo-lei-le* *timu*

she do–tired–ASP drill

'She did the drills and as a result she was tired.'

A further issue to be noticed is that, subject/agent–oriented resultatives with a postverbal NP are not equally acceptable when combined with 把 *ba*. For example, it seems to me as a native speaker that (8b) is acceptable, (9b) is marginally acceptable and (10b) is unacceptable, though the examples without 把 *ba* are all well accepted. A possible explanation will be stated in Section 5.4 and 5.5. I argue that the higher degree of semantic transitivity a sentence is interpreted with, the more acceptable it is when combined with 把 *ba*, as the fomrer is compatible with the function of 把 *ba* as a marker of high transitivity.

(8) a. 他 想–明白–了 这 一切 (CCL 116.1)

ta 想*-mingbai-le* *zhe* *yiqie*

he think–understand–ASP this everything

'He thought about everything and as a result he understood it.'

b. 他 把 这 一切 想–明白–了

ta *ba* *zhe* *yiqie* *xiang-mingbai-le*

he *ba* this everything think–understand–ASP

'He thought about everything and as a result he understood it.'

(9) a. 观众 看–懂–了 剧情 (CCL 62.1)

guanzhong *kan-dong-le* *juqing*

audience watch–understand–ASP plot

'The audience watched (the play) and as a result understood the plot.'

b. ?观众 把 剧情 看–懂–了

guanzhong *ba* *juqing* *kan-dong-le*

audience *ba* plot watch–understand–ASP

'The audience watched (the play) and as a result understood the plot.

(10) a. 我 坐－惯－了 电车 (CCL 22.1)

renmen *zuoguan-le* *dianche*

people sit– used to–ASP tram

'I had taken the tram for so many times that I was used to it.'

b. *我 把 电车 坐－惯－了

wo *ba* *dianche* *zuoguan-le*

I *ba* tram sit– used to–ASP

'I had taken the tram for so many times that I was used to it.'

5.1.3 Structure of the chapter

The remainder of this chapter is composed of the following parts: a literature review (Section 5.2), methodology (Section 5.3), results and discussion (Section 5.4), further implications (Section 5.5) and concluding remarks (Section 5.6). This chapter not only explains why some subject–oriented resultatives can take a postverbal NP and the acceptability of *ba* + subject–oriented resultatives, but also sheds light on the study of the 把 *ba*–construction itself, suggesting that it functions as a marker of high transitivity. This cast doubt on the traditional analysis of regarding 把 *ba* as expressing disposal (Wang 1947, Li 1974, Song 1981, Wang 2003), or causativity (Guo 1999, Xiong 2004, Ye 2004). In addition, the application of the method magnitude estimation (cf. Bard et al. 1996; see more information in Chapter 3, Section 3.3.3) to Chinese is a novel way of studying grammar in Chinese.

5.2 The 把 *ba*-construction: more about high semantic transitivity

As discussed in Chapter 2, Seciton 2.3.2, semantically the 把 *ba*–construction has been analyzed as expressing disposal (Wang 1947, Li 1974, Wang 2003), causation (Guo 1999, Xiong 2004, Ye 2004), or high transitivity (Hopper & Thompson 1980, Sun 1995, Næss 2007) in the literature. As shown in Chapter 2, the first two views are problematic and the last one may account for many phenomena but its possible usefulness for explaining 把 *ba* in resultatives has not yet been explored in depth. We shall come to see how this viewpoint hold for 把 *ba* + resultatives.

With respect to treating 把 *ba* as a marker of high transitivity, Hopper and Thompson (1980) propose ten parameters of transitivity as in (11). These parameters address the degree of semantic transitivity of a sentence, as has been discussed in detail in Chapter 2, Seciton 2.3.2. The more features a sentence possesses in the High column, the higher the semantic transitivity it is interpreted with.

(11) Parameters of Transitivity (Hopper and Thompson 1980: 252)

	High	Low
A Participants	2 or more participants A and O	1 participant
B Kinesis	action	non–action
C Aspect	telic	Atelic

D Punctuality	punctual	non–punctual
E Volitionality	volitional	non–volitional
F Affirmation	affimative	Negative
G Mode	realis	Irrealis
H Agency	A high in potency	A low in potency
I Affectedness of O	O totally affected	O not affected
J Individuation of O	O highly individuated	O non–individuated

Næss (2007) also adopts the transitivity analysis to account for the 把 *ba*–construction. She states that the NP after 把 *ba* must be affected, which designates the high–transitivity semantics of the sentence.

She proposes that "a prototypical transitive clasue is one where the two participants are maximally semantically distinct in terms of their roles in the event described by the clause" (Næss 2007: 30). Except from the parameter proposed by Hopper and Thompson (1980), she argues that "affected agent" is also a feature of Transitivity. She defines affected agent as 'the effect is the main goal of the agent's act' (Næss 2007: 56). Prototypically the agent is unaffected (cf. Langacker 1991). However, crosslinguistic evidence for the Affected Agent has been found, which is predicated by a class of verbs, namely ingestive verbs, like 'eat' and 'drink'. In addition, according to Haspelmath (1994:160), an effect could be achieved on the agent rather than the patient. The verbs include 'eat', 'drink', 'learn', 'see' and 'wear'. Therefore, an agent can be affected in an event.

In line with Næss (2007:53), eating is a typical example of an agent being affected by an act. To be specific, A (the most agent–like argument in a sentence) volitionally carries out the act of eating in the event, also causing itself to be affected by the event. When A eats, though it is the food that is consumed, A itself is also influenced inherently in that it becomes full because of the action of eating. For example, 'eat' in English can be transitive (*he ate a banana*) and intransitive (*he ate in 5 minutes*). In the former example, the affectedness of the patient is stated, with the apple eaten by him. However, since there is no P in the latter, it could be interpreted as expressing that he is full at the endpoint of eating. Then the affectedness of A can be construed.

Verbs like these have the properties of expressing an action which affects the agent. Sentences with such an A should also be viewed as bearing a degree of transitivity. This not only supplements the theory proposed by Hopper and Thompson (1980), but also shed light on the Chinese subject–oriented resultatives. In the corpus data collected from the LCMC, as stated in Section 5.1.2, there are agent–oriented resultatives, such as 学/背–会 *xue/bei-hui* 'learn/recite–can' (e.g. 12a), 看–懂 *kan-dong* 'see–understand' (see 12b), 听/过–惯 *ting/guo-guan* 'listen/live–be used to' (e.g. 12c), and 吃–够 *chi-gou* 'eat–enough' (see 12d). This is in line with what Haspelmath (1994) proposes about the affected agent. If A carries out an action, it could be affected by the event. The words include not only 'eat', 'learn', 'see', but also 'live'. Therefore the degree of transitivity of resultatives with such verbs can be analyzed in terms of affectedness of A, and the acceptability with 把 ba will be considered further.

(12) a. 呆少爷 学–会–了 这 句 话 (LCMC R03)
dai shaoye *xue-hui-le* *zhe* *ju* *hua*

dull master learn–can–ASP this CL sentence

'Dull master learned this sentence and as a result he could speak it.'

b. 我 就是 无法 看–懂 水 是 由

wo jiushi wufa kan-dong shui shi you

I just cannot see–understand water is by

什么 组成 (LCMCG27)

shenme zucheng

what compose

'I just canot see so as to understand what water is composed of.'

c. 老浦 过–惯–了 公子少爷 的 生活 (LCMCK08)

Laopu guo-guan-le gongzishaoye de shenghuo

Laopu (name) live–be used to childe POSS life

'Laopu (name) lived a childe's life and as a result he was used to this kind of life.'

d. 中国 早 已 吃–够–了 闭关锁国 的

zhongguo zao yi chi-gou-le biguansuoguo de

China early already eat–enough–ASP seclusion POSS

苦头 (LCMC E08)

kutou

hardship

'China had already tasted the hardship of seclusion and as a result had had enough of it.'

5.3 Methodology

Though subject–oriented resultatives with a postverbal NP can be found in the corpus (see Section 5.1), their numbers are too low to carry out further analysis. As discussed in Chapter 3, Section 3.3.4, my additional research adopts a two–fold methodology. First, I looked for subject–oriented resultatives with postverbal NPs in the corpora (for more, see Section 5.3.1). Second, due to the infrequency of certain patterns, I carried out a questionnaire survey to examine the acceptability judgements of these patterns. For this I employed the technique of magnitude estimation.

5.3.1 Corpus

Based on the ODVRC, data concerning Chinese resultatives will be taken from two corpora: the CCL and the LCMC.

Firstly, I picked out the subject–oriented result XPs which could take a postverbal NP from the complements in the ODVRC. Then based on the examples of subject–oriented resultatives with a postverbal NP, I looked for the combinations of verb + result XP and such combinations with 把 *ba* in the CCL and LCMC to get more examples. As the subject–oriented resultatives that can take a postverbal NP are not all well accepted by native speakers, the examples are used as source for the questionnaire survey. Examples from previous studies on Chinese resultatives will also be mentioned when necessary. To sum up, my corpora provide examples of subject–oriented resultatives with a postverbal NP as well as of ba + these resultatives, which could offer evidence for the issues mentioned in Section 5.1.2. Moreover, the patterns found in the corpus, namely subject–oriented resultatives which can take a postverbal NP, could be used as a basis for the questionnaire survey.

5.3.2 Questionnaire survey

As stated in Chapter 3, Section 3.3.3, the technique of magnitude estimation is adopted as a technique to conduct a questionnaire survey in order to test the acceptability of 把 *ba* + subject–oriented resultatives in Chinese. The survey is based on seven subject–oriented resultatives which corpus data found in the ODVRC, the CCL and the LCMC suggest may take a postverbal NP. These patterns are classified into three groups based on my intuition of compatibility with 把 *ba*, namely the acceptable group (V–会 *hui* 'can', V–明白 *mingbai* 'understand'),[2] the marginally acceptable group (V–懂 *dong* 'understand'), and the least acceptable group (V–腻 *ni* 'be tired of', V–烦 *fan* 'bored with', V–惯 *guan* 'be used to'and V–够 *gou* 'enough'). Moreover, two verbs (想 *xiang* 'think' and 弄 *nong* 'do')were used in V–明白 *mingbai* 'understand', so in all there are eight patterns as test sentences.

The eight test patterns are 想–明白 *xiang-mingbai* 'think–understand', 弄–明白 *nong-mingbai* 'do–understand', 练–会 *lian-hui* 'practice–can', 听–懂 *ting-dong* 'listen–understand', 喝–腻 *he-ni* 'drink–be tired of', 看–惯

2 V–会 *hui* 'can' used to be considered as marginally acceptable when combined with 把 *ba*. However, after analyzing the data, the rating of *ba* + V–会 *hui* 'can' was almost as high as *ba* + V–明白 *mingbai* 'understand' in the acceptable group, hence I moved it to this group in the final data analysis.

kan-guan 'see–be used to', 听–烦 *ting-fan* 'listen–bored with' and 喝–够 *he-gou* 'drink–enough'. The parameter is with or without 把 *ba*. As 把 *ba* is regarded as a marker of high transitivity (Hopper and Thompson 1980, Sun 1995), another parameter was added, the adverb 终于 *zhongyu* 'finally'. 终于 *zhongyu* 'finally' is construed as 'A has a purpose and finishes it eventually'. So volitionality of the agent can increase by adding such an adverb, and the degree of transitivity of the sentence will be enhanced.

The reason for choosing 终于 *zhongyu* 'finally' is that it has the highest corpus frequency of all the adverbs with the same meaning. In the LCMC, after getting all the tokens with 把 *ba*, I searched 'd (adverb), 1 to left' which means the adverb occurring immediately to the left of 把 *ba*, and obtained 121 different types of adverbs with 381 tokens. Among these adverbs, most are time–related, such as 就 *jiu* 'then' (54 items), 又 *you* 'again' (12 items), 再 *zai* 'again' (12 items), 便 *bian* 'then' (12 items), or negation 不 *bu* 'not' (13 items). These are the top five adverbs used with 把 *ba*.

Since semantic transitivity is a crucial factor, I looked for adverbs expressing meanings related to high semantic transitivity. Among those 'd (adverb), 1 to left' with an interpretation of high volitionality of the agent are 终于 *zhongyu* 'finally', 总算 *zongsuan* 'finally' and 最终 *zuizhong* 'finally', the first two occurding three times and the latter once. Only one case with 终于 *zhongyu* 'finally' is a resultative as in (13a). The sentences with 总算 *zongsuan* 'finally' and 最终 *zuizhong* 'finally' are like (13b) and (13c) respectively, which are not resultatives. Similarly, I searched for 'd (adverb), 2/3/4/5 to left', to examine the adverbs preceding 把 *ba*. The only other adverb associated with high semantic transitivity uncovered this way is 故意 *guyi* 'intentionally', as in

(13d).

(13) a. 我们 终于 把 债务 都 还–清–了 (LCMC R04)
women zhongyu ba zhaiwu dou huan-qing-le
we finally *ba* debt all repay–clear–ASP
'We repaied the debt and as a result, finally, the debt was clear.'

b. 总算 把 一 间 房子 分 成 了
zongsuan ba yi jian fangzi fen cheng le
finally *ba* one CL house devide become ASP
两 份 (LCMC F17)
liang fen
two CL
'Finally divide a house into two.'

c. 最终 把 全 世界 变 成 '社会主义
finally ba quan shijie bian cheng 'shehuizhuyi
zuizhong *ba* whole world change become 'socialism
的 天国' (LCMC G68)
de tianguo'
POSS heaven'
'Finally change the whole world into a heaven of socialism.'

d. 故意 从 身 后 把 驴 绳
guyi cong shen hou ba lü sheng
intentionally from body behind ba donkey rope
割–断 (LCMCR06)

ge-duan

cut–broken

'(One person) intentionally cut the rope linking the donkey from behind, and as a result the rope was broken.'

Moreover, under the condition 'd, 2/3/4/5 to left +把 *ba*', there are two resultatives, one with 终于 *zhongyu* 'finally' and one with 最终 *zuizhong* 'finally'. Taking into account all the adverbs with 把 *ba*, 终于 *zhongyu* 'finally' is the most frequently used in terms of high transitivity (see Table 5.1).

Table 5.1: Adverbs related to high transitivity used with 把 *ba*

Adverb	终于 *zhongyu* 'finally'	总算 *zongsuan* 'finally'	最终 *zuizhong* 'finally'	故意 *guyi* 'intentionally'
Token frequency	4	3	2	1

As mentioned in Section 5.3.1, based on the ODVRC, 8 patterns of result XPs which can take a postverbal NP with examples are obtained from the LCMC and the CCL. In order to eliminate other factors which may affect subjects' acceptability judgements, all the sentences take a third person singular as their subject (also the agent), half masculine and half feminine; the article of the nouns are 这 *zhe* 'this' or 那 *na* 'that'.

The testing sentences are listed in (14–21), and the two variables 把 *ba* and 终于 *zhongyu* 'finally' were added in the survey, resulting in 32 test sentences altogether. That is, the four variations are within each token set, namely without 把 *ba* or 终于 *zhongyu* 'finally', with 把 *ba*, with 终于 *zhongyu* 'finally', and with both 把 *ba* and 终于 *zhongyu* 'finally'.

(14)	他	想–明白–了	这	个	问题
	ta	*xiang-mingbai-le*	*zhe*	*ge*	*wenti*
	he	think–understand–ASP	this	CL	question

'He thought about this question and as a result he understood it.'

(15)	她	弄–明白–了	这	个	道理
	ta	*nong-mingbai-le*	*zhe*	*ge*	*wenti*
	she	do–understand–ASP	this	CL	question

'She thought about this principle and as a result she understood it.'

(16)	她	练–会–了	这	首	歌
	ta	*lian-hui-le*	*zhe*	*shou*	*ge*
	she	practice–can–ASP	this	CL	song

'She practised this song and as a result she could sing it.'

(17)	她	听–懂–了	小宇	的	话
	ta	*ting-dong-le*	*Xiaoyu*	*de*	*hua*
	she	listen–understand–ASP	Xiaoyu(name)	POSS	words

'She listened to Xiaoyu's words and as a result she understood them.'

(18)	他	喝–腻–了	这	种	茶
	ta	*he-ni-le*	*zhe*	*zhong*	*cha*
	he	drink–be tired of–ASP	this	kind	tea

'He had drunk this kind of tea so many times that he was tired of it.'

(19)	她	看–惯–了	那	种	微笑
	ta	*kan-guan -le*	*na*	*zhong*	*weixiao*
	she	see–be used to–ASP	that	kind	smile

'She had seen that kind of smile so many times that she was used to it.'

(20) 他 听–烦–了 老师 的 话

ta *ting-fan-le* *laoshi* *de* *hua*

he listen– bored with –ASP teacher POSS words

'He listened to the teacher's words and as a result he was bored with them. ('He was bored with the teacher's words.')

(21) 她 喝–够–了 那 种 药水

ta *he-gou-le* *na* *zhong* *yaoshui*

she drink–enough–ASP that kind portion

'She had drunk that kind of portion so many times that she had enough of it.'

As mentioned in Chapter 3, Seciton 3.3.4, to avoid the informants figuring out the purpose of the survey, I use the same number of fillers. Their format is similar to that of the test sentences: some have 把 *ba* and some have 终于 *zhongyu* 'finally'. We have an even distribution of acceptable, marginally acceptable and the least acceptable sentences.

There are, in other words, 64 sentences in total. If all these sentences were given in one survey, it would be too much for the subjects. Therefore, the eight patterns were divided into two groups, 想–明白 *xiang-mingbai* 'think–understand', 听–懂 *ting-dong* 'listen–understand', 看–惯 *kan-guan* 'see–be used to' and 喝–腻 *he-ni* 'drink–be tired of' in one group (survey 1.1) and 弄–明白 *nong-mingbai* 'do–understand', 练–会 *lian-hui* 'practice–can', 喝–够 *he-gou* 'drink–enough' and 听–烦 *ting-fan* 'listen–be bored with' in the other (survey 1.2). Each survey thus contains 16 test sentences and 16 fillers. As suggested in Chapter 3, Section 3.3.4, a version with a reversed order of the sentences is used to ensure the validity of the results. So there are four versions of the questionnaire survey in total. The complete questionnaires can be found in Appendix A and B.

The survey was conducted among 71 undergraduate students at Minzu University of China with the method of magnitude estimation, 35 of which did survey 1.1 and 36 survey 1.2. A few of the informants did not reveal their age or gender on the information sheet.[3] Among those who did provide all the demographical information, there are 6 men and 61 women. The average age of the participants is 20.33 years old.

The task for the subjects was to practice magnitude estimation first, and then judge the 32 sentences based on their intuitions. After the data were obtained and normalized, as discussed in Chapter 3, Secton 3.3.4, I calculated and analyzed mean, median, standard deviation, and p–values of t–tests (two groups in Excel and more than 2 in SPSS along with post hoc tests). In order to obtain valid data, a z–score >3 or <–3 is excluded, as it is viewed as an extreme outlier. Nevertheless, no outlier was found in this survey.

5.4 The questionnaire survey: results and discussion

I first present and discuss the results for the variable 把 *ba* across and within the three sets of sentences mentioned in Section 5.3.2. The results for the variable 终于 *zhongyu* 'finally' are discussed next.

3 The results suggest that age, gender and dialects do not affect acceptability judgements at any rate

5.4.1 Resultatives with and without 把 *ba*

5.4.1.1 Results

The results are given in Table 5.2. ANOVA suggests significant differences between the 8 items (p<.05). Moreover, there are differences among 1–3, 4, and 5–8, the scores decreased from 94 to 75 and to 50.

Table 5.2: Eight items with 把 *ba*

	with *ba*			
	Number	Mean	Median	Std. Deviation
1 'think–understand'	35	94.71	100	11.44
2 'do–understand'	36	90.00	100	20.70
3 'practice–can'	36	92.64	100	13.39
4 'listen–understand'	35	75.29	80	25.29
5 'drink–be tired of'	35	66.14	65	27.17
6 'see–be used to'	35	57.29	60	26.47
7 'listen–be bored with'	36	51.44	50	32.49
8 'drink–enough'	36	54.28	50	26.97
Total	284	72.72	72.5	29.10
ANOVA p–value	1.19×10^{-21}			

As the questionnaire surveys were designed based on a preliminary distinction among the eight items. That is, Group 1 (G1) contains 1–3, Group 2 (G2) 4, and Group 3 (G3) includes 5–8. So post hoc tests within groups were conducted, with the results displayed in Table 5.3 and 5.4. We can see there is no significant difference within G1 and G3 respectively (p>.05).

Table 5.3: Post hoc tests for Group 1 (with 把 *ba*)

(I) group	(J) group	Mean Difference (I–J)	Std. Error	Sig.	95% Confidence Interval	
					Lower Bound	Upper Bound
1	2	4.71	3.73	.63	–4.36	13.79
	3	2.07	3.73	1.00	–7.00	11.16
2	1	–4.71	3.73	.63	–13.79	4.36
	3	–2.63	3.70	1.00	–11.65	6.38
3	1	–2.07	3.73	1.00	–11.15	7.00
	2	2.63	3.70	1.00	–6.38	11.65

Table 5.4: Post hoc tests for Group 3 (with 把 *ba*)

(I) group	(J) group	Mean Difference (I–J)	Std. Error	Sig.	95% Confidence Interval	
					Lower Bound	Lower Bound
5	6	8.85	6.78	1.00	–9.31	27.03
	7	14.69	6.74	.19[4]	–3.34	32.74
	8	11.86	6.74	.48	–6.18	29.91
6	5	–8.85	6.78	1.00	–27.03	9.31
	7	5.84	6.74	1.00	–12.20	23.88
	8	3.00	6.74	1.00	–15.03	21.05
7	5	–14.69	6.74	.19	–32.74	3.34
	6	–5.84	6.74	1.00	–23.88	12.20
	8	–2.83	6.69	1.00	–20.75	15.08
8	5	–11.86	6.741	.48	–29.91	6.18
	6	–3.00	6.741	1.00	–21.05	15.03
	7	2.833	6.69	1.00	–15.08	20.75

4 According to Hollmann (2013), a p–value higher than .05 but lower than .2 is viewed as "nearly significant" . This suggests a trend in data, which means that if the sample size is large enough, the difference may be significant. Data like this may be relevant for potential follow–up research, but I shall leave them for now.

Since no significant differences appear among patterns within each group, the following results will be discussed regarding acceptability with 把 *ba*, namely acceptable groups (G1), marginally acceptable group (G2) and the least acceptable group (G3). We can see that when with 把 *ba*, G1 was rated with very high scores (mean 92.43), G2 received lower scores (75.29) than G1, and G3 had very low scores (57.23) in Table 5.5. There is a significant difference between the three groups when combined with 把 *ba*, which is confirmed by the post hoc tests in Table 5.6.

Table 5.5: Three groups (with 把 *ba*)

with *ba*	G1	G2	G3
Mean	92.43	75.29	57.23
Median	100	80	50
Std	15.70	25.29	28.64
p–value (Anova)	5.4×10^{-24}		

Table 5.6: Post hoc tests for the three groups (with 把 *ba*)

(I) group	(J) group	Mean Difference (I–J)	Std. Error	Sig.	95% Confidence Interval	
					Lower Bound	Upper Bound
1	2	17.14*	4.69	.001	5.83	28.46
	3	35.20*	3.08	1.6×10^{-24}	27.77	42.64
2	1	–17.14*	4.69	.001	–28.46	–5.83
	3	18.06*	4.55	2.8×10^{-4}	7.10	29.02
3	1	–35.20*	3.08	1.6×10^{-24}	–42.64	–27.77
	2	–18.06*	4.55	2.8×10^{-4}	–29.02	–7.10

The differences of the three groups between with and without 把 *ba* care displayed in Table 5.7. All are acceptable without 把 *ba* (mean >90 in all three groups), while the sentences in G1 is still highly acceptable when with 把 *ba*, the scores of the sentences decrease in the other groups: from 97.86 to 75.29 in G2, and 90.77 to 57.23 in G3. The latter two are significantly different with把 *ba* from their counterparts without 把 *ba* (p<.05).

Table 5.7: Three groups with vs. without 把 *ba*

	G1		G2		G3	
	without *ba*	with *ba*	without *ba*	with *ba*	without *ba*	with *ba*
Mean	93.90	92.43	97.86	75.29	90.77	57.23
Median	100	100	100	80	100	52
Std	14.92	15.70	6.33	25.29	18.95	28.64
p–value	0.48		2.7×10^{-6}		7.6×10^{-26}	

5.4.1.2 Discussion

Based on the stance of viewing the 把 *ba*–construction as a marker of high semantic transitivity in Section 5.2 (cf. Hopper and Thompson 1980, Sun 1995), we will discuss the sentences individually to determine their degrees of transitivity so as to explain why there are differences in acceptability when combined with 把 *ba*. According to Hopper and Thompson (1980), ten parameters are used to rank high transitivity: (a) participants, (b) kinesis, (c) aspect, (d) punctuality, (e) volitionality, (f) affirmation, (g) mode, (h) agency, (i) affectedness of O and (j) individuation of O. Moreover, , affectedness of A plays a role as well (Næss, 2007).

With respect to these parameters, all sentences in the three groups (see 22–28) could be analyzed as highly transitive in some features: they all involve two participants and describe actions (in some cases, of a mental type like 'think/

listen' and, in other cases, of a physical, like 'practise'); they are all telic (with the perfective particle marker 了 *le*), affirmative, realis and have an A high in potency (A as a third person singular). Some features are irrelevant, though. Punctuality cannot be construed from these sentences, neither for 'think' in G1, nor for 'drink' in G3. As these examples are subject-oriented, affectedness of O will not be discussed either. In yet other features, finally, the sentences exhibit variation, causing differences in their overall degrees of semantic transitivity.

First, with regard to volitionality, according to), the effect on the patient is more overt if A is stated as behaving purposefully (Hopper and Thompson, 1980).[5] In line with construction grammar, a resultative construction is viewed as a whole, and the degree of volitionality of A regarding each construct is analyzed as follows. In (22), the subject/agent 他 *ta* 'he' carries out the action 想 *xiang* 'think' volitionally such that he thought (about the question) aiming to understand it. Therefore (22) is high in the volitionality of the agent. As regards (23), though 弄 *nong* 'do' means 'do' literally, it is interpreted as 'think' in (22), both with the purpose of 'understand'. So (23) also involves high volitionality of the agent. In terms of (24), the action 练 *lian* 'practice' is conducted by the agent volitionally and purposefully so as to be able to sing the song. Therefore, it also has high volitionality. Regarding (25) in G2, the sentence is also interpreted as A carrying out the action 'listen' to understand the principle and

5 One may ask what the relationship of volitionality with weak resultative is. The two notions reflect different perspectives of the semantics of resultatives. A resultative with a high degree of volitionality does not mean it is weak, as the result/goal is not necessarily led to by the action. For example, in (22), it has high volitionality and is strong, as he thought about the question, but may not understand it. On the other hand, a weak resultative is not necessarily high in volitionality. If the A is inanimate (e.g. *the pond froze solid*), there is no volitionality involved

hence A is highly volitional. To conclude, the sentences in G1 and G2 are all construed with high volitionality of the agent.

(22)	他	想-明白-了	这	个	问题
	ta	*xiang-mingbai-le*	*zhe*	*ge*	*wenti*
	he	think–understand–ASP	this	CL	question

'He thought about this question and as a result he understood it.'

(23)	她	弄-明白-了	这	个	道理
	ta	*nong-mingbai-le*	*zhe*	*ge*	*wenti*
	she	do–understand–ASP	this	CL	question

'She thought about this principle and as a result she understood it.'

(24)	她	练-会-了	这	首	歌
	ta	*lian-hui-le*	*zhe*	*shou*	*ge*
	she	practice–can–ASP	this	CL	song

'She practised this song and as a result she could sing it.'

(25)	她	听-懂-了	小宇	的	话
	ta	*ting-dong-le*	*Xiaoyu*	*de*	*hua*
	she	listen–understand–ASP	Xiaoyu(name)	POSS	words

'She listened to Xiaoyu's words and as a result she understood them.'

However, the examples in G3 are interpreted with low volitionality of A. For example, in (26) the agent 他 *ta* 'he' performed the action 喝 *he* 'drink', but he did not do it with the intention of being tired of this kind of tea. Therefore, A in (26) is non–volitional. Likewise, A did not see the smile in order to be used to it (as in 27), or listen to the words to be tired of them (see 28), or drink that kind of portion in order to be fed up with it (see 29). So all the sentences in G3 are construed as non–volitional.

(26)	他	喝–腻–了	这	种	茶
	ta	*he-ni-le*	*zhe*	*zhong*	*cha*
	he	drink–be tired of–ASP	this	kind	tea

'He had drunk this kind of tea so many times that he was tired of it.'

(27)	她	看–惯–了	那	种	微笑
	ta	*kan-guan –le*	*na*	*zhong*	*weixiao*
	she	see–be used to–ASP	that	kind	smile

'She had seen that kind of smile so many times that she was used to it.'

(28)	他	听–烦–了	老师	的	话
	ta	*ting-fan-le*	*laoshi*	*de*	*hua*
	he	listen– bored with –ASP	teacher	POSS	words

'He listened to the teacher's words and as a result he was bored with them. (He was bored with the teacher's words.)

(29)	她	喝–够–了	那	种	药水
	ta	*he-gou-le*	*na*	*zhong*	*yaoshui*
	she	drink–enough–ASP	that	kind	portion

'She had drunk that kind of portion so many times that she had enough of it.'

Secondly, with regards total affectedness, as these are subject/agent–oriented examples, according to Næss (2007), it is A that is affected. Considering the result XPs in G1, 明白 *mingbai* 'understand' in (22) is interpreted as knowing something thoroughly. So he fully understood the question after thinking. That is, he was totally affected by the action. So 明白

mingbai ‘understand’ is be regarded as involving the total affectedness of A. The same hods true with 会 hui ‘can’ in (24) as she could sing the song.

Regarding 听－懂 *ting-dong* ‘listen–understand’ in G2, an issue to be mentioned is that 明白 *mingbai* ‘understand’ and 懂 *dong* ‘understand’ differ in semantics. With similar meaning, the former is higher in degree of understanding than the latter. In Chinese, both (30a) and (30b) are acceptable. However, (31a) is acceptable and (31b) is not.

This could be explained by our world knowledge. In cognitive process, the degree of understanding through listening and thinking differs. If one listens to something, the result of listening is not necessarily deep in terms of understanding. Nevertheless, if one thinks about something, the result of thinking usually is thorough understanding. So the combination of 明白 *mingbai* ‘understand’ and 听 *ting* ‘listen’ and the combination of 懂 *dong* ‘understand’ and听 *ting* ‘listen’ are both acceptable, as the action of ‘listerning’ does not involve a high level of understanding and both明白 *mingbai* ‘understand’ and 懂 *dong* ‘understand’ are compatible with such a meaning. However, the combination of 懂 *dong* ‘understand’ and 想 *xiang* ‘think’ is not acceptable – unlike that of 明白 *mingbai* ‘understand’ and 想 *xiang* ‘think’ – because the meaning of 懂 *dong* ‘understand’ is not compatible with the high level of understanding involved in 想 *xiang* ‘think’. Therefore, (31a) is acceptable, while (31b) is not. Consequently, 听－懂 *ting-dong* ‘listen–understand’ in G2 has a lower degree of understanding than 想－明白 *xiang-mingbai* ‘think–understand’ in G1 and hence also a lower degree of affectedness of A.

(30) a. 听－明白

ting-mingbai

listen–understand

b. 听－懂

ting-dong

listen–understand

(31) a. 想－明白

xiang-mingbai

think–understand

b. *想－懂

xiang-dong

think–understand

Concerning the sentences in G3 then, the predicates are action verbs like 'drink' in 喝－腻 *he-ni* 'drink–be tired of' (see 26) and 喝－够 *he-gou* 'drink–enough' (as in 29), as well as mental verbs 'see' and 'listen' in 看－惯 *kan-guan* 'see–be used to' (27) and 听－烦 *ting-fan* 'listen–bored with' (28). Either drinking or seeing/ listening, A is tired of or bored with P, which can be perceived as total affectedness of A cognitively.

Finally with regard to the feature individuation of O, according to Hopper and Thompson (1980: 253), it refers both to the distinctness of the patient from the A, and to its distinctness from its own background. The authors suggest further properties to judge the degree of individuation as in Table 5.8. The more features that O has in the first column, the more individuated it is.

Table 5.8: Individuation of OHopper and Thompson (1980: 253)

INDIVIDUATED	NON–INDIVIDUATED
proper	common
human, animate	inanimate
concrete	abstract
singular	plural
count	mass
referential, definite	non–referential

As regards the Os in the sentences (22–29), they are all common and definite, but inanimate. The Os in G1 are like 'this question' as in (32a), which is singular, countable but abstract. The O in G2 is 'words' (see 33a), which is countable but abstract and plural. The Os in G3 are either 'this kind of tea' in (34a), which is concrete, singular and countable, or 'that kind of smile' in (35a), which is singular, countable but abstract. In addition, the Os in G3 are singular in form (that kind of tea/smile), but not singular in meaning, as they refer to that kind of tea or smile, which is mass/ plural cognitively.

One thing to be noted is that if the number of the Os in the items is changed, as in (32b–35b), the acceptability judgements remain the same as their counterparts in (a). For example, the plural counterpart of (32a) in (32b) is equally acceptable. Similarly, if (33a) is changed from plural to singular as in (33b), it is still marginally acceptable. As for the sentences in G3, acceptability judgements between (34/35a) and the plural counterparts do not differ (34/35b). They are all unacceptable. So we may see an issue which matters here is whether O is individuated in an action from beginning to end. As long as O is related to a single action rather than repeated actions, it can be construed as individuated. Individuation of O in the three groups is stated in (36).

(32) a. 他 把 这 个 问题 想–明白–了

ta ba zhe ge wenti xiang-mingbai-le

he *ba* this CL question think–understand–ASP

'He thought about this question and as a result he understood it.'

b. 他 把 这 些 问题 想–明白–了

ta ba zhe xie wenti xiang-mingbai-le

he *ba* this some question think–understand–ASP

'He thought about these questions and as a result he understood them.'

(33) a. ?她 把 小宇 的 话 听–懂–了

ta ba Xiaoyu de hua ting-dong-le

she *ba* Xiaoyu (name) POSS words listen–understand–ASP

'She listened to Xiaoyu's words and as a result she understood them.'

b. ?她 把 那 句 话 听–懂–了

ta ba na ju hua ting-dong-le

she *ba* that CL word listen–understand–ASP

'She listened to that sentence and as a result she understood it.'

(34) a. *他 把 这 种 茶 喝–腻–了

ta ba zhe zhong cha he-ni-le

he *ba* this kind tea drink–be tired of–ASP

'He had drunk this kind of tea so many times that he was tired of it.'

b. *他 把 这些 种类 的 茶 喝-腻-了

ta ba zhexie zhonglei de cha he-ni-le

he *ba* these kind POSS tea drink–be tired of–ASP

'He had drank these kinds of tea so many times and as a result he was tired of them.'

(35) a. *她 把 那 种 微笑 看-惯-了

ta ba na zhong weixiao kan-guan -le

she *ba* that kind smile see–be used to–ASP

'She had seen that kind of smile so many times that she was used to it.'

b. *她 把 那些 种类 的 微笑 看-惯-了

ta ba naxie zhonglei de weixiao kan-guan -le

she *ba* those kind POSS smile see–be used to–ASP

'She had seen those kinds of smiles so many times and as a result she was used to them.'

(36) Individuation of O:

G1: high; single action (singular, count, though abstract)

G2: high; single action (count, though abstract and plural)

G3: low; repeated actions (concrete, singular and count for 'tea/potion'; abstract, singular and count for 'smile' ; abstract, plural and count for 'words')

Considering the parameters discussed above, all other factors being equal, the semantic transitivity of the sentences in the three groups can be analyzed as in (37). According to Hopper and Thompson (1980), the more 'high' features a clause has, the more transitive it is. We can see the sentences in G1 have 3 features, those in G2 2, and those in G3 1. Thereby, the sentences can be ranked in terms of semantic transitivity as G1>G2>G3, from more transitive to less transitive. In view of the fact that 把 *ba* is a marker of high transitivity, we can see that the more semantic transitive a sentence is , the more acceptable it is when combined with 把 *ba*.

(37) G1 volitionality: volitional
affectedness of O: totally affected
individuation of O: high
G2 volitionality: volitional
individuation of O: high
G3 affectedness of A: totally affected

5.4.2 把 *ba* + resultatives with and without 终于 *zhongyu* 'finally'

5.4.2.1 Results

The adverb 终于 *zhongyu* 'finally' was tested here as another parameter. Table 5.9 demonstrates that in 把 ba+ resultatives, if 终于 *zhongyu* 'finally' is added, the scores rise in all three groups, which suggest higher acceptability. Significant differences can be found between with 把 *ba* and 把 ba + 终于 *zhongyu* 'finally' in both G1 and G2 ($p</=.05$). However, the scores do not vary much in G3 (both are very low).

Table 5.9: Three groups with 把 *ba*: with vs. without 终于 *zhongyu* 'finally'

	G1		G2		G3	
	with *ba*	with *ba* and *zhongyu* 'finally'	with *ba*	with *ba* and *zhongyu* 'finally'	with *ba*	with *ba* and *zhongyu* 'finally'
Mean	92.43	97.20	75.29	87.14	57.23	58.18
Median	100	100	80	100	50	50
Std	15.70	10.99	25.29	24.59	28.64	29.56
p–value	0.01		0.05		0.78	

If the parameters were compared together within groups, as shown in Table 5.10, the sentences in G1 are judged high with and without 把 *ba*. The cases with 终于 *zhongyu* 'finally' scored significantly higher than the cases without it ($p<.05$). There is also a significant difference between sentences with 把 *ba* and with 把 *ba* + 终于 *zhongyu* + 'finally' (p<.05), the mean raising from 92.43 to 97.2.0

Table 5.10: G1: acceptable group with vs. without 把 *ba*/ 终于 *zhongyu* 'finally'

	without *ba*	with *ba*	without *zhongyu* 'finally'	with *zhongyu* 'finally'	with *ba*	with *ba* and *zhongyu* 'finally'
Mean	93.90	92.43	93.90	97.90	92.43	97.20
Median	100	100	100	100	100	100
Std.	14.92	15.69	14.920	9.59	15.70	10.99
p–value	0.48		0.02		0.01	

Considering G2, we can see in in Table 5.11 that the sentences becomes less acceptable when with 把 *ba*, the mean decreasing significantly from 97.86 to 75.29 ($p<.05$). The sentences are equally acceptable with and without 终于

zhongyu ‘finally’ (p>.05). However, if 终于 *zhongyu* ‘finally’ is added with 把 *ba*, the score increases significantly to 87.14 (p=.05).

Table 5.11: Marginally acceptable group with vs. without 把 *ba*/ 终于 *zhongyu* ‘finally’

	without *ba*	with *ba*	without *zhongyu* ‘finally’	with *zhongyu* ‘finally’	with *ba*	with *ba* and *zhongyu* ‘finally’
Mean	97.86	75.29	97.86	96.29	75.29	87.14
Median	100	80	100	100	80	100
Std.	6.32	25.29	6.32	12.15	25.29	24.59
p–value	2.7×10^{-6}		0.5		0.05	

With regards G3 (Table 5.12), there is a significant difference between with and without 把 *ba* (p<.05): the mean of the former is much higher than the latter (90.77 vs. 57.23). If combined with 终于 *zhongyu* ‘finally’, the mean with 把 *ba* rises just a little and remains very low (from 57.23 to 58.19), with no significant difference between the two cases (p>.05).

Table 5.12: G3: the least acceptable group with vs. without 把 *ba*/ 终于 *zhongyu* ‘finally’

	without *ba*	with *ba*	without *zhongyu* ‘finally’	with *zhongyu* ‘finally’	with *ba*	with *ba* and *zhongyu* ‘finally’
Mean	90.77	57.23	90.77	74.16	57.23	58.18
Median	100	52	100	82.5	52	50
Std.	18.95	28.64	18.95	28.56	28.64	29.56
p–value	7.6×10^{-26}		2.02×10^{-8}		0.78	

To conclude, all sentences are well accepted without 把 *ba*, but the results suggest significant differences between the three groups. When combined with

把 *ba*, G1 is acceptable, G2 marginally acceptable and G3 the least acceptable. If 终于 *zhongyu* 'finally' is added, there is no significant difference between with and without 终于 *zhongyu* 'finally', and significant differences between with 把 *ba* and with 把 *ba* + 终于 *zhongyu* 'finally' in the first two groups, but not in G3. That is, G3 differs significantly between with and without 终于 *zhongyu* 'finally', yet not between with 把 *ba* and 把 *ba* + 终于 *zhongyu* 'finally'.

5.4.2.2 Discussion

The differences between sentences with 把 *ba* plus 终于 *zhongyu* 'finally' and sentences with 把 *ba* but without 终于 *zhongyu* 'finally' can also be explained in terms of semantic transivity. As mentioned in Section 5.3.2.2, 终于 *zhongyu* 'finally' expresses high volitionality of the agent, which can increase the degree of transitivity of the sentence. Therefore, the semantics of 终于 *zhongyu* 'finally' coincide with the function of 把 *ba*， both indicating high transitivity.

Regarding the sentences in the three groups, the mean for 把 *ba* + 终于 *zhongyu* 'finally' is higher than for 把 *ba* without 终于 *zhongyu* 'finally' in G1 ($p<.05$). The sentences are equally acceptable between with and without 把 *ba*, but the score varies significantly between with and without 终于 *zhongyu* 'finally', though all are well accepted (>90). This is caused by the fact that all the factors are relevant to high transitivity: semantics of the sentences, 把 *ba* and 终于 *zhongyu* 'finally'. Already highly acceptable, when the sentences are combined with 终于 *zhongyu* 'finally', they become more acceptable (from 93.90 to 97.90), as 终于 *zhongyu* 'finally' enhances the degree of transitivity. This also holds true for with 把 ba, adding 终于 *zhongyu* 'finally' makes the sentences with 把 *ba* and 终于 *zhongyu* 'finally' even more acceptable (mean from 92.43 to 97.20; p<.05 in Table 5.10).

As for G2, the sentences are marginally acceptable with 把 *ba* due to their lower degree of transitivity than the G1 sentences. However, there is a certain degree of transitivity in G2, so no significant difference appears between with and without 终于 *zhongyu* 'finally'. Nevertheless, since 终于 *zhongyu* 'finally' can increase transitivity of a clause, after adding the adverb, the sentence with 把 *ba* and 终于 *zhongyu* 'finally' becomes more acceptable (mean from 75.3 to 87.1; p=.05). This is caused by the consistence of the semantics of 把 *ba* and 终于 *zhongyu* 'finally' in term of high transitivity. Combining the two markers strengthens the level of transivitiy and hence increases acceptability.

With respect to G3, the mean of the sentences with 把 *ba* and 终于 *zhongyu* 'finally' is still very low. This is due to the semantics of the patterns in this group (e.g. 喝–腻 *he-ni* 'drink–be tired of', 看–惯 *kan-guan* 'see–be used to'). These patterns are interpreted as repeated actions leading to unpleasant consequences, so the interpretation that someone tries to achieve such results (e.g. trying hard to see a kind of smile so as to be used to it) is not common in our daily life. This makes the sentences unnatural. In fact, the mean for the patterns with zhongyu 'finally' in G3 is relatively low compared to those without 终于 *zhongyu* 'finally'; there is a significant difference between the two (p<0.05). So the low ratings for the sentences with 把 *ba* and 终于 *zhongyu* 'finally' in G3 are reasonable.

5.5 Further implications

5.5.1 Subject/agent-oriented resultatives with postverbal NP

As mentioned in Section 5.1.2, there are subject/agent–oriented resultatives found in the corpus with a postverbal NP. Among the examples we can see these sentences occur in two situations. First, syntactically, if the verb is transitive and the result XP is a two–place predicate when used independently, then the V–result XP combination is agent–oriented and can take a postverbal NP. For instance, in (38a) 学–会 *xue-hui* 'learn–can' is a subject/agent–oriented resultative taking a postverbal NP. 学 *xue* 'learn' is transitive (see 38b) and 会 *hui* 'can' is a two–place predicate as in (38c). When the two are combined together to express 'she learned to swim and as a result she could swim' as in (38a), P 游泳 *youyong* 'swim' can still be kept, and the result XP is predicated of the subject (also the agent). Similarly, (39a) is a subject/agent–oriented resultative which takes a P because 想 *xiang* 'think' is transitive (see 39b), and 明白 *mingbai* 'understand' is a two–place predicate (e.g. 39c).

(38) a. 她　终于　学–会–了　游泳　(LCMC P10 7)

ta　*zhongyu*　*xue-hui-le*　*youyong*

she　finally　learn–can–ASP　swim

'She learned to swim and finally as a result she could swim.'

b. 她　学　游泳

ta　*xue*　*youyong*

She learn swim

'She learned to swim.'

c. 她 会 游泳

ta *hui* *youyong*

she can swim

'She could swim.'

(39) a. 他 想–明白–了 这 个 问题 (CCL 7.1)

ta *xiang-mingbai-le* *zhe* *ge* *wenti*

he think–understand–ASP this CL question

'He thought about this question and as a result he understood it.'

b. 他 想 这 个 问题 (CCL 7.1)

ta *xiang* *zhe* *ge* *wenti*

he think this CL question

'He thought about this question.'

c. 他 明白 这 个 问题 (CCL 7.1)

ta *mingbai* *zhe* *ge* *wenti*

he understand this CL question

'He understood this question.'

The reason for the P being able to occur in subject/agent–oriented resultatives like (38/39a) is that both the verb and the result XP are syntactically transitive, so the combination of the two can also be used transitively. In contrast, the V–result XP pattern in (40a) cannot take a postverbal NP. Recall the examples mentioned in Section 5.1.2, which are repeated below as in (40). Though the verb is transitive (see 40b), the result XP 累 *lei* 'tired' is a one–

place predicate. So (40c) is acceptable, whereas (40d) is not if a patient follows, as the ability of such a combination to take object is not as high as that of the transitive verb + two–place result XP. Furthermore, if a verb is intransitive and the result XP is a one–place predicate (e.g. 41), there is no need to add a postverbal NP since the object is not relevant at all.

(40) a. *她 做–累–了 题目

ta *zuo-lei-le* *timu*

she do–tired–ASP drill

'She did the drills and as a result she was tired.'

b. 她 做 题目

ta *zuo* *timu*

she do drill

'She did the drills.'

c. 她 累 了

ta *lei* *le*

she tired ASP

'She was tired.'

d. *她 累 题目

ta *lei* *timu*

she tired drill

'She was tired drill.'

(41) 他 走–累–了 (CCL2.1)

ta *zou-lei-le*

he walk–tired–ASP

'He walked and as a result he was tired.'

Secondly, semantically, if the combination of V + result XP is interpreted as repeated actions, then even though the result XP is a one–place predicate, the resultative construction can still take a postverbal NP. Although the verb 喝 *he* 'drink' is transitive as in (42b), the result XP 腻 *ni* 'be tired of' cannot take P independently (see 42c), the postverbal NP can still follow the combination 喝–腻 *he-ni* 'drink–be tired of' as in (42a). This is because (42a) is construed as repeated actions: he had drunk this kind of tea for so many times that he was tired of it.

(42) a. 他 喝–腻–了 这 种 茶
ta he-ni-le zhe zhong cha
he drink–be tired of–ASP this kind tea
'He had drunk this kind of tea for so many times that he was tired of it.'

b. 他 喝 这 种 茶
ta he zhe zhong cha
he drink this kind tea
'He drank this kind of tea.'

c. *他 腻 这 种 茶
ta ni zhe zhong cha
he be tired of this kind tea
'He was tired of this kind of tea.'

When the verb is intransitive and the result XP is one–place, if V + result XP is construed as repeated actions, the combination can still take a postverbal

NP. In (43b) 走 *zou* 'walk' is intransitive,[6] and 惯 *guan* 'be used to' is a one–place predicate (see 43c). Since the combination of the two is interpreted as repeated actions (people walked on the mountain roads so many times that they were used to it), there is a postverbal NP. Compare (43a) and (43b): both with intransitive verb and one–place result XP, the former cannot take P, whereas the latter takes P because of its semantics of repeated actions.

(43) a. *他　　走－累－了　　山路

ta　　*zou-lei-le*　　*shanlu*

he　　walk–tired–ASP　　mountain road

'He walked on the mountain road and as a result he was tired.'

b. 山里人　　走－惯－了　　山路 (CCL18.1)

shanliren　　*zou-guan-le*　　*shanlu*

mountain in people　　walk– be used to –ASP　　mountain road

'People in the mountain walked on the mountain road (so many times) and as a result they were used to it.'

c. *山里人　　惯　　山路

shanliren　　*guan*　　*shanlu*

mountain in people　　be used to　　mountain road

'People in the mountain were used to the mountain roads.'

With respect to the reasons, as mentioned in Chapter 2, Section 2.2.6,

6 走 *zou* 'walk' may be viewed as transitive as in (iii) below, where a postverbal NP follows. However, in semantics P is not patient, but a theme or location. So generally 走 *zou* 'walk' is intransitive.

(iii) 山里人　　走　　山路

shanliren　　*zou*　　*shanlu*

mountain in people　　walk　　mountain road

'People in the mountain walked on the mountain roads.'

Broccias (2013: 181) claims that if the postverbal NP is not a subcategorized object of the verb, the verbal event should be carried out in an above–the–norm fashion so as to form a resultative construction. This is because there is an energy flow between the two subevents. The action is carried out sufficiently so as to cause change to the postverbal NP which is not the verb's subcategorized object. Therefore the NP has the above–the–norm reading with regard to change of state. For instance, in (44) feet is an unsubcategorized object of the verb run, and they became sore as a result of too much running. The above–the norm interpretation suggests the energy flow coded by the action, which enables the verb to take a non–subcategorized object and form a resultative construction. In line with Broccias's (2013) idea, it can be argued that if an action is repeated (e.g. 43b), it designates a sufficient energy flow, which causes a change of state of the NP. Although it is subject–oriented, a postverbal NP is able to occur in the resultative.

(44) John danced his feet sore.

As mentioned in Section 5.1, the postverbal NP in subject/agent–oriented resultatives provides the possibility for the combination with 把 *ba*. As to the V–result XP construction, either the verb is transitive and the result XP a two–place predicate, or the V–result XP is interpreted as repeated actions, in which case a P can occur.

5.5.2 The acceptability of 把 *ba* + subject-oriented resultatives

Generally, the resultative constructions with the interpretation that the subject makes efforts to achieve something thoroughly are acceptable when combined with 把 *ba*. The cognitive explanation I propose is that high transitivity of a sentence construed in the resultative construction is compatible with the high transitivity function of 把 *ba*.

To be specific, as mentioned in Section 5.4, patterns in G1 (e.g. 想–明白 *xiang-mingbai* 'think–understand', 练–会 *lian-hui* 'practice–can') have high semantic transitivity, which are compatible with the function of ba, so the combination of 把 *ba* and these patterns are fully acceptable with high ratings. With respect to the pattern 听–懂 *ting-dong* 'listen–understand' in G2, its degree of semantic transitivity is lower than the items in G1, which makes it partly acceptable with 把 *ba* and explains its lower score than G1. Finally, in G3 (e.g. 喝–腻 *he-ni* 'drink–be tired of', 看–惯 *kan-guan* 'see–be used to'), the patterns are interpreted with a low degree of transitivity, which is in contrast to the semantics of 把 *ba*, and hence the sentences are the least acceptable with 把 *ba*, receiving the lowest scores. The significant differences in G2 and G3 between with and without 把 *ba* reflect the incompatibility of the sentences' low transitivity in semantics and the function of 把 *ba* as a marker of high transitivity. The higher score of 把 *ba* + sentences with 终于 *zhongyu* 'finally' than those without the adverb ($p<.05$) in G1 and G2 provides further evidence for the compatibility of the semantics of these particular resultatives, the adverb 终于 *zhongyu* 'finally' and the function of 把 *ba* , all construed as or indicating high semantic transitivity.

The reasons for the varying acceptability of 把 *ba* in subject/agent-oriented resultatives endorse the general analysis of 把 *ba* as a marker of high semantic transitivity in the literature. As stated in Chapter 2, Section 2.3, the function of 把 *ba* has been widely discussed since the 1940s from various perspectives, but no agreement has been reached. The results of the questionnaire surveys and discussion in this chapter suggest that 把 *ba* should be analyzed as marking high transitivity.

5.6 Concluding remarks

In this chapter I mainly focus on the acceptability of prototypical 把 *ba* + subject/agent–oriented resultatives in Chinese. Though the combination of the 把 *ba*–construction and the resultative construction has been discussed in the literature (e.g. Huang 1996, Wang 2001, Song 2004, Ye 2004, Zhao 2009), the acceptability of 把 *ba* + subject/agent–oriented resultative has so far received very little scholarly attention, with the exception of a few problematic discussions (e.g. Ye 2004, Zhao 2009). The 把 *ba*–construction requires a postverbal NP, whereas most subject/agent–oriented resultatives take no P. However, in the LCMC and the CCL some examples of subject/agent–oriented resultatives are found to take a postverbal NP, which makes it possible for them to be combined with把 ba. I propose two circumstances under which the subject/agent–oriented resultatives can take a postverbal NP: the verb is transitive and the result XP is a two–place predicate, or the V–result XP is interpreted as repeated actions. In other words, syntactic and semantic factors determine whether a subject–oriented resultative can take a postverbal NP.

The combinations of a subject/agent–oriented resultative and 把 *ba* do differ in acceptability. Due to the infrequency of corpus examples, I carried out a questionnaire survey among 71 Chinese college students to test the acceptability of 把 *ba* + subject/agent–oriented resultatives in Chinese. The technique of magnitude estimation (see Bard et al. 1996) was adopted in the survey, which could detect small but significant differences in acceptability.

The results suggest that the acceptability of 把 *ba* + subject–oriented resultative depends on the degree of semantic transitivity of sentences. In general, the more transitively a resultative construction is expressed, the more acceptable it is when combined with 把 *ba*. The cognitive explanation I propose is that high transitivity expressed by the sentence (including the volitionality of the agent, a high degree of affectedness of A, and a highly individuated O) is compatible with the function of 把 *ba* as marking high transitivity.

The research in this chapter fills in the gap in the literature about the acceptability of 把 *ba* + subject/agent–oriented resultatives. It also provides evidence for considering the affectedness of A as a parameter of Transitivity (Næss 2007), which is not mentioned by Hopper and Thompson (1980). The conclusion sheds light on the study of the semantics of the 把 *ba*–construction in previous scholarship and supports its analysis as a marker of high semantic transitivity. The adoption of magnitude estimation for the study of Chinese grammar is relatively innovative in the Chinese context, and the results suggest that it may indeed be useful for the study of other grammatical phenomena in Chinese.

Chapter 6 The acceptability of 把 *ba* + object-oriented resultatives

6.1 Introduction

6.1.1 把 *ba* + object-oriented resultatives in Chinese

As mentioned in Chapter 4, Chinese resultatives can be classified according to the overlapping criteria of marginal/prototypical, subject–/object–oriented and agent–/ patient–/location–oriented. This chapter mainly focuses on the prototypical type. All object–oriented resultatives are patient–oriented in the Lancaster Corpus of Mandarin Chinese (LCMC), for instance (1).

(1)	她	用	力	吹–灭–了	蛋糕	上	的
	ta	*yong*	*li*	*chui-mie-le*	*dangao*	*shang*	*de*
	she	use	strength	blow–quench–ASP	cake	on	POSS
	蜡烛		(LCMC A14)				
	lazhu						
	candle						

'She blew the candles on the cake with strength and as a result the candles were quenched.' (She blew out the candles on the cake with strength)

As mentioned in Chapter 1, Section 1.1.1, 'wipe–clean' in (2a) is a commonly discussed example in the scholarship (e.g. Goldberg 1995, Washio 1997, Rappaport Hovav and Levin 2001, Croft 2012). Its literal translation into Chinese does not sound natural (see 2b), and it seems more acceptable when combined with 把 *ba* (as in 2c). More generally, the combinations of 把 *ba* and object–oriented resultative constructions in Chinese also have different degrees of acceptability. Of all such constructions, some appear to be acceptable both with and without 把 *ba* as in (3), whereas some are better with 把 *ba* (e.g. 2c). It is observed that all object–oriented resultative constructions, both (3a) and its counterpart with 把 *ba* in (3b) are well accepted. There are also cases like (4), where the variant with 把 *ba* seems to be less acceptable. So a question arises as to why some object–oriented resultatives are equally acceptable with and without 把 *ba*, whereas others are not. In other words, recall Question 6: What determines the acceptability of object–oriented resultatives with and without 把 *ba*?

(2) a. She wiped the table clean. (Washio 1997:10)

b. ?她 擦–干净了 桌子

ta *ca-ganjing-le* *zhuozi*

she wipe–clean–ASP table

'She wiped the table clean.'

c. 她 把 桌子 擦–干净了

ta *ba* *zhuozi* *ca-ganjing-le*

she	*ba*	table	wipe–clean–ASP

'She wiped the table clean.'

(3) a.

他	擦－干－了	头发	(CCL 89.1)
ta	*ca-gan-le*	*toufa*	
he	wipe–dry–ASP	hair	

'He wiped her hair dry.'

b.

他	把	头发	擦－干了
ta	*ba*	*toufa*	*ca-gan-le*
he	*ba*	hair	wipe–dry–ASP

'He wiped his hair dry.'

(4) a.

妹妹	哭－湿－了	手绢	(CCL 1.1)
meimei	*ku-shi-le*	*shoujuan*	
younger sister	cry–wet–ASP	handkerchief	

'The younger sister cried and as a result the handkerchief was wet.' (The younger sister cried the handkerchief wet)

b.

?妹妹	把	手绢	哭－湿－了
meimei	*ba*	*shoujuan*	*ku-shi-le*
younger sister	*ba*	handkerchief	cry–wet–ASP

'The younger sister cried and as a result the handkerchief was wet.' (The younger sister cried the handkerchief wet.)

6.1.2 Methodology

As mentioned in Chapter 3, Section 3.3.4, a second questionnaire survey

(Survey 2) was designed for testing the acceptability of object–oriented resultatives with and without 把 *ba* (e.g. 5a). In addition, subject–oriented ones (see 5b) were also included in Survey 2 for comparisons between subject/agent– and object–oriented patterns. The parameters in Survey 2 include subject– and object–oriented resultatives, with and without 把 *ba*. Six object–oriented resultative patterns taken from the CCL and the LCMC are used as test sentences, namely 弄–坏 *nong-huai* 'do–broken', 哭–湿 *ku-shi* 'cry–wet', 唱–红 *chang-hong* 'sing–popular', 擦–干 *ca-gan* 'wipe–dry', 擦–干净 *ca-ganjing* 'wipe–clean' and 叠–整齐 *die-zhengqi* 'fold–neat'. In addition, four subject–oriented resultatives used in Survey 1 were retained in Survey 2: 想–明白 *xiang-mingbai* 'think–understand', 练–会 *lian-hui* 'practise–can', 听–懂 *ting-dong* 'listen–understand' and 听–烦 *ting-fan* 'listen–bored with'.

(5) a. 他　擦–干–了　头发

ta　*ca-gan-le*　*toufa*

he　wipe–dry–ASP　hair

'He wiped his hair dry.'

b. 她　练–会–了　这　首　歌

ta　*lian-hui-le*　*zhe*　*shou*　*ge*

she　practice–can–ASP　this　CL　song

'She practised this song and as a result she could sing it.'

In total there are ten sentences, each with and without 把 *ba*. An equal number of fillers are used, which takes the total number of questionnaire items to 40. As mentioned in Chapter 3, Section 3.3.4, due to the limit of participants' attention span, a version with a reversed sequence is provided. So there are two versions of the questionnaire in Survey 2. The full survey can be found in the Appendix A and B.

Different from the method of data collection in Survey 1, I went to the library and classrooms at Lancaster University and several universities in China for Survey 2, asking native students of Chinese whether they would like to take part in the project. If so, I handed out the questionnaire surveys and waited until they finished. Eighty–four participants completed Survey 2, using the technique of magnitude estimation. They first practised with the method, and then judged 40 sentences. There are 30 males and 54 females, with a mean age of 21.25 years.

After collecting and normalizing the data, as mentioned in Chapter 3, Section 3.4, the process includes the calculation of data which satisfy the condition $-3 <= z\text{-}score$ (standard deviation) $<= 3$ for the mean, median, standard deviation and p–value via t–tests and ANOVA.

6.1.3 Structure of the chapter

The remainder of this chapter comprises the following parts: the acceptability of 把 *ba* + object–oriented resultatives (Section 6.2), the acceptability of 把 *ba*+ subject–oriented resultatives (Section 6.3), the acceptability of 把 *ba* + subject–/ object–oriented resultatives (Section 6.4), further implications (Section 6.5) and concluding remarks (Section 6.6).

This chapter discusses Question 6 and provides possible explanations. Furthermore, by comparing the acceptability of subject–and object–oriented resultatives with and without 把 *ba*, the acceptability of Chinese resultatives, as well as the combination with 把 *ba*, is integrated as a whole. The capability of resultative constructions to take a postverbal NP is a crucial factor for the acceptability of subject– and object–oriented types, although constraints differ for the two. The number of syllables of the pattern 'verb + result XP', the status of the main verb and result XP, as well as the interpretation of resultatives affect acceptability. Regarding 把 *ba* + resultatives, the degree of semantic transitivity of a sentence plays a role in acceptability judgements. Since 把 *ba* is a marker of high semantic transitivity, a sentence interpreted with high transitivity is fully acceptable when combined with 把 *ba*.

6.2 The acceptability of object-oriented resultatives with and without 把 *ba*

6.2.1 Results

In Table 6.1 we can see that acceptability varies between with and without 把 *ba* among the six object–oriented resultatives, with examples as in (6a–f). Four patterns suggest no significant difference (p>.05), namely 弄–坏 *nong-huai* 'do–broken', 哭–湿 *ku-shi* 'cry–wet', 唱–红 *chang-hong* 'sing–popular' and 擦–干 *ca-gan* 'wipe–dry'. There are significant differences (*p*<.05) between with and without 把 *ba* regarding two patterns, 擦–干净 *ca-ganjing* 'wipe–clean' and 叠–整齐 *die-zhengqi* 'fold–neat'. Five patterns with 把 *ba* receive higher scores than without 把 *ba*, and one pattern is rated lower with 把 *ba* than without 把 *ba*, although the difference is not significant (哭–湿 *ku-shi* 'cry–wet' from 87.4 to 83.4; *p*=.14). But there is a trend in the data (.05< *p*<0.2), which means that if the sample size is large enough, there might be a significant difference.

(6) a.

他	弄–坏–了	小	火车
ta	*nong-huai-le*	*xiao*	*huoche*
he	do–broken–ASP	small	train

'He played with the model train and as a result the train was broken.'

b.

她	哭–湿–了	手绢
ta	*ku-shi-le*	*shoujuan*
she	cry–wet–ASP	handkerchief

'She cried and as a result the handkerchief was wet.' (She cried the handkerchief wet.)

c.

她	唱–红–了	那	首	歌
ta	*chang-hong-le*	*na*	*shou*	*ge*
she	sing–popular–ASP	that	CL	song

'She sang that song and as a result the song was popular.'

d.

他	擦–干–了	头发
ta	*ca-gan-le*	*toufa*
he	wipe–dry–ASP	hair

'He wiped her hair dry.'

e.

他	擦–干净了	桌子
ta	*ca-ganjing-le*	*zhuozi*

he wipe–clean–ASP table

'He wiped the table clean.'

f. 她 叠–整齐–了 衣服

ta die-zhengqi-le yifu

she fold–neat–ASP clothes

'She folded the clothes and as a result the clothes were neat.'

Table 6.1: Object–oriented resultatives with and without 把 *ba*

		Number	Mean	Median	Std	*p*–value
nong-huai 'do–damage'	without *ba*	84	94.93	100	11.88	0.28
	with *ba*	83	96.65	100	8.31	
ku-shi 'cry –wet'	without *ba*	83	87.43	94	15.97	0.14
	with *ba*	81	83.37	90	19.37	
chang-hong 'sing–popular'	without *ba*	83	83.33	88.5	19.43	0.07
	with *ba*	78	87.67	92.5	16.04	
ca-gan 'wipe–dry'	without *ba*	83	91.82	100	18.80	0.37
	with *ba*	83	94.06	100	12.66	
ca-ganjing 'wipe–clean'	without *ba*	84	82.87	90	19.85	2.33×10^{-7}
	with *ba*	84	95.73	100	9.11	
die-zhengqi 'fold–neat'	without *ba*	81	77.37	80	20.46	5.62×10^{-9}
	with *ba*	84	93.71	100	12.94	

From a different perspective, the patterns can be compared with each other (see Table 6.2). Since four without 把 *ba* (except for the two with significant differences between with and without 把 *ba*) are all taken from the corpus, comparisons are carried out when combined with 把 *ba*. ANOVA presents significant differences (*p*<.05) among the six 把 *ba* + object-oriented resultatives (*p*<.05). In Table 6.2 we can see that most ratings are quite high (>85), whereas only one is comparatively lower than the others ('cry –wet' 83.4). Recall that this pattern is judged lower with 把 *ba* than without 把 *ba* (the difference is not significant, but there is a trend in the data), and this will be discussed below in Section 6.2.2.

Table 6.2: Six object-oriented resultatives with 把 *ba*

	N	Mean	Std. Deviation	Std. Error
1 'do-damage'	83	96.65	8.31	0.91
2 'cry-wet'	81	83.37	19.37	2.15
3 'sing-popular'	78	87.67	16.03	1.82
4 'wipe-dry'	83	94.06	12.65	1.39
5 'wipe-clean'	84	95.73	9.10	0.99
6 'fold-neat'	84	93.71	12.94	1.41
Total	493	91.95	14.28	0.64

In addition, post hoc tests show significant differences between some pairs (see Table 6.3). As in Table 6.4, significant differences mainly exist between two patterns (哭–湿 *ku-shi* 'cry–wet', 唱–红 *chang-hong* 'sing-popular') and the other four sentences. However, there is no significant difference between the two patterns with 把 *ba*.

Table 6.3: Post hoc tests for 哭 – 湿 *ku–shi* 'cry–wet' and 唱 – 红 *chang–hong* 'sing–popular' and other patterns with 把 *ba*

(I) group	(J) group	Mean Difference (I–J)	Std. Error	Sig.	95% Confidence Interval	
					Lower Bound	Upper Bound
2 'cry–wet'	1	−13.28*	2.11	.00	−19.52	−7.04
	3	−4.29	2.14	.69	−10.64	2.04
	4	−10.69*	2.11	.00	−16.93	−4.45
	5	−12.35*	2.11	.00	−18.58	−6.13
	6	−10.34*	2.11	.00	−16.57	−4.12
3'sing–popular'	1	−8.98*	2.13	.00	−15.29	−2.68
	2	4.29	2.14	.69	−2.04	10.64
	4	−6.39*	2.13	.04	−12.70	−.09
	5	−8.06*	2.13	.00	−14.34	−1.78
	6	−6.04	2.13	.071	−12.33	.24

Table 6.4: *ba* + object–oriented resultative pairs that are significantly differences (p<.05)

Pattern a (with mean)	Pattern b (with mean)	Pattern c (with mean)
ba+ku-shi 'cry –wet' 83.37	*ba+nong-huai* 'do–damage' 96.65	*ba+chang-hong* 'sing–popular' 87.67
	ba+ca-gan 'wipe–dry' 94.06	
	ba+ca-ganjing 'wipe–clean' 95.73	
	ba+die-zhengqi 'fold–neat' 93.7`	

6.2.2 Discussion

6.2.2.1 Degree of semantic transitivity of sentences

As discussed in Chapter 5, since 把 *ba* is analyzed as a marker of high semantic transitivity, we can see why there are such differences when combined with object–oriented resultatives. In general, object–oriented resultatives are highly transitive semantically, since it is in line with the concept of transitivity, namely "an activity is 'carried–over' or 'transferred' from an agent to a patient" (Hopper and Thompson 1980: 251). To be specific, as introduced in Chapter 2, Section 2.3.2.3, ten parameters are suggested, namely (a) participants, (b) kinesis, (c) aspect, (d) punctuality, (e) volitionality, (f) affirmation, (g) mode, (h) agency, (i) affectedness of O (O for object) and (j) individuation of O.[1]

The sentences in (7–12) are construed as having high transitivity with some common features. All take two participants, describe actions (e.g. 'cry' in 8, 'sing' in 9, 'wipe' in 10 and 11), telic (all with the perfective particle marker 了 le), affirmative, realis, and A high in potency (A as third person singular). The feature (d) punctuality is irrelevant, since all the actions described in the sentences cannot be interpreted as punctual (e.g. 'play' in 7, 'cry' in 8, or 'wipe' in 10 and 11).

(7)	他	弄–坏–了	小	火车
	ta	*nong-huai-le*	*xiao*	*huoche*
	he	do–broken–ASP	small	train

'He played with the model train and as a result the train was broken.'

(8)	她	哭–湿–了	手绢
	ta	*ku-shi-le*	*shoujuan*
	she	cry–wet–ASP	handkerchief

'She cried and as a result the handkerchief was wet.' (She cried the handkerchief wet.)

1 As discussed in Chapter 5, Section 5.2, Næss (2007) includes Affectedness of A as a factor contributing to high transitivity. Since the sentences are object–oriented, this parameter will not be included here.

(9)	她	唱－红－了	那	首	歌
	ta	*chang-hong-le*	*na*	*shou*	*ge*
	she	sing–popular–ASP	that	CL	song

'She sang that song and as a result the song was popular.'

(10)	他	擦－干－了	头发
	ta	*ca-gan-le*	*toufa*
	he	wipe–dry–ASP	hair

'He wiped her hair dry.'

(11)	他	擦－干净了	桌子
	ta	*ca-ganjing-le*	*zhuozi*
	he	wipe–clean–ASP	table

'He wiped the table clean.'

(12)	她	叠－整齐－了	衣服
	ta	*die-zhengqi-le*	*yifu*
	she	fold–neat–ASP	clothes

'She folded the clothes and as a result the clothes were neat.'

Regarding the individuation of O, as mentioned in Chapter 5, Section 5.4.1.2, Hopper and Thompson (1980: 253) propose further properties to judge the degree of individuation of O (see 13). Among the features of O, what the six patterns have in common as 'individuated' is referential. Although only one takes demonstrative 那 *na* 'that' (see 9), the other Os are construed as definite. For instance, 手绢 *shoujua* 'handkerchief' in (8) is interpreted as the handkerchief she used, 头发 *toufa* 'hair' in (10) refers to his hair, and 桌子 *zhuozi* 'table' in (11) indicates the table he wiped. The Os are common, inanimate, which are viewed as being more typical of non–individuated according to (13). One notable difference is that only the O 歌 *ge* 'song' in (9) is an abstract referent, whereas the other Os are concrete, such as 手绢 *shoujua* 'handkerchief' in (8) and 头发 *toufa* 'hair' in (10). This makes (9) lower in individuation of O than the other sentences.

(13) Individuation of O   Hopper and Thompson (1980: 253)

INDIVIDUATED	NON–INDIVIDUATED
proper	common
human, animate	inanimate
concrete	abstract
singular	plural
count	mass
referential, definite	non–referential

However, as suggested in Chapter 5, Section 5.4.1.2, formal features may partially account for the degree of individuation of O. The issue which matters here is O as a concept, especially for Chinese which lacks abundant morphological changes (Li and Thompson 1989: 11; e.g. the morphological change of adding –s/–es to form countable plural nouns in English). Since there are not many differences in form between singular vs. plural, count vs. mass nouns in Chinese, the individuation of O can only be judged conceptually. For instance, provided an activity is construed as a single action rather than repeated ones, O can be regarded as high individuation. Viewed in this way, all the sentences express a single event. For instance, in (8) she cried and as a result the handkerchief was wet, or in (12) she folded the clothes and subsequently the clothes were neat. Therefore, all the sentences are construed as having individuation of O.

Nevertheless, there are slight differences among these examples regarding some parameters. To begin with, the volitionality of A varies among the sentences. In (7), although the agent 'he' played with the model train volitionally, he did not intend to damage it, thereby no volitionality of A is construed. Similarly, the agent 'she' in (8) did not cry so as to make the handkerchief wet, so again there is no volitionality of A. The other items are all interpreted with high volitionality of A as the agent carries out the action purposefully. For instance, in (9) she sang the song with the intention of making it popular.[2] In (10) and (11) he 'wiped' his hair/ the table so as to make it clean/dry; in (12) she 'folded' the clothes aiming to make them neat. So the volitionality of A is ranked as 唱–红 *chang-hong* 'sing–popular', 擦–干 *ca-gan* 'wipe–dry', 擦–干净 *ca-ganjing* 'wipe–clean' and 叠–整齐 *die-zhengqi* 'fold–neat'>弄–坏 *nong-huai* 'do–broken' and 哭–湿 *ku-shi* 'cry–wet'.

One issue to be noticed is that although both are construed as having low volitionality of A, there is a difference between 弄–坏 *nong-huai* 'do–broken' in (14) and 哭–湿 *ku-shi* 'cry–wet' in (15a). The main verb in the

---

2 In the CCL, all the examples with 唱–红 *chang-hong* 'sing–popular' are interpreted as the singer sang a song and as a result the song was popular, for instance (iv). So the volitionality of A is high in this pattern.

(iv) 十多 年 前, 一 香港 歌星 唱–红–了 一 首 狼 歌 (CCL 52.1)

十多	年	前,	一	香港	歌星	唱–红–了	一	首	狼	歌
shi duo	*nian*	*qian,*	*yi*	*xianggang*	*gexing*	*chang-hong-le*	*yi*	*shou*	*lang*	*ge*
ten more	year	ago,	one	Hongkong	singer	sing–popular–ASP	one	CL	wolf	song

'More than ten years ago, a singer in Hongkong sang a song about a wolf and as a result the song was popular.'

former is transitive, while that in the latter is intransitive. Though semantically (15a) is analyzed with a certain degree of semantic transitivity, since it is interpreted with low volitionality of A, it is lower in transitivity than the other patterns. In addition, the verb 哭 *ku* 'cry' is intransitive syntactically, so (15b) is unacceptable. Then, formed as a resultative construction 哭–湿 *ku-shi* 'cry–wet', a postverbal NP can occur due to the meaning of the construction under the framework of construction grammar. However, the intransitive status of the main verb remains, which in some sense restricts the property of the sentence and marks it with comparatively lower syntactic transitivity. Although it could take a postverbal NP, the low syntactic transitivity led to by the intransitive verb have impacts on the semantics in this regard. When combined with 把 *ba* as in (15c), its low transitivity in both semantics and syntax is not fully compatible with the function of 把 *ba* as a marker of high semantic transitivity. Consequently, (15c) is rated with a lower score compared to (15a) without 把 *ba*.

(14) 他　弄–坏–了　小　火车

ta　*nong-huai-le*　*xiao*　*huoche*

he　do–broken–ASP　small　train

'He played with the model train and as a result the train was broken.'

(15) a. 她　哭–湿–了　手绢

ta　*ku-shi-le*　*shoujuan*

she　cry–wet–ASP　handkerchief

'She cried and as a result the handkerchief was wet.' (She cried the handkerchief wet.)

b. *她 哭-了 手绢

ta *ku-le* *shoujuan*

she cry–ASP handkerchief

'She cried the handkerchief.'

c. 她 把 手绢 哭-湿-了

ta *ba* *shoujuan* *ku-shi-le*

she *ba* handkerchief cry–wet–ASP

'She cried the handkerchief wet.'

In addition, the affectedness of O also differs between 'cry–wet the handkerchief' and the other examples. The former is construed such that only some bits of the handkerchief end up wet. Thus it is not totally affected. As for the other Os, for instance in 'wipe–dry the hair', all individual hairs are conceptualized as being dried by the towel; or the model train was 'generally' broken, the 'full' song was popular: all the Os are affected highly. So the affectedness of O in (15c) is not very high compared to the other five patterns. Especially regarding the pattern 'do–broken the model train' as in (14), the affectedness of the 'broken model train' is much higher than that of the 'partly wet handkerchief'. So for both there is low volitionality of A, and with all the other parameters equal, the semantic transitivity of 'do–broken' in (14) is construed as higher than that of 'cry–wet' in (15a).

Nevertheless, if the sentence of 'cry–wet the handkerchief' is interpreted as having high affectedness of O, it will be acceptable with 把 *ba*. There are examples in the CCL of 把 + 哭–湿 *ba* + *ku-shi* 'cry–wet', such as (16a) and (16b). There are some adverbs in the sentences which indicate a high degree of affectedness of O. For instance, the adverb 都 *dou* 'all; even' in (16a) suggests strong and total affectedness of O, which increases the degree of semantic transitivity of the sentence. Therefore (16a) with 把 *ba* is acceptable. Similarly, 全 *quan* 'all' in (16b) is also interpreted with high transitivity, which makes the sentences more acceptable. In addition, among the 20 哭–湿 *ku-shi* 'cry–wet' resultatives found in the CCL, if without 把 *ba*, none contain such adverbs. However, all five items with 把 *ba* take adverbs with the interpretation of the total affectedness of O. This increases the degree of semantic transitivity of the sentence, which is in line with the function of 把 *ba*. Therefore, the sentences are fully acceptable.

(16) a. (太太) 把 小 手帕 都 哭–湿–了 (CCL 8.1)

(taitai) ba xiao shoupa dou ku-shi-le

(madam) *ba* small handkerchief all cry–wet–ASP

'The madam cried and as a result the small handkerchief was all wet.' (The madam cried the small handkerchief all wet.)

b. (文秀) 把 他的 衣襟 全 哭–湿–了 (CCL 14.1)

(wenxiu) ba tade yijin quan ku-shi-le

(wenxiu; name) *ba* his edge of clothes all cry–wet–ASP

'(Wenxiu; name) cried and as a result his edge of clothes was all wet.' (Wenxiu cried his edge of clothes all wet.)

In addition, as stated in Chapter 4, Section 4.3.3, among the 500 sample examples in the LCMC, all 39 resultatives with 把 *ba* are formed with transitive verbs. On the other hand, intransitive–based resultatives (without 把 *ba*) typically do not take a postverbal NP (89.5%). However, there are two examples formed with typical intransitive verbs that take a postverbal NP as in (17a) and (18a). (17a) takes the intransitive verb 笑 *xiao* 'laugh' and P 腰 *yao* 'waist'. If combined with 把 *ba* as in (17b), its lower acceptability than (17a) can be anticipated, as the intransitive verb is construed as having low syntactic transitivity, which is incompatible with the function of 把 *ba* to mark high semantic transitivity.

Moreover, 56 examples of 笑–弯–了 腰 *xiao-wan-le yao* 'laugh–bent–ASP waist' (laugh so as to bend over) are found in the CCL, among which two are used with 把 ba as in (17c/d). Noticeably, the two sentences are both interpreted with a high degree of transitivity. In (17c) the adverb 都 *dou* 'even' indicates that she laughed heavily so that even the waist was highly affected, being bent (normally if someone laughs, the waist will not be affected and be bent). In (17d) the adverbs 就已经 *jiu yijing* 'then already' also suggest that before she read, she already began to laugh so much that she bent her waist, which is also construed as having a high degree of affectedness of O. As the interpretation of (17c/d) with high semantic transitivity is compatible with the function of 把 *ba*, the sentences are acceptable.

(17) a. 她 几乎 笑–弯–了 腰 (LCMC P03)

ta *jihu* *xiao-wan-le* *yao*

she almost laugh–bend–ASP waist

'She laughed and as a result she almost bent her waist.' (She laughed so much that she almost bent over)'

b. ?她 几乎 把 腰 笑-弯-了

ta jihu ba yao xiao-wan-le

she almost *ba* waist laugh-bend-ASP

'She laughed and as a result she almost bent her waist.' (She laughed so much that she almost bent over.)

c. 她们 把 腰 都 笑-弯-了 (CCL 31.1)

tamen ba yao dou xiao-wan-le

they *ba* waist even laugh-bend-ASP

'They laughed and as a result they even bent their waist.' (They laughed so heavily that they even bent over.)

d. (她 还 没 念), 就 已经 把 腰 笑-弯-了 (CCL 9.1)

(ta hai mei nian), jiu yijing ba yao xiao-wan-le

(she yet not read), then already ba waist laugh-bend-ASP

'(She hadn't read yet), then had already laughed and as a result bent her waist.' (She hadn't read yet, then had already laughed so heavily that she bent over.)

Regarding (18a), another resultative in the LCMC with intransitive verb + postverbal NP, there are no similar patterns with 把 *ba* found in the corpora. If combined with 把 *ba* as in (18b), it will be less acceptable than without 把 *ba* in (18a). So generally, if an object-oriented resultative (without 把 *ba*) is formed with an intransitive verb following a postverbal NP, it will be less acceptable when used with 把 *ba*, as the degree of transitivity is not compatible between syntax and semantics. However, if the sentence with 把 *ba* is expressed with elements denoting a high degree of semantic transitivity (e.g. adverbs like 全

quan 'all'), then its acceptability will be enhanced.

(18) a. 他 游-碎-了 月色 (LCMC P10)

ta *you-sui-le* *yuese*

he swim-break-ASP moonlight

'He swam and as a result broke the moonlight (in the pond).'

b. ?他 把 月色 游-碎-了

ta *ba* *yuese* *you-sui-le*

he *ba* moonlight swim-break-ASP

'He swam and as a result broke the moonlight (in the pond).'

Taking all these into account, and with the other parameters equal, the degree of transitivity of the six sentences is ranked as follows in Table 6.5:

Table 6.5: Degree of transitivity of the six object-oriented resultatives

Pattern	Volitionality of A	Status of verb	Affectedness of O	Degree of transitivity
nong-huai 'do-broken'	low	transitive	total	high
chang-hong 'sing-popular'	high	transitive	total	high
ku-shi 'cry -wet'	low	intransitive	part	middle
ca-gan 'wipe-dry'	high	transitive	total	high
ca-ganjing 'wipe-clean'	high	transitive	total	high
die-zhengqi 'fold-neat'	high	transitive	total	high

Since 把 *ba* is analyzed as a marker of high semantic transitivity, if a pattern is interpreted with high transitivity semantically, it will be more acceptable when combined with 把 *ba*, due to the coherence in semantics. 弄-坏 *nong-huai* 'do-broken' (from 94.9 to 96.7), 擦-干 *ca-gan* 'wipe-dry' (91.8

to 94.1), 唱－红 *chang-hong* 'sing–popular' (from 82.4 to 87.7; p=0.07) are still rated with high (or even higher) scores when combined with 把 *ba* as they are construed as having high semantic transitivity. 哭－湿 *ku-shi* 'cry–wet' (from 87.4 to 83.4), on the other hand, is interpreted with lower transitivity caused by the semantics of the sentence and the status of the verb. Therefore, its combination with 把 *ba* is lower than without 把 *ba*. Nevertheless, the difference is not significant as the degree of transitivity of the whole sentence is at a middle level, which is still in line with the function of 把 *ba* as a marker of high semantic transitivity. Yet the difference is not significant, only with a trend in the data (p=.14), which means if the data are large enough in size, there could be significant differences.

6.2.2.2 Number of syllables of resultative constructions

The degree of transitivity, however, does not explain all the differences between with and without 把 ba. One issue to be noted is the phenomenon that 擦－干净 *ca-ganjing* 'wipe–clean' and 叠－整齐 *die-zhengqi* 'fold–neat' are judged lower without 把 *ba* than with 把 *ba* (p<.05). Since they are interpreted with high transitivity, this is not the reason for the significant difference. We may note the difference in number of syllables between these two patterns and the others. The two result XPs are disyllabic words (干净 *gan'jing* 'clean', 整齐 *zheng'qi* 'neat'), whereas the other result XPs are monosyllabic (e.g. 坏 *huai* 'broken', 红 *hong* 'popular', 干 *gan* 'dry').

In the history of the Chinese language, there is a trend of words changing from monosyllables to disyllables, which is called disyllabification (Wang 1989, Shi 2002). Historically, Chinese words started as monosyllabic but changed into disyllabic or having yet more syllables. For instance, in ancient Chinese, the sun is called 日 ri (one syllable), whereas nowadays it is referred to as 太阳 *tai'yang* (two syllables).

The result of disyllabification is that 80% of Chinese words are now disyllabic (Shi 2002:2), which is much more than in the past. According to Lü (1961: 423; cited by Shi 2002: 2), among the 3,000 Chinese words most frequently used in Mandarin Chinese, most are composed of two syllables, as stated in Table 6.6. If the word category is not considered, 75% of the 3,000 words are disyllabic. This reflects a regulation that words with two syllables are used the most in Mandarin.

Table 6.6: Distribution of word types in disyllabic words

(Lü 1961: 423; cited by Shi 2002: 2)

	Total	Disyllabic words	Percentage
Nouns	1621	1379	85%
Adjectives	451	311	69%
verbs	941	573	61%

Some scholars argue that the disyllable is the basic phonological pattern of Chinese (Hu 1981; cited by Shi 2002: 3). The form of a word is dependent on the number of syllables (Shi 2002: 3). For example, regarding the translated names of countries used in Chinese, if the name is monosyllabic, the word 国 *guo* 'country' will be added after the name, such as 英国 *ying'guo* 'England', 法国 *fa'guo* 'France'. If the name is disyllabic, there is no 国 *guo* 'country', and it is unnatural if 国 *guo* 'country' is used when referring to the country. For example Japan is called 日本 *ri'ben* in Chinese, and 日本国 *ri'ben'guo* 'Japan country' is seldom used.

Considering the relation between disyllabification and resultative constructions in Chinese, Shi (2002: 7) argues that disyllabification is one motivation for the grammaticalization of resultatives (formed as verb + result XP) in Chinese.[3] Originally, the verb and the result XP (both monosyllabic) were independent. During the disyllabification process, as the two items were monosyllabic and adjacent to each other, the combination contained two syllables. This fits the disyllabic preference of words in Chinese. In addition, there was a cause–result relation between the verb and the result XP. Consequently, the verb and the result XP were prone to fusion (morpheme boundary loss; cf. Hopper and Traugott 2003: 157), and the pattern verb + result XP behaved like an entity, or a disyllabic verbal phrase, which could take a postverbal NP. This is also when the resultative construction began to evolve.

For instance, according to Shi (2002: 9), in ancient Chinese V–死 *si* 'die' could not take an object. If 死 *si* 'die' was interpreted as the result of an action, the P had to be placed after (see 19a) or before the main verb (as in 19b), but not after 死 *si* 'die'. Then, later there could be a postverbal NP after V–死 *si* 'die' as in (19c). In (19a) the main verb and 死 *si* 'die' are separated by P in the middle. (19b) may signal the emergence of the resultative construction,

3 According to Hopper and Traugott (2003: 2), grammaticalization is defined as the change of relatively lexical items to more grammatical ones through time. For example, *be going to* was used as a purposive directional phrase, e.g. I *am going to visit Bill* (i.e. *I am leaving in order to visit Bill*). Over time, it developed into a future auxiliary, e.g. *I am going to like Bill*. In this case it does not have a purposive meaning but denotes futurity (i.e. 'I will like Bill in the future'). So *be going to* is grammaticalized.

According to Shi (2002), Chinese resultatives have undergone a process of grammaticalization, from independent verb and adjective/verb to a fixed construction as verb + result XP. The process can be exemplified as in (19), below.

as the verb 压 *ya* 'crush' and the result XP 死 *si* 'die' remain adjacent, the former causing the latter. However, P still cannot follow the result XP. (19c) indicates the formation of the resultative construction, as 'die' is the result of 'freeze'. Meanwhile, as the construction 冻–死 *dong-si* 'freeze–die' is disyllabic, it sounds like a verbal phrase phonologically, which makes it able to take a postverbal NP. So P 'people' was put after the resultative 冻–死 *dong-si* 'freeze–die'.

(19) a. 击 陈柱国房君 死(史记; cited from Shi 2002: 9)
ji *chenzhuguofangjun* *si* (*ShiJi*; around 100 B.C.)
hit *Chenzhuguofangjun* (name) die (Records of the historian)
'(Someone) hit Chenzhuguofangjun (name) and he (Chen) died.'

b. 百 余 人 炭 崩 尽 压 死(论衡; ibid.)
bai *yu* *ren* *tan* *beng* *jin* *ya* *si* (*LunHeng*; around 86 A.D.)
hundred more people coal collapse all crush die (On balance)
'The coal collapsed, and more than a hundred people were crushed to death.'

c. 秦时 六月 皆 冻–死 人(朱子语类; ibid.)
qinshi *liuyue* *jie* *dong-si* *ren* (*Zhuzi yulei*; 1263 A.D.)
Qin dynasty July all freeze–die people (Classified conversations of Zhuxi)
'In the Qin Dynasty, all its people froze to death in July.'

The ability of resultatives (verb + result XP) to take postverbal NP, however, is limited to patterns with two syllables. If the XP is disyllabic (or has even more syllables), the combination of verb + result XP contains at least three syllables. This does not accord with the basic phonological form of Chinese words with two syllables. As the trisyllabic combination does not with fit the preference for disyllabic words, it cannot be regarded as a verbal phrase, which further restricts the usage of these resultative constructions, for instance the capability to take a postverbal NP. In addition, it is observed by Li (1994), Ma and Lu (1996) and Shi (2002) that if the syllable count of the verb or result XP is more than one, then the combination of the two (a resultative) cannot take a postverbal NP. For instance, the result XP in (20a) and the verb in (20b) are disyllabic. If there are postverbal NPs following, the two sentences are less acceptable.

(20) a. ?我们 改–合理–了 制度 (Li 1994: 37)

women gai-he'li-le zhidu

we change–reasonable–ASP system

'We changed the system and as a result it was reasonable.'

b. ?她 收集– 齐–了 材料 (Ma and Lu 1996: 9)

ta shou'ji-qi-le cailiao

she ccollect–all–ASP document

'She collected the documents and as a result the documents were all collected.' (She finished collecting all the documents.[4])

This explains the low ratings of the sentences in Survey 2 as in (21a) and

4 Though the translation of (20b) makes it like a completive (see more in Chapter 4, Section 4.3.1.1.1) rather than a resultative, 齐 *qi* 'all' refers to the object 材料 *cailiao* 'document' rather than the action.

(22a). The two result XPs are disyllabic words, namely 干净 *gan'jing* 'clean' and 整齐 *zheng'qi* 'neat'. When combined with a verb, even monosyllabic, the construction contains three syllables in total, which makes it unlike a usual disyllabic word. The restriction on this type is its incapability to take a postverbal NP. Therefore, examples of this kind are judged as less acceptable (mean 82.87 for 21a and 77.37 for 22a), which are significantly lower than their counterparts with 把 *ba* (i.e. 21b and 22b).

(21) a.	他	擦-干净了	桌子	
	ta	*ca-ganjing-le*	*zhuozi*	
	he	wipe–clean–ASP	table	
	'He wiped the table clean.'			
b.	他	把	桌子	擦-干净了
	ta	*ba*	*zhuozi*	*ca-ganjing-le*
	he	*ba*	table	wipe–clean–ASP
	'He wiped the table clean.'			
(22) a.	?她	叠-整齐-了	衣服	
	ta	*die-zhengqi-le*	*yifu*	
	she	fold–neat–ASP	clothes	
	'She folded the clothes and as a result the clothes were neat.'			
b.	她	把	衣服	叠-整齐-了
	ta	*ba*	*yifu*	*die-zhengqi-le*
	she	*ba*	clothes	fold–neat–ASP
	'She folded the clothes and as a result the clothes were neat.'			

When combined with 把 *ba* as in (21b) and (22b), the postverbal NP 桌子

zhuozi 'table' and 衣服 *yifu* 'clothes' are fronted before the verb. As there are no postverbal NPs after three–syllable resultatives, the sentences become much more acceptable with significant differences (mean 95.73 for 21b, 93.71 for 22b; p<.05 compared to 21/22a).

Nevertheless, there are a few examples in the CCL formed with disyllabic result XPs such as 干净 *gan'jing* 'clean' in (23a). Meanwhile, Shi (2002:12) provides examples with more than two syllables in the combination of verb + result XP (e.g. 23b). According to him, this happens very late, until the resultative construction is fully grammaticalized. Then the restriction on the number of syllables becomes loose, which explains a certain degree of acceptability of (23a/b). He argues that most resultatives with more than two syllables are still in low fusion, hence taking no postverbal NP. To sum up, the acceptability of (23a/b) shows the gradience of the phenomenon whereby verb + result XP with more than two syllables is able to take a postverbal NP. However, recall that there is a significant difference of 擦–干净 *ca-ganjing* 'wipe–clean' between without 把 *ba* (82.9) and with 把 ba (95.7); the capability of such patterns to take P is still limited.

(23) a. 她 擦–干净了 茶炉 (CCL 192)

ta *ca-ganjing-le* *chalu*

she wipe–clean–ASP water boiler

'She wiped the water boiler clean.'

b. 我 理解–错–了 那 个 问题 (Shi 2002:12)

wo *li'jie-cuo-le* *na* *ge* *wenti*

I understand–wrong–ASP that CL question

'I thought about that question and as a result I was wrong.' (I misunderstood that question.)

Corpus data provide further evidence for the relationship between the number of syllables and the acceptability of resultatives. Based on the data obtained from the LCMC mentioned in Chapter 4,138 result XPs with 1,332 examples of resultatives were extracted. Among the 138 patterns, only 16 are disyllabic, such as 明白 *ming'bai* 'understand', 干净 *gan'jing* 'clean', 到手 *dao'shou* 'get hand' (get). Then, among the 99 sentences with disyllabic result XPs, only 11 (11.11%) take a postverbal NP. The other examples are either combined with 把 *ba* in which P precedes the main verb (e.g. 24a), or P is fronted as in (24b).

(24)	a. 他	派	人	把	办公室	打扫–干净 (LCMC G76)
	ta	*pai*	*ren*	*ba*	*bangongshi*	*da'sao-gan'jing*
	he	send	people	*ba*	office	sweep–clean

'He sent people to sweep the office clean.'

b. 地	没	扫–干净	(LCMC P11)
di	*mei*	*sao-gan'jing*	
floor	not	sweep–clean	

'The floor was not swept clean.'

Regarding the 500 examples discussed in Chapter 4, there are 453 (90.6%) resultatives formed with two syllables which consist of a one–syllable verb and a one–syllable result XP (see 25a). In contrast, 47 (9.4%) sentences are formed with more than two syllables, either a monosyllabic verb and a disyllabic result XP (e.g. 25b), or a disyllabic verb and a monosyllabic result XP (such as 25c), or both verb and result XP are disyllabic (e.g. 25d).

(25) a. 她 终于 学–会–了 游泳 (LCMC P10 7)

ta zhongyu xue-hui-le youyong

she finally learn–can–ASP swim

'She learned to swim and finally as a result she could swim.'

b. 老 狱卒 终于 想–清楚–了 (LCMC N14)

lao yuzu zhongyu xiang-qingchu-le

old jailer finally think–clear–ASP

'The old jailer thought and finally as a result he was clear.'

c. 他 申请–到 公司 赞助 (LCMC K20)

ta shenqing- dao gongsi zanzhu

he apply–get company grant

'He applied for a grant from the company and as a result got it.'

d. 衣服 会 很 容易 地 清洗–干净 (LCMC E06)

yifu hui hen rongyi de qingxi-ganjing

clothes will very easy de[5] wash–clean

'The clothes will be easily washed clean.'

To be specific, the relations between syllables and postverbal NP are stated in Table 6.7. Regarding two–syllable resultative constructions, the ones with a postverbal NP (59.4%) number slightly more than those without a postverbal NP (40.6%). Comparatively, among 3–syllable resultatives, the number of patterns with a postverbal NP (19.1%) is much lower than that without a postverbal NP (80.9%). Comparing these two in terms of distribution by means

5 地 de is a particle suggesting the modification of verb.

of a chi–square test, there is a significant difference ($p<.0001$). This suggests that most Chinese resultatives are disyllabic, whether they take a postverbal NP or not. Nevertheless, those with patterns of more than two syllables seldom take a postverbal NP. There is either no P (e.g. 25b), or P is fronted before the main verb (see 25d).

Table 6.7: Relation between syllables and postverbal NP

Number of syllables (verb+result XP)	With postverbal NP (percentage)	Without postverbal NP (percentage)	Total
2 (453)	269 (59.4%)	184 (40.6%)	100%
More than 2 (47)	9 (19.1%)	38 (80.9%)	100%
p–value (chi–square)	<.0001		

In addition, among nine examples with multi–syllabic verb + result XP (more than two syllables), seven are marginal resultatives with 到 *dao*'get' (e.g. 26) or 住 *zhu* 'hold'. This further suggests that resultatives with more than two syllables and a postverbal NP are very limited and infrequent in Chinese, mostly belonging to the marginal type. Prototypically patterns taking a postverbal NP are disyllabic.

(26) 他 申请–到 公司 赞助 (LCMC K20)

ta *shenqing- dao* *gongsi* *zanzhu*

he apply–get company grant

'He applied for a grant from the company and as a result got it.'

Moreover, although there are examples of 擦–干净 *ca-ganjing* 'wipe–clean' found in the CCL, its mean (82.9) suggests lower acceptability than others such as 弄–坏 *nong-huai* 'do–broken' (94.9) with a significant difference (*p*<.05). In terms of 叠–整齐 *die-zhengqi* ‘fold–neat’, there are no examples in the corpus taking a postverbal NP, and the lowest score (77.4) among the six patterns with a significant difference (*p*<.05) indicates its low acceptability. Apart from some exceptions of resultative constructions with more than two syllables taking a postverbal NP, the majority of resultatives in this form still come with no postverbal NP.

6.3 The acceptability of 把 *ba* + subject-oriented resultatives

As stated in Section 6.1.1, since Survey 2 also aims to compare the acceptability between subject–oriented and object–oriented resultatives with and without 把 *ba*, four subject–oriented patterns used in Survey 1 are retained here, namely 想–明白 *xiang-mingbai* ‘think–understand (as in 27a), 练–会 *lian-hui* ‘practise–can’ (see 27b), 听–懂 *ting-dong* ‘listen–understand’ (see 27c) and 听–烦 *ting-fan* ‘listen–bored with’ (in 27d). To be specific, the first two patterns belong to an acceptable group (with 把 *ba*) (G1), and the last two form a marginally acceptable group (G2) and the least acceptable group (G3), respectively.

(27) a. 他　想–明白–了　这　个　问题

ta　*xiang-mingbai-le*　*zhe*　*ge*　*wenti*

he　think–understand–ASP　this　CL　question

'He thought about this question and as a result he understood it.'

b.	她	练–会–了	这	首	歌
	ta	*lian-hui-le*	*zhe*	*shou*	*ge*
	she	practice–can–ASP	this	CL	song

'She practised this song and as a result she could sing it.'

c.	她	听–懂–了	小凯	的	话
	ta	*ting-dong-le*	*Xiaokai*	*de*	*hua*
	she	listen–understand–ASP	Xiaokai(name)	POSS	words

'She listened to Xiaoyu's words and as a result she understood them.'

d.	他	听–烦–了	老师	的	话
	ta	*ting-fan-le*	*laoshi*	*de*	*hua*
	he	listen– bored with–ASP	teacher	POSS	words

'He listened to the teacher's words and as a result he was bored with them.' (He was bored with the teacher's words.)

In Table 6.8, the three groups are still judged differently when including 把 *ba*. In G1, ratings for with and without 把 *ba* are both high (mean above 90), and there is no significant difference between the two ($p>.05$). In G2, ratings for with 把 *ba* are lower than without 把 *ba*, dropping from 95.20 to 79.05, with a significant difference ($p<.05$). In G3, ratings for with 把 *ba* are even lower than without 把 ba, decreasing from 86.51 to 63.52 with a significant difference ($p<.05$).

Table 6.8: Three groups of subject–oriented resultatives with and without 把 *ba*

	G1		G2		G3	
	without *ba*	with *ba*	without *ba*	with *ba*	without *ba*	with *ba*
Number	165	168	84	84	78	80
Mean	92.35	93.29	95.20	79.05	86.51	63.52
Median	100	100	100	80	90	60
Std	14.82	12.44	12.10	21.19	16.58	25.23
p–value	0.5		8.5×10^{-9}		2.7×10^{-10}	

This could still be accounted for by the analysis in Chapter 5. Since 把 *ba* is a marker of high semantic transitivity, the more transitive a sentence is, the more acceptable it is when combined with 把 *ba*. The degree of semantic transitivity of the three groups varies from high (G1) through middle (G2) to low (G3), therefore the degree of acceptability decreases from fully acceptable (G1) through marginally acceptable (G2) to the least acceptable (G3).

The reason for the differences among the three groups in 把 *ba* + subject–oriented resultatives rests with the degree of transitivity expressed by the sentences, which has been fully discussed in Chapter 5.

6.4 The acceptability of 把 *ba* + subject-/object-oriented resultatives

6.4.1 Results

There are some distinctions of subject–oriented resultatives with and without 把 *ba* regarding the data between the two surveys. If the data are analyzed in terms of three groups, there is no significant difference between with and without 把 *ba* for G1 (see Table 6.8). If done in terms of four patterns, there is a significant difference between with and without 把 *ba* for a pattern in G1 in survey 2, 想–明白 *xiang-mingbai* 'think–understand' (p<.05; see Table 6.10), though it is still highly acceptable when used without 把 *ba* (mean 91.41). It should be noted that for the two patterns in G1 想–明白 *xiang-mingbai* 'think–understand' and 练–会 *lian-hui* 'practise–can' in survey 2, as stated in Table 6.10, there is no significant difference between the two regarding use without 把 *ba*, yet they differ significantly when used with 把 *ba*. Comparatively, 想–明白 *xiang-mingbai* 'think–understand' and 练–会 *lian-hui* 'practise–can' in survey 1 are equally acceptable with high ratings (p>.05; see Table 6.10).

Table 6.9: Subject-oriented resultatives with and without 把 *ba* in the two surveys

	Survey 2				Survey 1			
	'think-understand'		'practise-can'		'think-understan'		'practise-can'	
	without *ba*	with *ba*	without *ba*	with *ba*	without *ba*	with *ba*	without *ba*	with *ba*
Number	81	84	81	84	34	35	36	36
Mean	91.41	96.00	93.25	90.58	96.76	94.71	95.19	92.64
Median	100	100	100	100	100	100	100	100
Std	16.64	9.98	12.85	14.04	9.76	11.44	12.78	13.39
p-value	0.03		0.2		0.49		0.41	

Table 6.10: 想 – 明白 *xiang-mingbai* 'think-understand' and 练 – 会 *lian-hui* 'practise-can' with and without 把 *ba* in the two surveys

	Survey 1		Survey 2	
	without *ba*	with *ba*	without *ba*	with *ba*
p-value ('think-understand' vs. 'practise-can')	0.49	0.57	0.47	0.004

If the pattern 想–明白 *xiang-mingbai* 'think-understand' is compared between the two surveys as in Table 6.11, we can see that the ratings for without 把 *ba* in the two surveys are all over 90, so there is a trend of significant difference between the two (*p*=.08). In terms of 把 *ba* + 想–明白 *xiang-mingbai* 'think-understand', they are equally acceptable.

Table 6.11: 想 – 明白 *xiang-mingbai* 'think-understand' with and without 把 *ba* in the two surveys

'think-understand'	without *ba*		with *ba*	
	Survey 1	Survey 2	Survey 1	Survey 2
mean	96.76	91.41	94.71	96.00
p-value	0.08		0.54	

6.4.2 Discussion

One reason for the slight difference for 想–明白 *xiang-mingbai* 'think–understand' between with and without 把 *ba* may be that 明白 *ming'bai* 'understand' is disyllabic, as in (28a). Recall that for result XP 干净 *gan'jing* 'clean' and 整齐 *zheng'qi* 'neat' in object–oriented resultatives, the differences between with and without 把 *ba* are significant, and the ratings vary a lot. We may surmise that the reason for the significant difference for 想–明白 *xiang-mingbai* 'think–understand' in survey 2 is due to the disyllabic result XP. Because words with two syllables are used the most frequently in Mandarin Chinese, the combination of verb + disyllabic result XP will end up with three syllables. One constraint on patterns like this is its low capability to take a postverbal NP. In (28a) there is a postverbal NP after the trisyllabic resultative, but when combined with 把 *ba* as in (28b), the NP is fronted. In addition, the compatibility of semantic transitivity expressed by the sentence and the function of 把 *ba* also makes (28b) more acceptable than (28a).

(28) a. 他 想–明白–了 这 个 问题

ta *xiang-mingbai-le* *zhe* *ge* *wenti*

he think–understand–ASP this CL question

'He thought about this question and as a result he understood it.'

b. 他 把 这 个 问题 想–明白–了

ta *ba* *zhe* *ge* *wenti* *xiang-mingbai-le*

he *ba* this CL question think–understand–ASP

'He thought about this question and as a result he understood it.'

However, this situation does not arise in survey 1, in which the disyllabic result XP 明白 *mingbai* 'understand' is used with two verbs (想 *xiang* 'think' and 弄 *nong* 'do'). There are no significant differences between with and without 把 *ba* in terms of the verb–result XP patterns mentioned above. This may be due to the size of the data sample. In survey 1 the data were obtained from 35/36 participants, whereas 84 subjects completed survey 2. Nevertheless, the main results with respect to the different acceptability of subject–oriented resultatives in survey 1 are attested to in survey 2. In addition, though the judgements of the sentence 想–明白 *xiang-mingbai* 'think–understand' in survey 2 between with and without 把 *ba* differ significantly, they are fully acceptable with high ratings (all over 90).

If compared with the patterns discussed in Section 6.2.1, we can see that the effect of the number of syllables on the capability of resultatives to take a postverbal NP varies between subject–oriented and object–oriented resultatives. Although the score for the disyllabic pattern 明白 *ming'bai* 'understand' is higher with 把 *ba* than without 把 *ba*, both of them are rated over 90 with full acceptability. In contrast, the object–oriented resultatives with disyllabic result XPs 干净 *gan'jing* 'wipe–clean' and 整齐 *zheng'qi* 'neat' without 把 *ba* are judged much lower than with 把 *ba*, which are regarded as marginally acceptable (see Table 6.12). Subject–oriented resultatives with a disyllabic result XP are more acceptable than object–oriented ones in the pattern of disyllabic result XP + NP. In other words, subject–oriented resultatives with a two–syllable result XP are more able to take a postverbal NP than object–oriented resultatives.

Table 6.12: Subject–oriented vs. object–oriented resultatives with disyllabic result XPs

	'think–understand'		'wipe–clean'		'fold–neat'	
	without *ba*	with *ba*	without *ba*	with *ba*	without *ba*	with *ba*
Number	81	84	81	84	81	84
Mean	91.41	96.00	82.87	95.73	77.37	93.71
Median	100	100	90	100	80	100
Std	16.64	9.98	19.85	9.10	20.46	12.94
p–value	0.03		2.33×10^{-7}		5.62×10^{-9}	

This signals a difference between subject– and object–oriented resultatives. An explanation postulated is that, in subject–oriented resultatives that can take a postverbal NP, the result XP is a two–place predicate, like 明白 *ming'bai* 'understand' in (29). Therefore, its capability to take a postverbal NP is strong, although it is a disyllabic word. Nevertheless, the result XP in object–oriented resultatives is a one–place predicate, for instance 干净 *ganjing* 'clean' in (30), which restricts the capability of 擦–干净 *ca-ganjing* 'wipe–clean' to take a postverbal NP.

(29) 他 明白 这 个 问题

ta *mingbai* *zhe* *ge* *wenti*

he understand this CL question

'He understood this question.'

(30) *他 干净 桌子

ta *ganjing* *zhuozi*

he clean table

'He cleaned the table.'

In addition, as discussed in Section 6.2.2.2, multi–syllabic (more than two) resultatives with a postverbal NP only appear in a few patterns, for instance marginal resultatives which are limited to a few instances. In terms of prototypical resultatives, there are only two examples, namely V–明白 *ming'bai* 'understand/clear' (as in 31a) and V–清楚 *qing'chu* 'clear' (see 31b) in the 500 corpus samples. However, 说–明白 *shuo ming'bai* 'speak–clear' in (31a) is different from 想–明白 *ming'bai* 'think–understand' in (31c). The former may be viewed as spurious, whereas the latter is subject–oriented. Similarly, (31b) can be regarded as object–oriented. To sum up, resultatives of more than two syllables generally do not take a postverbal NP. Those with P are restricted to the marginal type, and limited prototypical types like V–明白 *ming'bai* 'understand/clear', V–清楚 *qing'chu* 'clear' and probably V–干净 *ganjing* 'clean'. Alternatively, these patterns may be views as semi–lexicalized, though they are still resultative constructions.

(31) a.

我	正	盘算	着	怎么	说–明白	女孩子
wo	*zheng*	*pansuan*	*zhe*	*zenme*	*shuo-mingbai*	*nühaizi*
I	current	consider	ASP	how	speak–clear	girl
也	可以	玩	枪	(LCMC G59)		
ye	*keyi*	*wan*	*qiang*			
also	can	play	gun			

'I was considering how to speak so as to make it clear that girls can also play with guns.'

b.

你	先	交代–清楚	来路	(LCMC N05)
ni	*xian*	*jiaodai-qingchu*	*lailu*	

you first tell–clear source

'You first tell (us) so as to make the source clear.' (You first tell the source clearly.)

c. 他 想–明白–了 这 个 问题

ta xiang-mingbai-le zhe ge wenti

he think–understand–ASP this CL question

'He thought about this question and as a result he understood it.'

6.5 Further implications

6.5.1 The acceptability of subject-/object-oriented resultatives

Regarding subject–oriented resultatives, as stated in Chapter 5, Section 5.5.1, either the verb is transitive and the result XP is a two–place predicate syntactically (e.g. 32a/b), or the sentences is interpreted as repeated actions semantically (e.g. 32c), the resultative constructions can take a postverbal NP. The number of syllables is not a deciding factor in the acceptability of subject–oriented resultatives. A result XP can be monosyllabic (as in 32a/c) or disyllabic (32b). The results of the two questionnaire surveys suggest the full acceptability of subject–oriented resultatives with these features, all with high ratings (over 90).

(32) a.

她	终于	学–会–了	游泳
ta	*zhongyu*	*xue-hui-le*	*youyong*
she	finally	learn–can–ASP	swim

'She practised this song and as a result she could sing it.'

b.

他	想–明白–了	这	个	问题
ta	*xiang-mingbai-le*	*zhe*	*ge*	*wenti*
he	think–understand–ASP	this	CL	question

'He thought about this question and as a result he understood it.'

c.

他	喝–腻–了	这	种	茶
ta	*he-ni-le*	*zhe*	*zhong*	*cha*
he	drink–be tired of–ASP	this	kind	tea

'He had drunk this kind of tea so many times that he was tired of it.'

Taking into account everything discussed above, some constraints on the capability of resultative constructions to take a postverbal NP can be observed. Generally, subject–oriented resultatives do not take a postverbal NP, whereas object–oriented resultatives do. Nevertheless, as suggested in Chapter 5, Section 5.5.1, some subject–oriented resultatives do take P, hence the possibility to be combined with 把 ba. I suggest that the factors which affect the acceptability of resultatives with a postverbal NP in Mandarin Chinese include the number of syllables in a resultative (disyllabic or more than two syllables), the status of the verb (transitive or intransitive), the status of the result XP (one–place or two–place predicate) and the interpretation of the resultative construction (single event or repeated actions). These factors vary in terms of subject– and object–oriented resultatives phonologically, syntactically and semantically.

6.5.2 The acceptability of 把 *ba*+subject-/object-oriented resultatives

Recall the acceptability of 把 *ba* + subject–oriented resultatives discussed in Chapter 5; it depends on the degree of semantic transitivity of a sentence. If a sentence is construed as having high transitivity, it is more acceptable when combined with 把 *ba*, as 把 *ba* is a marker of high transitivity.

With respect to object–oriented resultatives, since they are generally interpreted as having high semantic transitivity, the combination with 把 *ba* is by and large high in acceptability (mean >80). However, a pattern is rated lower after being combined with 把 *ba*, namely 哭–湿 *ku-shi* 'cry–wet' (from 87.43 to 83.37; *p*=.14). As proposed in Section 6.2.2.1, it is low in volitionality of A and total affectedness of O, and the verb is intransitive, which marks its low degree of syntactic transitivity. Since low syntactic transitivity is not fully compatible with the function of 把 *ba*, it is less acceptable when combined with 把 *ba*. However, the difference is not significant, and the combination is acceptable, although there is a trend in the data. So the acceptability of 把 *ba* + object–oriented resultatives hinges on the semantics of a sentence regarding transitivity, as well as the status of the verb. If a verb is normally intransitive, its combination with 把 *ba* is less acceptable than without 把 *ba*, yet still to a certain extent acceptable (mean over 80).

Evidence for this argument can also be found in the corpus data collected from the LCMC. Among the 38 out of 500 resultatives with 把 *ba* , all are formed with transitive verbs, for instance 打 *da* 'beat', 放 *fang* 'put'. Intransitive verbs do not appear frequently in 把 *ba* + resultative constructions, unless adverbs with the interpretation of a deep degree of semantic transitivity are express by the sentence. Recall that there are examples found in the CCL such as 把 + 哭–湿 *ba* + *ku-shi* 'cry–wet'. However, adverbs such as 都 *dou* 'all; even', 全 *quan* 'all' are used simultaneously to increase the degree of semantic transitivity of sentences, which makes the items more acceptable. This again provides evidence for analyzing 把 *ba* as a marker of high semantic transitivity. Nevertheless, syntactic transitivity and semantic transitivity should be viewed independently, and the former affects the latter in terms of acceptability in some sense.

6.5.3 Subject-oriented resultatives vs. object-oriented resultatives: 唱–红 *chang-hong* 'sing-popular'

A final issue regarding object–oriented resultatives is the pattern 唱–红 *chang-hong* 'sing–popular' as in (33). Its semantics accords with the function 把 *ba*, which makes the combination with 把 ba more acceptable than without 把 *ba* (from 83.33 to 87.67; *p*=.07). However, as stated in Section 6.2.1, this pattern differs significantly from the other four patterns (expect for 哭–湿 *ku-shi* 'cry–wet') when used with 把 *ba*. Although it is viewed as acceptable with 把 *ba*, the degree of acceptability is comparatively lower than the other patterns.

(33)	她	把	那	首	歌	唱–红–了
	ta	*ba*	*na*	*shou*	*ge*	*chang-hong-le*
	she	*ba*	that	CL	song	sing–popular–ASP

'She sang that song and as a result the song was popular.'

Actually, 唱–红 *chang-hong* 'sing–popular' is judged lower than the other patterns, even without 把 *ba* (see Table 6.13). ANOVA suggests significant differences among the six patterns (p<.05). According to the post hoc tests in Table 6.14, significant differences exist in patterns 3, 5 and 6. Since the reason for patterns 5 and 6 is the number of syllables in the pattern verb + result XP, we come to pattern 3 唱–红 *chang-hong* 'sing–popular' for further discussion.

Table 6.13: Six object–oriented resultatives without 把 *ba*

	N	Mean	Std. Deviation	Std. Error
1 'do–damage'	84	94.93	11.88	1.30
2 'cry–wet'	83	87.43	15.97	1.75
3 'sing–popular'	82	83.37	19.43	2.15
4 'wipe–dry'	83	91.82	18.80	2.06
5 'wipe–clean'	84	82.87	19.85	2.17
6 'fold–neat'	81	77.37	20.47	2.27
Total	497	86.30	18.81	.84

Table 6.14: Post hoc tests for object–oriented resultatives

Dependent Variable	(I) group	(J) group	Mean Difference (I–J)	Std. Error	Sig.
socre	1	2	7.49	2.77	.11
		3	11.59*	2.78	.00
		4	3.10	2.77	1.00
		5	12.06*	2.77	.00
		6	17.55*	2.79	.00
	2	1	–7.49	2.77	.11
		3	4.10	2.79	1.00
		4	–4.38	2.78	1.00
		5	4.56	2.77	1.00

Table 6.14 (Continued)

Dependent Variable	(I) group	(J) group	Mean Difference (I–J)	Std. Error	Sig.
socre	2	6	10.06*	2.80	.01
	3	1	–11.59*	2.78	.00
		2	–4.10	2.79	1.00
		4	–8.49*	2.79	.038
		5	.46	2.78	1.00
		6	5.95	2.81	.52
	4	1	–3.10	2.77	1.00
		2	4.38	2.78	1.00
		3	8.49*	2.79	.038
		5	8.95*	2.77	.020
		6	14.44*	2.80	.00
	5	1	–12.06*	2.77	.00
		2	–4.56	2.77	1.00
		3	–.46	2.78	1.00
		4	–8.95*	2.77	.02
		6	5.49	2.79	.75
	6	1	–17.55*	2.79	.00
		2	–10.06*	2.80	.01
		3	–5.95	2.81	.52
		4	–14.44*	2.80	.00
		5	–5.49	2.79	.75

唱–红 *chang-hong* 'sing–popular' is different from the other patterns in that it refers to abstract notions, with the result of the action being 'the song became popular'. In contrast, other object–oriented resultatives describe concrete actions and results, such as 'wipe the hair dry' and 'cry and as a result the handkerchief was wet'. 唱–红 *chang-hong* 'sing–popular' is similar to the sentences in Group 1 (G1) in Survey 2 (e.g. 34a/b), the only difference is that the former is object–oriented and the latter subject–oriented. Although 唱–红 *chang-hong* 'sing–popular' is regarded as acceptable for both with and without 把 *ba*, if compared to the sentences in G1 (see Table 6.15), it is lower than the latter with a significant difference (p<.05) for both with and without 把 *ba* .

(34) a. 他 把 这 个 问题 想–明白–了
ta ba zhe ge wenti xiang-mingbai-le
he *ba* this CL question think–understand–ASP
'He thought about this question and as a result he understood it.
b. 她 把 这 首 歌 练–会–了
ta ba zhe shou ge lian-hui-le
she *ba* this CL song practise–can–ASP
'She practised this song and as a result she could sing it.'

Table 6.15: 把 *ba* + object–oriented resultative 唱 – 红 *chang–hong* 'sing–popular' vs. subject–oriented resultative in G1

	chang-hong 'sing–popular'	G1 ('think–understand' and 'practise–can')	*ba*+*chang-hong* 'sing–popular'	*ba*+G1 ('think–understand' and 'practise–can')
Number		165	78	168
Mean	83.33	92.35	87.67	93.29
Median	90	100	92.5	100
Std	19.43	14.82	16.04	12.44
p–value	1.85×10^{-5}		0.002	

This also indicates a difference between subject–oriented and object–

oriented resultatives. It is possible that if both are acceptable with and without 把 *ba*, and construed as abstract notions (e.g. formed with verbs like 想 *xiang* 'think', 唱 *chang* 'sing'), then subject–oriented patterns are better than object–oriented ones. That is, subject–oriented resultatives suggest the result or affectedness of the subject/agent, and results like these are mostly related to abstract conceptions and mental verbs. As discussed in Chapter 5, Section 5.2, in terms of Affected Agent (cf. Næss 2007), Haspelmath (1994: 160) argues that verbs like 'learn', 'see' tend to occur with an Affected Agent. So subject–oriented resultatives are more frequent and acceptable with mental verbs, both with and without 把 *ba*.

In contrast, object–oriented resultatives describe the effect on the object, hence they relate more to concrete actions like 'wipe', 'do'. Moreover, as observed from the corpus data (Section 4.4.2.3.1), subject–oriented resultatives are more frequent using mental verbs, whereas object–oriented ones are more frequent with action verbs. So in terms of abstract notions, subject–oriented patterns are more acceptable than object–oriented ones. Although it is acceptable to combine mental verbs and abstract results (such as 唱–红 *chang-hong* 'sing–popular) in object–oriented resultatives, the degree of acceptability is lower than subject–oriented resultatives (e.g. 想–明白 *xiang-mingbai* 'think–understand') and object–oriented resultatives interpreted with real actions (e.g. 擦–干 *ca-gan* 'wipe–dry'), both with and without 把 *ba*.

6.6 Concluding remarks

In this chapter, based on survey 2, I have discussed the acceptability of 把 *ba* + object–oriented resultative constructions in Mandarin Chinese. As 把 *ba* functions to mark high transitivity, object–oriented resultatives are expected to be highly acceptable when combined with 把 *ba*, due to the high–transitivity interpretation of this type. The results of survey 2, carried out among 84 Chinese college students verify this expectation. Among the six test sentences, five are rated high in acceptability when combined with 把 *ba* (mean >85).

One pattern哭–湿 *ku-shi* 'cry–wet' receives lower scores with 把 *ba* than without 把 *ba*. This is caused by the comparatively lower degree of semantic transitivity (non–volitionality of A, part affectedness of O) and syntactic transitivity (intransitive main verb) than the other patterns, which are not fully compatible with the function of 把 *ba*. Nevertheless, the difference between with and without 把 *ba* is not significant (p=.14) as the pattern is still construed as having a medium degree of semantic transitivity.

Furthermore, one factor that affects the acceptability of object–oriented resultatives is the number of syllables of the pattern V + result XP. As suggested in Section 6.2.2.2, disyllabic words are the ones most frequently used in Mandarin, therefore resultative constructions with more than two syllables (e.g. 擦-干净 *ca-gan'jing* 'wipe–clean', 叠–整齐 *die-zheng'qi* 'fold–neat') are less acceptable with a postverbal NP. When combined with 把 ba, the P is fronted, which makes the combination of 把 *ba* and such resultatives more acceptable.

By comparing the acceptability of subject–/object–oriented resultatives with and without 把 *ba*, the capability of taking a postverbal NP is a crucial factor, which differs in two regards. Taking the two issues mentioned above, namely the capability of a result XP to take a postverbal NP, and the acceptability of 把 *ba* + resultatives, the constraints on subject–/ object–oriented resultatives are in accordance with some perspectives, but differ in other aspects. In terms of the capability of a result XP to take a postverbal NP, subject–oriented resultatives should be composed with a transitive verb and a two–place–predicate result XP, or interpreted as repeated actions. The number of syllables of the pattern 'V+result XP' plays little role in their acceptability. In contrast, object–oriented resultatives are more acceptable with disyllabic pattern 'V+result XP'. The status of the main verb and result XP, as well as the interpretation of the resultative construction, is irrelevant. Subject–oriented resultatives with P are more acceptable in expressing abstract notions and mental verbs than object–oriented resultatives.

Considering the acceptability of 把 *ba* + resultatives, the constraint that both types of resultatives require is that if a resultative is interpreted with high semantic transitivity, it will be fully acceptable when combined with 把 *ba*. The higher transitivity a sentence is construed with, the more acceptable it is with 把 *ba*. However, object–oriented resultatives with an intransitive main verb are less acceptable with 把 *ba* than without 把 *ba*. This rule does not apply to subject–oriented resultatives. More can be seen in Table 6.16, where sentences with the conditions met are fully acceptable, and '/' represents that the factor is irrelevant. Further discussion will follow in Chapter 7, Section 7.1.

Table 6.16: Factors related to acceptability of resultatives and with and without *ba*

	With a postverbal NP		With 把 *ba*	
Factor	subject-oriented	object-oriented	subject-oriented	object-oriented
Number of syllables of 'verb+result XP'	/	Two	/	/
Status of the verb	Transitive	/	/	Transitive
Status of the result XP	Two-place	/	/	/
Semantics of the result XP	Repeated actions /		/ /	
Degree of semantic transitivity involved in the sentence	/	/	High	High
Conception expressed by the sentence	Abstract	Concrete	/	/

The research in this chapter fills a gap regarding the acceptability of resultatives with a postverbal NP, which is related with phonological, syntactic and semantic factors. It should be noticed that subject- and object-oriented resultatives are viewed differently in terms of constraints, which suggests a distinction between the two types of resultatives. In addition, the acceptability of 把 *ba* + object-oriented resultatives again provides evidence for analyzing 把 *ba* as a marker of high semantic transitivity (Hopper and Thompson 1980, Sun 1995). Both subject- and object-oriented resultatives verify the argument that the higher semantic transitivity a sentence is interpreted with, the more acceptable it is when combined with 把 *ba*. This answers Question 7 as for the function of 把 *ba* in a resultative construction.

Chapter 7 Conclusion

7.1 Summary

In this book, I have discussed the usage of Chinese resultatives by adopting two approaches on the basis of the usage–based model, namely a corpus–based one and a questionnaire–based one. First, I collected data on Chinese resultatives from a corpus and analyzed their frequency in terms of various parameters, which gave us an accurate and empirically based sense of the actual usage of resultatives. Second, I investigated the acceptability of subject–/object–oriented resultatives with and without 把 *ba* via two questionnaire surveys, which suggested that there is a continuum of acceptability.

In Chapter 4, I answered Questions 1–3, namely 1) What qualifies as a Chinese resultative construction? 2) What do Chinese resultatives look like in actual usage? 3) How are Chinese resultatives viewed from a typological perspective? To begin with, I proposed two tests to identify Chinese resultatives, leading to a distinction between marginal and prototypical resultatives. An overview of Chinese resultatives based on the Lancaster Corpus of Mandarin Chinese (LCMC) and the Online Database on Verb–resultative Constructions in Contemporary Chinese (ODVRC) was provided considering type and token frequency in terms of various classifications, such as subject– versus object–oriented, weak versus strong versus spurious, transitive– versus intransitive–based. Regarding the properties of Chinese resultatives, a dimension of agent– versus patient– versus location–oriented resultatives was postulated. Resultatives with 把 *ba* as well as 终于 *zhongyu* 'finally' were also analyzed with respect to frequency.

My findings are the following. The two tests are found to be crucial for the classification of Chinese resultatives. Prototypical Chinese resultatives are highly productive with high type and token frequency, in contrast to marginal resultatives, which have high token frequency but low type frequency. Most resultatives have the following characteristics: subject–oriented, strong, patient–oriented, transitive–based, without 把 *ba* and without 终于 *zhongyu* 'finally'. Typologically, Chinese belongs to the same type as English, both of which permit strong and weak resultatives. They are different from languages only allowing weak resultatives (e.g. French, Italian and Japanese).

In Chapters 5 and 6, I answered the following Questions: 4) What determines the capacity of subject/agent–oriented resultatives to take a postverbal NP? 5) What determines the acceptability of subject/agent–oriented resultatives with and without 把 *ba*? 6) What determines the acceptability of object–oriented resultatives with and without 把 *ba*? 7) What is the function of 把 *ba* in a resultative construction? To test the acceptability of Chinese resultatives, two questionnaire surveys were used, employing the technique of magnitude estimation (see Bard et al. 1996), which can detect small differences in acceptability. The first survey answered Question 5, the second survey Question 6 and the two together Question 7. The criteria used in the design were subject– versus object–oriented resultatives (survey 2), with versus without 把 *ba* (survey 1 and 2), with versus without 终于 *zhongyu* 'finally' (survey 1). This last parameter tests high semantic transitivity as put forward by Hopper & Thompson (1980). 终于 *zhongyu* 'finally' expresses the idea of an agent trying hard to achieve something, which implies a high degree of volitionality of A. If 把 *ba* is a marker of high transitivity in resultative constructions, then adding 终于 *zhongyu* 'finally' could increase the acceptability of 把 *ba* + resultatives, as 把 *ba* and 终于 *zhongyu* 'finally' are semantically compatible in terms of high semantic transitivity.

Question 4 is an issue connecting the corpus data and questionnaire surveys. A resultative can only occur with 把 *ba* if it can take a postverbal NP without 把 *ba*. Based on the analysis of the corpus data in Chapter 4, prototypically subject/agent–oriented resultatives do not take objects, whilst object–oriented ones do. This is due essentially to the differences between the two types. If the result XP is predicated of the subject, the object will not be closely linked to the expression, hence it need not occur in the sentence. In contrast, if the resultative is object–oriented, there should be an object.

However, in the LCMC, I found examples of subject/agent–oriented resultatives taking postverbal NPs, and of object–oriented resultatives with objects in the preverbal position without 把 *ba*. Therefore the acceptability of object–oriented resultatives without 把 *ba* turns out to be a question regarding whether it can take a postverbal NP. Taking into account the corpus data and the sentences in the surveys, I argue that the ability of resultatives to take postverbal NP depends on phonological, syntactic and semantic factors. To be specific, the acceptability of resultative+ postverbal NP is determined by the number of syllables of 'V+ result XP' (disyllabic or more than two syllables), the status of the verb (transitive or intransitive), the status of the result XP (one–place or two–place predicate) and the interpretation of the resultative construction (single event or repeated actions). Subject/agent–oriented resultatives differ from object–oriented ones in terms of these aspects. Of the former, those with transitive verbs and two–place–predicate result XPs, or with the interpretation of repeated actions, are able to take a postverbal NP (e.g. 想–明白 *xiang-mingbai* 'think–understand'). The number of syllables does not affect the acceptability of subject–oriented resultatives with a postverbal NP.

Restrictions on object–oriented resultatives taking a postverbal NP are fewer than subject–oriented patterns, as there are always objects in the sentences, but the positions may vary (i.e. postverbal or preverbal). The prototypical type is formed with disyllabic patterns (verb + result XP) and postverbal objects. In contrast, pattens with ore than two syllables cannot take a postverbal NP; the object should be put before the main verb.

Subject/agent–oriented patterns barely take a postverbal NP, but resultatives formed with a transitive verb and a two–place result XP, or construed as repeated actions are able to do so. In the first situation, the combination of transitive verb + two–place result XP boosts the ability of the construction to take objects postverbally, as long as the verb and the result XP are compatible with each other semantically. Regarding the second situation, repeated actions produces ample energy flow, and such an interpretation enhances the degree of the affected–subject meaning expressed by the resultative construction as a whole, which makes the construction able to take a postverbal NP. Therefore, the acceptability of subject–oriented resultatives mainly stems from syntactic and semantic factors.

Considering object-oriented resultatives, as argued by Shi (2002; Chapter 6), there is a preference for disyllabic words rather than monosyllabic ones in Mandarin Chinese. The format of verb + result XP is viewed as a unit, and the two parts are adjacent, each with one syllable, so the whole structure with two characters fits the disyllabic pattern. Thereby, the resultative construction is regarded as a verbal phrase cognitively, which can take a postverbal NP. If a result XP is disyllabic, then in a resultative together with a monosyllabic verb, there will be three syllables (e.g. 擦-干'净 *ca-gan'jing* 'wipe-clean'). The whole construction does not fit the conventional disyllabic pattern. Therefore, if a postverbal NP shall follow, the sentence will be ruled out. In order to make the sentence acceptable, the object must be fronted before the main verb, directly or by means of the 把 *ba*-construction. Viewed in this way, the acceptability of object-oriented resultatives lies in phonological facet.

The results of the questionnaires are as follows. In the first questionnaire survey (Chapter 5), all the test sentences are acceptable without 把 *ba*, the acceptability of ba + subject-oriented resultatives is scalar, namely fully acceptable, marginally acceptable and the least acceptable, these three being significantly different (p<.05). Subject-oriented resultatives with the interpretation of the subject making efforts to achieve something thoroughly are acceptable when used with 把 *ba*. In addition, 把 *ba* + subject-oriented resultatives with 终于 *zhongyu* 'finally' are rated significantly higher than those without 终于 *zhongyu* 'finally' in fully acceptable and marginally acceptable sentences, but not in the least acceptable ones (the latter are always low in acceptability).

In the second survey (Chapter 6), apart from the patterns with a disyllabic result XP which are marginally acceptable, my object–oriented sentences were found to be acceptable in general. When combined with 把 *ba*, their acceptability is still high. However, there are some differences. The patterns with disyllabic result XPs are significantly better when used with 把 *ba*, whereas no significant differences occur between monosyllabic result XP with and without 把 *ba*. The status of the main verb also affects the acceptability of 把 *ba* + object–oriented resultatives. If a resultative construction is formed with an intransitive verb, it is judged to be less acceptable when used with 把 *ba*, although not significantly so ($.2>p>.05$). This is different from those formed with transitive verbs: the latter are more acceptable with 把 *ba*

Consistent with a constructional/cognitive approach, the explanation I propose is that in general, a high degree of semantic transitivity represented by a sentence (a resultative construction) is compatible with the function of 把 *ba* as a marker of high semantic transitivity. This holds true for the acceptability of 把 *ba* + subject–/object–oriented resultatives. The more transitive a resultative is construed to be semantically, the more acceptable it is with 把 *ba*. This also accounts for 把 *ba* + subject–oriented resultatives with 终于 *zhongyu* 'finally'. Since 终于 *zhongyu* 'finally' expresses a high degree of semantic transitivity, it is compatible with the function of 把 *ba*. Therefore, fully acceptable and marginally acceptable 把 *ba* + subject–oriented resultatives are judged to be better with this adverb than without it. However, for those subject–oriented resultatives that are already very low in acceptability with 把 *ba*, adding 终于 *zhongyu* 'finally' cannot make the sentences better.

In addition, the acceptability of 把 *ba* + object–oriented resultatives depends on the number of syllables of the pattern 'V+ result XP' and the status of the main verb. The phonological factor, as illustrated before, stems from the disyllabification process and the preference for disyllabic words in Chinese. A resultative consisting of an intransitive verb marks it as low in syntactic transitivity, which is not fully compatible with the function of 把 *ba* as a marker of high semantic transitivity. So expressions formed with an intransitive verb plus a postverbal NP with 把 *ba* are less acceptable than those without 把 *ba*. Thus syntactic transitivity and semantic transitivity are independent of but related to each other. The degree of compatibility between the two determines the acceptability of 把 *ba* + resultatives.

To sum up, the acceptability of resultatives depends on whether there can be a postverbal NP. This lies in phonological, syntactic and semantic factors, and varies in terms of subject– and object–oriented types. The acceptability of 把 *ba* + resultatives is determined by the compatibility of degree of syntactic transitivity of the main verb and semantic transitivity involved in the sentence. If the two are compatible with each other (a transitive main verb and a construal with a high degree of semantic transitivity), a 把 *ba* + resultative will be acceptable.

7.2 Contribution

The findings of this work contribute to the study of Chinese resultatives with the usage–based approach from a cognitive–typological perspective in descriptive, theoretical and methodological ways.

First, the corpus study contributes to the study of Chinese resultatives in a descriptive way. Previous scholarship on the frequency and distribution of these constructions is non–existent. Or studies based on corpus data focus on comparisons between English and Chinese. This book mainly investigates the properties of Chinese resultatives, which sheds light on resultatives in the field of typology. The two tests clarify the definition of Chinese resultatives. This definition further demonstrates the characteristics of Chinese resultatives in terms of marginal patterns, which are distinct from European languages such as English. The majority of subject/agent–oriented resultatives are transitive–based, which casts doubt on what is argued by Rappaport Hovav and Levin (2001) that few subject–oriented resultatives are transitive–based.

Second, my claim about the relation between the acceptability of Chinese resultatives and postverbal NPs has not been discussed in the scholarship. Based on empirical data from the corpora and explained in line with cognitive linguistics mentioned in the previous section, my discussion fills a gap in this respect both descriptively and theoretically. In addition, although the topic of resultatives has been widely discussed in the literature (e.g. Sybesma 1992, Zou 1994, Huang 1996, Wang 2001, Shen 2003, Song 2003, 2004, Zhao 2009), research has mainly focused on the object–oriented type, with acceptability judged as binary and subject–oriented resultatives generally ignored. I have investigated the acceptability of the subject–oriented type, and a continuum in this regard is demonstrated. The findings also shed light on research on resultatives typologically. The subject–oriented type is uncommon in languages like English, so related discussions are rare, whereas my research goes some wayt towards filling this gap.

Third, my discussion about the acceptability of 把 *ba* in resultatives contributes to the debate about the function of the 把 *ba*-construction in the resultative construction, which further sheds light on general knowledge about 把 *ba*. Empirical evidence is provided for treating 把 *ba* as a marker of high semantic transitivity (cf. Hopper & Thompson 1980, Sun 1995) rather than expressing disposal (Wang 1947, Li 1974, Wang 2003) or causation (Guo 1999, Xiong 2004, Ye 2004). Moreover, the affectedness of A as a parameter of transitivity (Næss 2007) is evident in terms of 把 *ba* + subject-oriented resultatives, which is missed by Hopper and Thompson (1980).

A final contribution of this work is the combination of corpora and questionnaire surveys. These methodologies are not novel in the scholarship, but as far as I am concerned, the adoption of magnitude estimation to judge acceptability is the first attempt in the Chinese tradition. Different from judgements based on linguists' intuition, the empirical evidence obtained from questionnaire surveys is more reliable. Its capability to detect small but significant differences among sentences is meaningful to reveal fine-grained distinctions in grammar (e.g. a scalar system for the acceptability of subject-oriented resultatives with 把 *ba*). The findings shed light on future research into grammar and can be applied to linguistic phenomena already discussed in the literature, which means that some of the generally accepted views on those phenomena will need to be revised.

7.3 Limitations

First, I employed the LCMC for my corpus-based study. However, as mentioned in Chapter 4, this balanced corpus is fairly limited in size, with only one million words, and it may not paint the whole picture of resultatives in use. For instance, quite a few result XPs listed in the ODVRC, which can pass the tests for resultatives, are not attested to in the LCMC. Moreover, the data in the LCMC are written language, so spoken Chinese is not taken into account. The conclusions based on the LCMC may be revised if more data are collected.

Second, the weak/strong/spurious classification proposed by Washio (1997) is worth discussing. In my data set discussed in Chapter 4, it is quite clear to make judgements according to the context. However, the boundaries between these concepts blur and may be interpreted differently by various speakers. In other words, the distinctions he suggests among strong/weak/spurious resultatives are treated as discrete, but they are much more gradated than suggested, and some examples can be ambiguous. According to Washio (1997), the resultative wipe the table clean/dry is weak in that clean or dry is catergorized by the semantics of wipe. If we consider 'rinse', according to the Longman Dictionary of Contemporary English Online (following Washio's routine), it is defined as 'to remove soap, dirt etc. from something by washing it quickly with water'. Then the resultative construction rinse the gully clean can be viewed as weak, as the sense 'to remove dirt' (hence clean) is implied in the meaning of rinse. However, it may also be regarded as strong since rinse emphasizes the manner of 'washing quickly with water', which does not necessarily lead to the result of becoming clean. It may therefore be appropriate to modify this classification; for instance, by recognising the existence of gradience in this context.

Third, the acceptability–judgement questionnaires produced interesting results. They were not as stable as expected, however. The same pattern was judged differently in the two surveys (e.g. 想–明白 *ming'bai* 'think–understand' is fully acceptable in the two surveys but there is a significant difference between with and without 把 *ba* in survey 2, yet not in survey 1). The reason for this difference is unclear, but perhaps the environment in which the data were collected played a role. Survey 1 was carried out in a classroom, monitored by a professor at the beginning of a lecture. Survey 2 was done by inviting participants in study classrooms and libraries. It is hard to tell which group of subjects were more careful in which situation, but it may be a factor leading to the differences in the results. Perhaps it is best to make sure that the participants and the environment are more similar if the results of different surveys are to be compared.

7.4 Suggestions for further work

To begin with, the combinations of resultative constructions and other constructions should be investigated. This work mainly focuses on 把 *ba* + resultatives. However, many other constructions can also be combined with resultatives, such as the patient–subject clause, the 被 *bei*–construction (passive) and the verb–copying construction (Chapter 2, Section 2.4). The acceptability of combinations varies, and sometimes a resultative can only be combined with only one construction, not the others. Although there are discussions on this topic in the scholarship, they are problematic. (For example, in Chapter 2, Section 2.4, Song (2004) proposes the prominence hierarchy. According to him, a nonagentive resultative such as 吃–饱 *chi-bao* 'eat–full' can only be combined with the verb–copying construction, but not the 把 *ba*–construction. However, also construed as a nonagentive event, 想–明白 *xiang-mingbai* 'think–understand' can be used with both constructions.) Therefore, this is a direction I would like to speculate about via the methodology of a questionnaire survey, as this approach will give us a better idea of the differences in the acceptability of resultatives with different constructions than intuition–based studies. I have a preliminary idea that one aim for various constructions to be used with resultatives is to avoid P in the postverbal position when the restrictions on resultatives to take a postverbal NP are not met, namely, the number of syllables in the resultative, the status of verb, the status of the result XP and the interpretation of the resultative construction (as mentioned in Section 7.1, these constraints vary in terms of subject–/object–oriented types). So the problem is that P should occur in a sentence for a more comprehensible meaning, but it cannot meet the requirements of being in a postverbal position. The solutions also differ in terms of the subject–/ object–oriented type. For a subject–oriented resultative, if P shall appear, it tends to be combined with the verb–copying construction so that P will follow the main verb rather than a result XP. Object–oriented resultatives, on the other hand, will be used with the 把 *ba*–construction, the patient–subject clause or the 被 *bei*–construction (passive), in all of which P will be fronted before the main verb. Whether there is a preference for the object–oriented type to be used with the three constructions, and the rationales for co–occurrence, shall be illuminated in follow–up research.

The second direction concerns the weak/strong/spurious resultatives proposed by Washio (1997). It is of significance to view resultatives from a typological perspective, as some languages allow all three types (e.g. English, Chinese), whereas others only sanction the weak type (e.g. French, Japanese). However, as mentioned in the previous section, the classification proposed by him is not that tenable. Then, how to deal with ambiguous examples requires fine–grained elaborations and explanations.

A third area of potential interest is a truly cross–linguistic study of resultatives. This book mainly focuses on Chinese and takes some typological insights into account. Research into more languages may lead to a better understanding of some of the parameters of variation and may even add new ones. Perhaps, this variation could be captured by some kind of semantic maps (e.g. Haspelmath 2003). That is, "a method for describing and illuminating the patterns of multifunctionality of grammatical morphemes that does not imply a commitment to a particular choice among monosemic and polysemic analyses" (Haspelmath 2003: 213). The basic form of a semantic map is a geometrical representation of functions in conceptual/semantic space that are linked by connecting lines and then constitute a network. The configuration of functions shown in the conceptual space is supposed to be universal, whereas various languages differ with respect to the boundaries of semantic maps that represent particular language categories. For instance, the categories of resultatives could be subject–/object–oriented, weak/strong, transitive–/intransitive–based, all presented on a semantic map. As different languages have distinct properties, diverse distributions of the categories will be stated on the map regarding languages (e.g. English has 'subject–oriented, object–oriented, weak, strong, transitive– and intransitive–based' features, whereas French has object–oriented, weak, transitive– and intransitive–based ones). Since this approach has not been applied to resultatives, a notable gap in this regard remains to be filled.

References

1. Bard, E. G., Robertson, D., & Sorace, A. (1996). Magnitude estimation of linguistic acceptability. Language, 72(1), 32–68. doi:10.2307/416793
2. Barðdal, J. (2006). Predicting the productivity of argument structure constructions. *Proceedingss of the 32nd Annual Meeting of the Berkeley Linguistics Society* (pp 467–478). doi:http://dx.doi.org/10.3765/bls.v32i1.343
3. Boas, H. C. (2003). *A constructional approach to resultatives*. Stanford: CSLI Publications.
4. Borjars, K., & Burridge, K. (2010). *Introducing English grammar* (2nd ed.). London: Routledge.
5. Bresnan, J. (1982). The passive in lexical theory. In J. Bresnan (Eds.), *The mental representation of grammatical relations* (pp. 3–86). Cambridge, Mass: MIT Press.
6. Broccias, C.. (2003). *The English change network: Forcing changes into schemas*. Berlin: Mouton de Gruyter.
7. Bybee, J. L. (1985). *Morphology: A study of the relation between meaning and form*. Amsterdam/ Philadelphia: John Benjamins Publishing.
8. Bybee, J. (2010). *Language, usage and cognition*. Cambridge: Cambridge University Press.

9. Bybee, J., Perkins, R., & Pagliuca, W. (1994). *The evolution of grammar: Tense, aspect, and modality in the languages of the world*. Chicago: University of Chicago Press.
10. Chao, Y. (1968). *A grammer of spoken Chinese*. Berkeley: University of California Press.
11. Chen, Q. (2008). *Hanyu timao yanjiu de leixingxue shiye* [A study on the aspectual system of Mandarin from a typological perspective]. Beijing: The Commercial Press.
12. Cheng, L. L.–S. & Huang, C.–T. J. (1994). On the argument structure of resultative compounds. In M. Chen & O. Tzeng (Eds.), *A Festschrift for William S.-Y. Wang: Interdisciplinary studies on language and language change* (pp. 187–221). Taipei: Pyramid Press.
13. Chomsky, N. (1981). *Lectures on government and binding*. Dordrecht: Foris Publications.
14. Chomsky, N. (1986). *Knowledge of language: Its nature, origin, and use*. New York: Praeger Publishers.
15. Chomsky, N. (1995). *The Minimalist Program*. Cambridge, Mass: MIT Press.
16. Clausner, T. C., & Croft, W. (1997). Productivity and schematicity in metaphors. *Cognitive Science*, 21(3), 247–82.
17. Comrie, B. (1976). *Apect*. Cambridge: Cambridge University Press.
18. Croft, W. (2002). *Typology and universals* (2nd ed.). Cambridge: Cambridge University Press.
19. Croft, W. & Cruse, D. A. (2004). *Cognitive linguistics*. Cambridge: Cambridge University Press.

20. Croft, W. (2012). *Verbs: Aspect and causal structure*. Oxford: Oxford University Press.

21. Dahl, Ö. (1985). *Tense and aspect systems*. Oxford: Basil Blackwell.

22. Featherston, S. (2005). Magnitude estimation and what it can do for your syntax: Some wh–constraints in German. *Lingua*, 115, 1525–1550. doi:10.1016/j.lingua.2004.07.003

23. Fillmore, C. J. (1982). Frame semantics. In I. Yang (Eds.), *Linguistics in the morning calm* (pp. 111–137). Seoul: Hanshin Publishing Co.

24. Gao, Q. (1997). Resultative cerb compounds and ba–construction in Chinese. *Journal of Chinese Linguistics*, 25(1), 84–130.

25. Goldberg, A. E. (1995). *A construction grammar approach to argument structure*. Chicago: The University of Chicago Press.

26. Goldberg, A. E. & Jackendoff, R. (2004). The English resultative as a family of constructions. *Language*, 80(3), 532–568.

27. Gordon, P. C., & Hendrick, R. (1997). Intuitive knowledge of linguistic co–reference. *Cognition*, 62(3), 325–370. doi:https://doi.org/10.1016/S0010–0277(96)00788–3

28. Cowart, W. (1997). *Experimental syntax: Applying objective methods to sentence judgements*. Thousand Oaks: Sage Publications.

29. Guo, R. (1999). *Baziju de peijia jiegou* [The valence structure of the Ba construction]. Paper presented at the Second Seminar of Valance Grammar in Contemporary Chinese, Shanghai.

30. Haegeman, L. (1994). *Introduction to government and binding theory* (2nd ed.). Oxford: Blackwell.

31. Han, J. (2013). *Constructional change and emergence in Chinese*

Expressions involving BA (Doctoral dissertation). The University of Edinburgh.

32. Halliday, M. A. K. (1985). *An introduction to functional grammar*. London: Edward Amold Pty Ltd.
33. Hashimoto, A. Y. (1971). Mandarin syntactic structures. *Unicorn (Chinese Linguistics Project and Seminar)*, 8, 1–146. Princeton University.
34. Haspelmath, M. (1994). Passive participles across languages. In B. Fox & P. Hopper (Eds.), *Voice: Form and function* (pp. 151–177). Amsterdam: John Benjamins.
35. Haspelmath, M. (2003). Geometry of grammatical meaning: semantic maps and cross–linguistic comparison. In M. Tomasello (Ed.), *The new psychology of language, Vol. 2* (pp. 211–242). Mahwah, N.J.: Erlbaum.
36. Hoekstra, T. A. (1988). Small clause results. *Lingua* ,74, 101–139.
37. He, Y. (2004). Dongqushi "v + qilai" de yuyi fenhua jiqi jufa biaoxian [Semantic types of verb–direction construction "v + up" and their syntactic features]. *Studies in Language and Linguistics*, 24(3), 23–31.
38. Hollmann, W. B. (2003). *Synchrony and diachrony of English periphrastic causatives: a cognitive perspective* (Doctoral dissertation). Manchester University.
39. Hollmann, W. B. (2006). Passivisability of English periphrastic causatives. In S. T. Gries & A. Stefanowitsch (Eds.), *Corpora in cognitive linguistics: corpus-based approaches to syntax and lexis* (pp. 193–223). Berlin/New York: Mouton de Gruyter.
40. Hollmann, W. B. (2013). *Ditransitive constructions in Lancashire dialect*. Paper presented at the LAGB Annual Meeting. SOAS, London.

41. Hopper, P. J. & Thompson, S. A. (1980). Transitivity in grammar and discourse. *Language*, 56, 251–299.

42. Hopper, P. J., & Traugott, E. C. (2003). *Grammaticalization* (2nd ed.). Cambridge: Cambridge University Press.

43. Hu, Y. & Xu, B. (1981). *Xiandai hanyu* [Contemporary Chinese]. Shanghai: Shanghai Educational Publishing House.

44. Huang, Y. (1996). Ba/bei jiegou yu dongci chongfu jiegou de hubu fenbu xianxiang [The complementary distribution of Ba construction, Bei construction and verb–copying construction]. *Studies of the Chinese Language*, 251(2), 92–99.

45. Jin, G., Xiao, H., Fu L., & Zhang, Y. (2005). Xiandai hanyu yuliaoku jianshe ji shenjiagong [The construction and development of the corpus of Contemporary Chinese.]. *Applied Linguistics*, 2, 111–120.

46. Keller, F., & Sorace, A. (2003). Gradient auxiliary selection and impersonal passivization in German: An experimental investigation. *Journal of Linguistics*, 39(1), 57–108. doi:10.1017/S0022226702001676

47. Koestenberger, M., et al. (2009). Right ventricular function in infants, children and adolescents: reference values of the tricuspid annular plane systolic excursion (TAPSE) in 640 healthy patients and calculation of z score values. *Journal of the American Society of Echocardiography*, 22(6), 715–719. doi:https://doi.org/10.1016/j.echo.2009.03.026

48. Lakoff, G. (1987). *Women, fire and dangerous things: What categories reveal about the mind*. Chicago: University of Chicago Press.

49. Lakoff, G., & Johnson, M. (1980). *Metaphors we live by*. Chicago: University of Chicago Press.

50. Langacker, R. W. (1987). *Foundations of cognitive grammar: Theoretical prerequisites*. Stanford: Stanford University Press.

51. Langacker, R. W. (1991). *Concept, image, and symbol: The cognitive basis of grammar*. Berlin: Moutun de Gruyter.

52. Levin, B. & Rappaport H. M. (1995). *Unaccusativity: At the syntax-lexical semantics interface*. Cambridge, Mass.: MIT Press.

53. Li, C. N., & Thompson, S. A. (1981). *Mandarin Chinese: A functional reference grammar*. Berkeley and Los Angeles: University of California Press.

54. Li X. (1994). Dui shujieshi dai binyu gongneng de kaocha [An investigation into the function of verb–resultative construction with object]. *Chinese Language Learning*, 83(5), 32–38.

55. Li, X. (2008). *Jieguo buyu yuyi zhixiang yanjiu* [On the semantic orientation of verb–resultative construction's complement] (Doctoral dissertation). Capital Normal University.

56. Li, Y. (1974). What does 'disposal' mean? Features of the verb and noun in Chinese. *Journal of Chinese Linguistics*, 2, 200–218.

57. Li, Y. (1990). On V–V compounds in Chinese. *Natural Language and Linguistic Theory*, 8(2), 177–207. doi:https://doi.org/10.1007/BF00208523

58. Li, Y. (1995). Thematic hierarchy and causativity. *Natural Language and Linguistic Theory*, 13(2), 255–282. doi:https://doi.org/10.1007/BF0099278

59. Luo, S., Wang, W. & Hong, M. (2010). Yinghan jieguo goushi RAP de yuliaoku yu leixingxue yanjiu [A corpus–based and typological approach to RAP constraints on English and Chinese resultative constructions]. *Foreign Language Teaching and Research*, 42(4), 268–274.

60. Lü, S. (1961). Xiandai hanyu danshuang yinjie wenti chutan [The research on monosyllabic and disyllabic issues in Contemporary Chinese.] *Studies of the Chinese Language*, 1, 10–22.

61. Lü, S. (1999 [1955]). *Hanyu yufa lunwenji* [Works on Chinese grammar] (2nd ed.). Beijing: The Commercial Press.

62. Lü, S. (Ed.). (1999). *Xiandai hanyu babai ci* [Eight hundred words in contemporary Chinese]. Beijing: The Commercial Press.

63. Lyons, J. (1977). *Semantics*. Cambridge: Cambridge University Press.

64. Ma, Z. & Lu, J. (1997). Xingrongci zuo jieguo buyu qingkuang kaocha (3) [An investigation into the adjectives as resultative (3)]. *Chinese Language Learning*, 102(6), 7–9.

65. McEnery, T., & Xiao, Z. (2004). The Lancaster Corpus of Mandarin Chinese: A Corpus for Monolingual and Contrastive Language Study. *Religion*, 17, 1175–1178.

66. McEnery, T., Xiao, R., & Tono, Y. (2006). *Corpus-based language studies: An advanced resource book*. London: Routledge.

67. Næss, Å. (2007). *Prototypical transitivity*. Amsterdam/ Philadelphia: John Benjamins Publishing.

68. Neeleman, A. & Van de Koot, H. (2002). Bare Resultatives. *The Journal of Comparative Germanic Linguistics*, 6(1), 353–406. doi:http://dx.doi.org/10.1023/A:1022852519378

69. Olsen, M. B. (1997). *A Semantic and Pragmatic Model of Lexical and Grammatical Aspect*. New York: Garland Press.

70. Pollard, C. & Sag, I. A. (1994). *Head-driven phrase structure grammar*. Stanford: CSLI.

71. Rappaport Hovav, M. & Levin, B. (2001). An event structure account of English resultatives. *Language*, 77(4), 766–797. doi:10.1353/lan.2001.0221
72. Rosch, E. H. (1973). Natural categories. *Cognitive Psychology*, 4(3), 328–350. doi:https://doi.org/10.1016/0010–0285(73)90017–0
73. Rosch, E. H. (1978). Principles of categorization. In E. H. Rosch & B. B. Lloyd (Eds.), *Cognition and categorization* (pp. 27–48). Hillside N.J: Erlbaum.
74. Shi, C. (2008a). Dongjieshi "V lei" de jufa yuyi jiqi lilun yunhan [The syntactic and semantic analysis of the VRC V–*lei* (累) and its theoretic implication. *Linguistic Sciences*, 34(3), 242–258.
75. Shi, C. (2008b). *Hanyu dongjieshi de jufa yuyi yanjiu* [The syntax and semantics of Chinese verb–resultative constructions]. Beijing: Peking University Press.
76. Shi, H. (2011). *Hanyu dongjieshi de zhenghe yu lishi yanbian* [The conceptual integration and historical development of the Chinese verb–resultative constructions]. Shanghai: Fudan University Press.
77. Shen, J. (2004). Dongjieshi "zhuilei" de yufa he yuyi [The syntax and semantics of the resultative 'chase tired']. *Linguistic Sciences*, 3(6), 3–15.
78. Shi, Y. (2002). Hanyu fazhanshi shang de shuangyinhua qushi he dongbu jiegou de dansheng [The motivation of the disyllabification for the emergence of the resultative construction]. *Linguistics Study*, 46(1), 1–14.
79. Simpson, J. (1983). Resultatives. In L. Levin, M. Rappaport & A. Zaenen (Eds.), *Papers in lexical-functional grammar* (pp. 143–157). Indiana: Indiana university linguistics club.
80. Song, H. & Wang, X. (2013). Jin shinian guonei yuliaoku yuyanxue yanjiu

zongshu [A review of corpus Linguistics studies in China in recent ten years]. *Shandong Foreign Language Teaching Journal*, 154(3), 41–47.

81. Song, W. (2003). *Xiandai hanyu dongjieshi peijia de renzhi yanjiu* [On the valence of Contemporary Chinese V–R Compounds: A study based on conceptual structures] (Doctoral dissertation). Graduate School of Chinese Academy of Social Sciences.
82. Song, W. (2004). Dongjieshi zai jige jushi zhong de fenbu [The distribution of the resultative construction in other constructions]. *Linguistic Research*, 92(3), 13–19.
83. Song, Y. (1981). Guanyu Baziju de liangge wenti [Two questions of the Ba construction]. *Linguistic Research*, 8(2), 39–43.
84. Sorace, A., & Keller, F. (2005). Gradience in linguistic data. *Lingua*, 115(11), 1497–1524.
85. Sprouse, J. (2011). A test of the cognitive assumptions of magnitude estimation: Commutativity does not hold for acceptability judgments. *Language* 87(2), 274–288.
86. Stevens, S. S. (1956). The direct estimation of sensory magnitudes: Loudness. *The American journal of psychology*, 69(1), 1–25. doi:10.2307/1418112
87. Stowell, T. (1981). *Origins of phrase structure* (Doctoral dissertation). Massachusetts Institute of Technology.
88. Sun, C. (1995). Transitivity, the ba construction and its history. *Journal of Chinese Linguistics*, 23(1), 159–195.
89. Sunaoka, K. (2013). Design of an online database for Chinese resultative verb compounds, In *Proceedings of the 63rd Annual Conference of The*

Chinese Linguistic Society of Japan (pp. 23–32).

90. Sybesma, R. (1992). *Causatives and accomplishments: The case of Chinese ba* (Doctoral dissertation). Holland Institute of Generative Linguistics.
91. Tai, J. H. (1999). Verb–copying in Chinese revisited. *Chinese Languages and Linguistics*, 5, 97–119.
92. Talmy, L. (1976). Semantic causative types. In M. Shibatani (Ed.), *Syntax and Semantics* (Vol. 6). *The grammar of causative constructions* (pp. 43–116). New York: Academic Press.
93. Talmy, L. (2000). *Toward a cognitive semantics* (Vol. 2). Cambridge, Mass.: MIT Press.
94. Tantucci, V. (2015). Traversativity and grammaticalization: The aktionsart of guo as a lexical source of evidentiality. *Chinese Language & Discourse*, 6(1), 57–100. doi:10.1075/cld.6.1.03
95. Thompson, S. A. (1973). Transitivity and some problems with the Ba construction in Mandarin Chinese. *Journal of Chinese Linguistics*, 1(2), 208–221.
96. Traugott, E. C., & Trousdale, G. (2013). *Constructionalization and constructional changes*. Oxford: Oxford University Press.
97. Travis, L. (1984). *Parameters and effects of word order variation*. Cambridge, Mass.: MIT Press.
98. Tsao, F. (1987). A topic–comment approach to the ba–construction. *Journal of Chinese Linguistics*, 15(1), 1–54.
99. Vendler, Zeno. (1967). *Linguistics in Philosophy*. Ithaca, N.Y.: Cornell University Press.
100. Verspoor, C. M. (1997). *Contextually-dependent lexical semantics*

(Doctoral dissertation). University of Edinburgh.

101. Wang, H. (1999). Dongqushi shubu jiegou peijia yanjiu [Valence studies of the verb–directional constructions]. *Studies in Language and Linguistics*, 36(1), 142–152.

102. Wang, H. (2001). Dongjieshi shubu jiegou zai baziju he chongdongju zhong de fenbu [The distribution of the resultative construction in the Ba construction and the verb–copying construction]. *Linguistic Research*, 78(1), 6–11.

103. Wang, H. (2003). *Baziju de yiyi jiujing shi shenme*? [What is the semantics of the Ba construction?] *Linguistic Research*, 87(2), 35–40.

104. Wang, L. (1947). *Zhongguo xiandai yufa* [Modern Chinese grammar]. Shanghai: Zhonghua Book Company.

105. Wang, L. (1989). *Hanyu yufa Shi* [The history of Chinese grammar]. Beijing: The Commercial Press.

106. Washio. (1997). Resultatives compositionality and language variation. *Journal of East Asian Linguistics*, 6(1), 1–49. doi:https://doi.org/10.1023/A:1008257704110

107. Wechsler, S. (1997). Resultative predicates and control. In *Texas linguistic forum*, 38 (pp. 307–321). Austin: University of Texas.

108. Weskott, T., & Fanselow, G. (2008). Variance and informativity in different measures of linguistic acceptability. In N. Abner & J. Bishop (Eds.), *Proceedings of the 27th West Coast Conference on Formal Linguistics* (pp. 431–439). Somerville, MA: Cascadilla Press.

109. Weskott, T., & Fanselow, G. (2011). On the informativity of different measures of linguistic acceptability. *Language*, 87(2), 249–273. doi:

10.1353/lan.2011.0041

110. Williams, E. (1983). Against Small Clauses. *Linguistic Inquiry*, 14(2), 287–308. Xiao, Z. (2002). *A corpus-based study of aspect in Mandarin Chinese*. (Doctoral dissertation). Lancaster University.

111. Xiong, Z. (2004). *Xiandai hanyu zhong de zhishi jushi* [The causative sentences in contemporary Chinese]. Hefei: Anhui University Press.

112. Xun, E., Rao, G., Xiao, X., & Zang, J. (2016). Da shuju beijing xia BCC yuliaoku de yanzhi [The construction of the BCC Corpus in the age of Big Data]. *Corpus Linguistics*, 3(1), 93–118.

113. Yang, D. (2004). 20 shiji 80 niandai zhongqi yilai de dongqushi yanjiu shiping [Researches on directiona complement since the middle of the 1980s]. *Language Teaching and Linguistics Studies*, 2, 54–62.

114. Yang, L. & Wang, Y. (2009). Jiyu yuliaoku hanyu dongjie goushi youjie/wujie yu jieguo buyu wu jiangeti xianzhi yanjiu [A research on the third aspectual constraint to Chinese resultatives based on the corpus]. *Journal of Changchun University of Science and Technology* (Social Sciences Edition), 22(6), 938–941.

115. Ye, X. (2004). “Ba”ziju de zhishixing jieshi [Causative interpretation of the Ba–sentence]. *Chinese Teaching in the World*, 68(2), 25–39.

116. Zhang, X. (2017). Guonei yuliaoku yuyanxue yanjiu: huigu yu zhanwang [The study on corpus linguistics in China: review and expectation]. *Journal of Xi'an International Studies University*, 25(2), 36–41.

117. Zhan, W., Guo R., Chen Y. (2003). *The CCL Corpus of Chinese Texts: 700 million Chinese Characters, the 11th Century B.C. – present*. Available online at the website of Center for Chinese Linguistics (abbreviated as

CCL) of Peking University, http://ccl.pku.edu.cn:8080/ccl_corpus.

118. Zhan, W., Ma T., Tian J. & Sunaoka K. (2015). Hanyu shubu jiegou shujuku de goujian jiqi keshihua yanjiu [Development of an online database on Chinese resultative verb compounds and its application based on data visualization technology]. *Journal of Technology and Chinese Language Teaching*, 6(1), 1–15.

119. Zhao, Q. (2009a). Yinghan dongjieshi de gongxing yu gexing [Similarities and differences of English and Chinese resultative constructions]. *Foreign Language Teaching and Research*, 41(4), 256–265.

120. Zhao, Q. (2009b). *Hanyu dongjie goushi de lunyuan shixian* [Argument realizations of English and Chinese resultative constructions] (Doctoral dissertation). Fudan University.

121. Zou, K. 1994. Resultative V–V Compounds in Chinese. *MIT Working Papers in Linguistics*, 22, 271–290.

122. The Longman Dictionary of Contemporary English Online website: https://www.ldoceonline.com/

Appendix A: Chinese Questionnaire surveys of acceptability of Chinese resultatives

Lancaster University
Linguistics and English Language

参与说明

项目名称：汉语语法研究

研究人：余烁 s.yu1@lancaster.ac.uk

Dept of Linguistics and English Language

County South

Lancaster University

Lancaster LA1 4YL

United Kingdom

您受邀参与此项研究。请在您确定是否参加以前，请仔细阅读以下说明。

此项研究的目的是什么?

此项研究是我在兰卡斯特大学语言学与英语学院攻读博士学位的一部分，研究目的是探究汉语语法。

研究包括什么？

此项研究包括问卷调查。

为什么邀请我参加？

我邀请您是因为我对母语为汉语的人群如何判断句子的可接受度感兴趣。

如果您同意参加我的研究，我将感到非常荣幸。

如果我参与此项目会怎样？

如果您同意参加，将参与以下一些活动：您拿出一支笔，阅读调查问卷上的说明，基于您的汉语语感判断所给句子是否自然。

我参与此项目有哪些好处？

如果您参加此项研究，您对句子的判断将有助于我们更好地理解汉语语法。

我参加后会有哪些可能的弊端和风险？

您参加此项研究不存在任何弊端。参与问卷调查只需要您10分钟的时间。

我如果不参加或者不想继续参加研究，会怎样？

如果您决定不参加此项研究，这将不会影响您的学业和您此门课程的成绩。

您有权在任何时候无条件退出项目。如果您在项目开始后或完成后两周之内退出，我将不会使用您提供的任何信息。如果您晚于上述时间退出，我将在我的研究中使用您提供的信息。

我参与此项目是保密的吗？

所有在项目进行期间收集的关于您的信息都会被严格保密。任何关于身份的信息，例如姓名，都将在我的博士论文或其他关于此项目的出版发表中进行匿名处理。我将安全保管收集到的数据。所有纸质文件都会存放在带锁的文件柜中。电子版数据将储存在设有密码的电脑中，存放个人信息的文件夹也将被加密。

研究结果将怎样处理?

此项研究的结果仅用于学术目的，包括我的博士论文和其他出版或发表，例如期刊文章。我也计划在学术会议上发表我的研究结果。

如果有其他问题怎么办?

如果您还有其他问题，或者如果您在参与此项目的过程中有任何不满，请联系我本人或我的导师。

Elena Semino	Willem Hollmann
Head of Department（系主任）	Supervisor（导师）
e.semino@lancaster.ac.uk	w.hollmann@lancaster.ac.uk
+44(0)1524594176	+44 (0)1524 94644

Dept of Linguistics and English Language

County South

Lancaster University

Lancaster LA1 4YT

United Kindom

此项研究已得到兰卡斯特大学伦理委员会（UREC）的批准。

非常感谢您参与此项目

同意书

项目名称：汉语语法研究

我已阅读了与此项目有关的说明。 □

我已了解此研究的目的及我要回答的问题。我同意参与项目说明中所列的安排。 □

我参与此项目完全出于本人意愿。我有权在任何时候退出此项目，但仅限于完成的两周之内。如果我在完成项目的两周之后退出，我提供的信息将会被用于研究。 □

我了解所有信息都是匿名的。 □

我收到了此同意书和项目说明。 □

姓名：

签名：

日期：

汉语语法调查研究

此项问卷调查是本人攻读博士学位期间关于汉语语法研究项目的一部分。如果您想了解更多信息，我将非常乐意告诉您更多关于此项研究的目的与结果。您可以通过以下方式联系我。

您的回答将完全被保密，任何通过此调查收集的信息都不会被泄露。非常感谢您的协助与支持。

Shuo Yu

s.yu1@lancaster.ac.uk

Dept of Linguistics and English Language

County South

Lancaster University

Lancaster LA1 4YL

United Kingdom

准备

为了完成此问卷调查，需要您自带一支笔。请将您的回答填在问卷右侧的表格中，并在实验结束后将问卷交给协助老师。

个人信息

请根据相关问题填写个人信息。如您不便回答部分问题，请忽略。

出生日期	
性别	
现居住地（市/县）	

您一直居住于此地吗？如果不是，请给出您此前居住地的信息，包括居住时长。	
除了普通话，您会说方言吗？如果是，您认为自己说的是哪种方言（例如北方方言，吴方言）？	

如没有问题，请继续

指示：

该实验旨在探究汉语语法。我们列出了一些句子，请根据语感判断这些句子是否自然，并用具体分数表明自己的判断。一个句子听起来越自然，所得分数越高；越不自然，所得分数越低。判断的分数高低没有限制，但请勿给出负数（如–5，–20等）。请注意，句子自然度应与其所得分数成正比。例如，您给句①打20分，句②的自然度在您看来是句①的一半，即您认为句②只有句①一半自然，那么句②得10分。如果句③的自然度是句②的一半，那么句③得5分。(类似地，如果您判断句①得200分，那么句②得100分，句③得50分。您所判断的句子分数高低没有限制。)

练习：

下面三个句子为判断练习。请将分数（取决于句子在你语感中的自然度）填在右侧的方框内。

	评分
①今天晚上特别冷。	
②小张等了就走了。	
③他苹果给。	

当您确定可以使用此方法进行判断之后，如没有问题，请正式开始测试。此项实验没有时间限制，请根据自己的实际情况进行判断。请注意，您所给的评分完全基于您的汉语语感。一旦您给一个句子评分后，请不要再做改动。

如没有问题，请继续

句子（问卷1.1）：

		评分
1.	他把桌子擦干净了。	
2.	她叠整齐了衣服。	
3.	她终于看累了小说。	
4.	他把这种茶喝腻了。	
5.	她终于把工作做完了。	
6.	她看惯了那种微笑。	
7.	她哭湿了手绢。	
8.	他把这个问题想明白了。	
9.	她听懂了小宇的话。	
10.	她终于看惯了那种微笑。	
11.	他想清楚这个问题。。	
12.	她终于看完了那本小说。	
13.	他喝腻了这种茶。	
14.	她终于把那种微笑看惯了。	
15.	他烦了老师的话。	
16.	他终于把这个问题想明白了。	
17.	她把那种微笑看惯了。	

续表

		评分
18.	他终于练熟了这首歌。	
19.	她把小宇的话听懂了。	
20.	他把这个问题想了。	
21.	她终于听懂了小宇的话。	
22.	他擦干净了桌子。	
23.	他终于把这种茶喝腻了。	
24.	她把小宇的话懂了。	
25.	他终于想明白了这个问题。	
26.	她看累了小说。	
27.	他终于喝腻了这种茶。	
28.	她终于把小宇的话听懂了.	
29.	他想明白了这个问题。	
30.	她把小说看累了。	
31.	他又终于听了这首歌。	
32.	他弄坏了小火车。	

再次感谢您的协助!

句子（问卷1.2）:

		评分
1.	他弄坏了小火车。	
2.	他又终于听了这首歌。	
3.	她把小说看累了。	
4.	他终于练会了这首歌。	
5.	她把这个道理弄明白了。	
6.	她哭湿了手绢。	
7.	他终于把老师的话听烦了。	

续表

		评分
8.	她喝够了那种药水。	
9.	她终于看完了那本小说。	
10.	他把这首歌练会了。	
11.	她弄明白了这个道理。	
12.	她终于把那种药水喝够了。	
13.	他烦了老师的话。	
14.	她终于把这个道理弄明白了。	
15.	他擦干净了桌子。	
16.	他终于听烦了老师的话。	
17.	她把小宇的话懂了。	
18.	他练会了这首歌。	
19.	她终于把工作做完了。	
20.	她把那种药水喝够了。	
21.	他听烦了老师的话。	
22.	他终于练熟了这首歌。	
23.	她看累了小说。	
24.	他把这个问题想了。	
25.	她终于弄明白了这个道理。	
26.	他终于把这首歌练会了。	
27.	他想清楚这个问题。	
28.	她终于喝够了那种药水。	
29.	他把老师的话听烦了。	
30.	她终于看累了小说。	
31.	她叠整齐了衣服。	
32.	他把桌子擦干净了。	

再次感谢您的协助！

句子（问卷2）：

		评分
1.	她洗衣服洗累了。	
2.	他把我打了。	
3.	他听了又这首歌。	
4.	她把手绢哭湿了。	
5.	他听烦了老师的话。	
6.	她讲述细致了这件事。	
7.	她把那首歌唱红了。	
8.	他想明白了这个问题。	
9.	她把小宇的话懂了。	
10.	他擦桌子擦干净了	
11.	她练会了这首歌。	
12.	他把这个问题想明白了。	
13.	她听懂了小凯的话。	
14.	他把菜炒咸了。	
15.	他听老师的话听烦了。	
16.	他踢偏了球。	
17.	她把衣服叠整齐了。	
18.	他弄坏了小火车。	
19.	她把被子叠好了。	
20.	他擦干净了桌子。	
21.	她把小明的话听懂了。	
22.	她弄了头发。	
23.	她把这首歌练会了。	
24.	他想这个问题想明白了。	
25.	她叠整齐了衣服。	

续表

		评分
26.	他把头发擦干了。	
27.	她哭湿了手绢。	
28.	她叠了衣服。	
29.	她听小夏的话听懂了。	
30.	他把桌子擦干净了。	
31.	她说清道理。	
32.	他把小火车弄坏了。	
33.	他炒咸了菜。	
34.	他把老师的话听烦了。	
35.	她唱红了那首歌。	
36.	他绳子拉。	
37.	他擦干了头发。	
38.	她把这个问题想了。	
39.	他烦了老师的话。	
40.	她叠好了被子。	

再次感谢您的协助！

Appendix B: English translation of questionnaire surveys of acceptability of Chinese resultatives

Lancaster University
Linguistics and English Language

Participant information sheet

Title: Research on Chinese grammar

Researcher: Shuo Yu s.yu1@lancaster.ac.uk

Dept of Linguistics and English Language

County South

Lancaster University

Lancaster LA1 4YL

United Kingdom

You are invited to take part in this research. Please take time to read the following information carefully before you decide whether or not you wish to take part in it.

What is the purpose of this study?

I am carrying out this study as part of my Doctoral studies in the Department of Linguistics and English Language. The aim of the study is to look into Chinese grammar.

What does the study entail?

My study will involve a questionnaire survey.

Why have I been invited?

I have approached you because I am interested in understanding how native speakers will judge some sentences in terms of acceptability.

I would be very grateful if you would agree to take part in my study.

What will happen if I take part?

If you decided to take part, this would involve the following: you take out a pen, read the instructions on the questionnaire survey, and make acceptability judgements of the sentences based on your intuition.

What are the possible benefits from taking part?

If you take part in this study, your judgements of the sentences will contribute to our understanding of Chinese grammar.

What are the possible disadvantages and risks of taking part?

It is unlikely that there will be any major disadvantages to taking part. Participation in the survey will only take 10 minutes.

What will happen if I decide not to take part or if I don't want to carry on with the study?

If you decide not to take part in this study, this will not affect your studies and the way you are assessed on your course.

You are free to withdraw from the study at any time and you do not have to give a reason. If you withdraw while the study takes place or until 1 month after it finishes, I will not use any of the information that you provided. If you withdraw later, I will use the information you shared with me for my study.

Will my taking part in this project be kept confidential?

Any identifying information, such as names and personal characteristics, will be treated as confidential and anonymised in the PhD thesis or any other publications of this research. All other data will be anonymised. The data I will collect will be kept securely. Any paper–based data will be kept in a locked cupboard in Minzu University of China. Only Professor Xiaoqun Lu will have access to the cupboard. Electronic data will be stored on a password protected computer and files containing personal data as well as the computer or laptop will be encrypted.

What will happen to the results of the research study?

The results of the study will be used for academic purposes only. This will include my PhD thesis and other publications, for example journal articles. I am also planning to present the results of my study at academic conferences. I will retain the data for 15 years.

What if there is a problem?

If you have any queries or if you are unhappy with anything that happens concerning your participation in the study, please contact myself or my supervisor.

Elena Semino	Willem Hollmann
Head of Department	Supervisor
e.semino@lancaster.ac.uk	w.hollmann@lancaster.ac.uk
+44(0)1524594176	+44 (0)1524 94644

Dept of Linguistics and English Language

County South

Lancaster University

Lancaster LA1 4YT

United Kindom

This study has been reviewed and approved by members of Lancaster University Research Ethics Committee (UREC).

Thank you for considering your participation in this project.

Lancaster University
Linguistics and English Language

Consent Form

Project title: Research on Chinese grammar

I have read the information sheet relating to this project. ☐

I have had explained to me the purposes of the project and what will be required of me, and any questions have been answered to my satisfaction. I agree to the arrangements described in the information sheet in so far as they relate to my participation. ☐

I understand that my participation is entirely voluntary and that I have the right to withdraw from the project any time, but no longer than 1 month after its completion. If I withdraw after this period, the information I have provided will be used for the project. ☐

I understand that all data collected will be anonymised and that my identity will not be revealed at any point. ☐

I have received a copy of this consent form and of the accompanying information sheet. ☐

Name:

Signed:

Date:

Chinese Grammar experiment

The experiment you're participating in is part of a project on Chinese grammar. If you'd like more information about the project, I'll be happy to tell you more about the goals of the work and the results we've achieved so far. You may get in touch with us at the address shown below.

We very much appreciate your willingness to assist us in this work. None of the information collected here will be associated with your name in any way.

Shuo Yu

s.yu1@lancaster.ac.uk

Dept of Linguistics and English Language

County South,

Lancaster University

Lancaster LA1 4YL

United Kingdom

Preliminaries

In order to complete this questionnaire all you need is a pen or pencil. Please let the experimenter know if you're missing this. You'll mark your responses to the test sentences on this questionnaire, and return it to the experimenter afterwards.

Demographic information

In this section we ask you to give some demographic information about you and your parents/caregivers. If there is any question you do not wish to answer, just leave the space provided blank.

About you

Date of birth	
Gender	
City or town of residence	
Have you lived in this city or town all your life? If not, please give details of the other places where you lived, including how long you lived there.	
Would you consider yourself a speaker of a regional dialect? If so, what dialect would you say you speak (for example Northern dialect, Xiang dialect)?	

Please do not turn over until you are asked to do so

Instructions

In this experiment we would like to find out about Chinese grammar. To do so, we will present you with a list of sentences, and we would like you to tell us how normal they would sound to you. We would like to ask you to express your judgements as numbers: the more normal a sentence sounds to you, the higher the number you give it; the less normal a sentence sounds to you, the lower the number. There is no limit to how high your ratings may go, but we would ask you not to go below zero (e.g. –5 or –20, etc.). Also, you should make sure that you rate every sentence exactly in proportion to the other sentences. In other words, if your rating for sentence 1 was 20, and you find sentence 2 only half as normal, then you should rate that 10. And if you find sentence 3 half as normal again, then you should rate that 5. (Alternatively, if you've given sentence 1 a rating of 200, then sentence 2 would be 100, and 3 would be 50. Remember that there's no limit to how high you may go in your scores.)

Practice

We will now give you 3 sentences to practise with. Please record your rating (the degree to which you feel the sentence would sound) in the boxes on the right hand side of the sentences. If you have any questions about the way in which we'd like you to rate the sentences, please ask the experimenter.

							Rating
①	*jintian*	*wanshang*	*tebie*	*leng*			
	today	evening	very	cold			
	'It was very cold this evening.'						
②	*Xiaozhang*	*deng*	*le*	*jiu*	*zou*	*le*	
	Xiaozhang (name)	wait	ASP	then	go	ASP	
	'Xiaozhang waited and then left.'						
③	*ta*	*pingguo*	*gei*				
	he	apple	give				
	'He apple gave.'						

Once you're sure that you feel comfortable with the procedure, please wait until the experimenter asks you to turn the page and start on the actual experiment. There is no time limit for this experiment so please take as long as you like. However, it's important that the ratings you give are your initial gut response: once you've assigned a number to a sentence please don't correct it but just leave it as it is.

Please do not turn over until you are asked to do so

The sentences (Survey 1.1)

Rating

1.

ta	*ba*	*zhuozi*	*ca-ganjing-le*
he	*ba*	table	wipe–clean–ASP

'He wiped the table clean.'

2.

ta	*die-zhengqi-le*	*yifu*
she	fold–neat–ASP	clothes

'She folded the clothes and as a result the clothes were neat.'

3.

ta	*zhongyu*	*kan-lei-le*	*xiaoshuo*
she	finally	read–tired–ASP	novel

'She read the novel and finally as a result she was tired.'

4.

ta	*ba*	*zhe*	*zhong*	*cha*	*he-ni-le*
he	*ba*	this	kind	tea	drink–be tired of–ASP

'He had drunk this kind of tea so many times that he was tired of it.'

5.

ta	*zhongyu*	*ba*	*gongzuo*	*zuo-wan-le*
she	finally	*ba*	work	do–finished–ASP

'She did her work and as a result she finished it finally.'

6.

ta	*kan-guan-le*	*na*	*zhong*	*weixiao*
she	see–be used to–ASP	that	kind	smile

'She had seen that kind of smile so many times that she was used to it.'

7.

ta	*ku-shi-le*	*shoujuan*
she	cry–wet–ASP	handkerchief

'She cried the handkerchief wet.'

8.

ta	*ba*	*zhe*	*ge*	*wenti*	*xiang-mingbai-le*
he	*ba*	this	CL	question	think–understand–ASP

'He thought about this question and as a result he understood it.'

		Rating
9.	*ta ting-dong-le Xiaoyu de hua* she listen–understand–ASP Xiaoyu (name) POSS word She listened to Xiaoyu's words and as a result understood them.	
10.	*ta zhongyu kan-guan-le na zhong weixiao* she finally see–be used to that kind smile 'She had seen that kind of smile so many times that she was used to it finally.'	
11.	*ta xiang-qingchu zhe ge wenti* he think–clear this CL question 'He thought about these questions and as a result he was clear about them.'	
12.	*ta zhongyu kan-wan-le na ben xiaoshuo* she finally read–finished–ASP that CL novel 'She read that novel and as a result she finished reading it finally.'	
13.	*ta he-ni-le zhe zhong cha* he drink–be tired of–ASP this kind tea 'He had drunk this kind of tea so many times that he was tired of it.'	
14.	ta *zhongyu ba na zhong weixiao kan-guan-le* she finally *ba* that kind smile see–be used to 'She had seen that kind of smile so many times that she was used to it finally.'	
15.	*ta fan le laoshi de hua* he bored with ASP teacher POSS word 'He was bored with the teacher's words.'	
16.	*ta zhongyu ba zhe ge wenti xiang-mingbai-le* he finally *ba* this CL question think–understand –ASP 'He thought about this question and as a result he understood it finally.'	

Rating

17. *ta* *ba* *na* *zhong* *weixiao* *kan-guan-le*

she *ba* that kind smile see–be used to

'She had seen that kind of smile so many times that she was used to it finally.'

18. *ta* *zhongyu* *lian-shu-le* *zhe* *shou* *ge*

he finally practice–skilled–ASP this CL song

'He practiced this song and finally as a result he could sing it skilfully.'

19. *ta* *ba* *Xiaoyu* *de* *hua* *ting-dong-le*

she *ba* *Xiaoyu* (name) POSS word listen–understand–ASP

'She listened to Xiaoyu's words and as a result understood them.'

20. *ta* *ba* *zhe* *ge* *wenti* *xiang* *le*

he *ba* this CL question think ASP

'He thought about this question.'

21. *ta* *zhongyu* *ting-dong-le* *Xiaoyu* *de* *hua*

she finally listen–understand–ASP Xiaoyu (name) POSS word

'She listened to Xiaoyu's words and as a result understood them.'

22. *ta* *ca-ganjing-le* *zhuozi*

he wipe–clean–ASP table

'He wiped the table clean.'

23. *ta* *zhongyu* *ba* *zhe* *zhong* *cha* *he-ni-le*

he finally *ba* this kind tea drink–be tired of–ASP

'He had drunk this kind of tea so many times that he was tired of it finally.'

24. *ta* *ba* *Xiaoyu* *de* *hua* *dong* *le*

she *ba* Xiaoyu (name) POSS word understand ASP

'She understood Xiaoyu's words.'

Rating

25. *ta* *zhongyu* *xiang-mingbai-le* *zhe* *ge* *wenti*

he finally think–understand–ASP this CL question

'He thought about this question and as a result he understood it finally.'

26. *ta* *kan-lei-le* *xiaoshuo*

she read–tired–ASP novel

'She read the novel and as a result she was tired.'

27. *ta* *zhongyu* *he-ni- le* *zhe* *zhong* *cha*

he finally drink–be tired of–ASP this kind tea

'He had drunk this kind of tea so many times that he was tired of it finally.'

28. *ta* *zhongyu* *ba* *Xiaoyu* *de* *hua* *ting-dong-le*

she finally *ba* Xiaoyu (name) POSS word listen–understand –ASP

'She listened to Xiaoyu's words and as a result understood them finally.'

29. *ta* *xiang-mingbai-le* *zhe* *ge* *wenti*

he think–understand–ASP this CL question

'He thought about this question and as a result he understood it.'

30. *ta* *ba* *xiaoshuo* *kan-lei-le*

she *ba* novel read–tired–ASP

'She read the novel and as a result she was tired.'

31. *ta* *you* *zhongyu* *ting* *le* *zhe* *shou* *ge*

he again finally listen ASP this CL song

'Finally he listened to this song again.'

32. *ta* *nong-huai-le* *xiao* *huoche*

he do–broken–ASP small train

'He played with the model train and as a result it was broken.'

Thank you again for your cooperation!

The sentences (Survey 1.2)

Rating

1. *ta ba zhuozi ca-ganjing-le*

   he *ba* table wipe–clean–ASP

   'He wiped the table clean.'

2. *ta you zhongyu ting le zhe shou ge*

   she again finally listen ASP this CL song

   'Finally he listened to this song again.'

3. *ta ba xiaoshuo kan-lei-le*

   she *ba* novel read–tired–ASP

   'She read the novel and as a result she was tired.'

4. *ta zhongyu lian-hui-le zhe shou ge*

   he finally practice–can–ASP this CL song

   'He practiced this song and as a result he could sing it finally.'

5. *ta ba zhe ge daoli nong-mingbai-le*

   she *ba* this CL principle do–understand–ASP

   'She thought about this principle and as a result she understood it.'

6. *she ku-shi-le shoujuan*

   she cry–wet–ASP handkerchief

   'She cried the handkerchief wet.'

7. *ta zhongyu ba laoshi de hua ting-fan-le*

   he finally *ba* teacher POSS word listen–bored with –ASP

   'He listened to the teacher's words and as a result he was bored with them finally.'

8. *ta he-gou-le na zhong yaoshui*

   he drink–enough–ASP that kind portion

   'She had drunk that kind of portion so many times that she had enough of it.'

							Rating
9.	*ta*	*zhongyu*	*kan-wan-le*	*na*	*ben*	*xiaoshuo*	
	she	finally	read–finished–ASP	that	CL	novel	

'She read that novel and as a result she finished reading it finally.'

10.	*ta*	*ba*	*zhe*	*shou*	*ge*	*lian-hui-le*	
	he	*ba*	this	CL	song	practice–can–ASP	

'He practiced this song and as a result he could sing it.'

11.	*ta*	*nong-mingbai-ke*	*zhe*	*ge*	*daoli*	
	she	do–understand–ASP	this	CL	principle	

'She thought about this principle and as a result she understood it.'

12.	*ta*	*zhongyu*	*ba*	*na*	*zhong*	*yaoshui*	*he-gou-le*	
	she	finally	*ba*	that	kind	portion	drink–enough–ASP	

'She had drunk that kind of portion so many times that she had enough of it finally.'

13.	*ta*	*fan*	*le*	*laoshi*	*de*	*hua*	
	he	bored with	ASP	teacher	POSS	word	

'He was bored with the teacher's words.'

14.	*ta*	*zhongyu*	*ba*	*zhe*	*ge*	*daoli*	*nong-mingbai-le*	
	she	finally	ba	this	CL	principle	do–understand–ASP	

'She thought about this principle and as a result she understood it finally.'

15.	*ta*	*ca-ganjing-le*	*zhuozi*	
	he	wipe–clean–ASP	table	

'He wiped the table clean.'

16.	*ta*	*zhongyu*	*ting-fan-le*	*laoshi*	*de*	*hua*	
	he	finally	listen–bored with–ASP	teacher	POSS	word	

'He listened to the teacher's words and as a result he was bored with them finally.'

Rating

17. *ta* *ba* *Xiaoyu* *de* *hua* *dong* *le*

she *ba* Xiaoyu (name) POSS word understand ASP

'She understood Xiaoyu's words.'

18. *ta* *lian-hui-le* *zhe* *shou* *ge*

he practice–can–ASP this CL song

'He practiced this song and as a result he could sing it.'

19. *ta* *zhongyu* *ba* *gongzuo* *zuo-wan-le*

she finally *ba* work do–finished–ASP

'She did her work and as a result she finished it finally.'

20. *ta* *ba* *na* *zhong* *yaoshui* *he-gou-le*

she ba that kind portion drink–enough–ASP

'She had drunk that kind of portion so many times that she had enough of it.'

21. *ta* *ting-fan-le* *laoshi* *de* *hua*

he listen–bored with–ASP teacher POSS word

'He listened to the teacher's words and as a result he was bored with them.'

22. *ta* *zhongyuhe* *lian-shu-le* *zhe* *shou* *ge*

he finally practice–skilled–ASP this CL song

'He practiced this song and finally as a result he could sing it skilfully.'

23. *ta* *kan-lei-le* *xiaoshuo*

she read–tired–ASP novel

'She read the novel and as a result she was tired.'

24. *ta* *ba* *zhe* *ge* *wenti* *xiang* *le*

he ba this CL question think ASP

'He thought about this question.'

								Rating
25.	*ta*	*die-zhengqi-le*	*yifu*					
	she	fold–neat–ASP	clothes					
	'She folded the clothes and as a result the clothes were neat.'							
26.	*ta*	*zhongyu*	*ba*	*zhe*	*shou*	*ge*	*lian-hui-le*	
	he	finally	*ba*	this	CL	song	practice–can–ASP	
	'He practiced this song and as a result he could sing it finally.'							
27.	*ta*	*xiang-qingchu*	*zhe*	*ge*	*wenti*			
	he	think–clear	this	CL	question			
	'He thought about these questions and as a result he was clear about them.'							
28.	*ta*	*die*	*le*	*yifu*				
	she	fold	ASP	clothes				
	'She folded the clothes.'							
29.	*ta*	*ba*	*laoshi*	*de*	*hua*	*ting-fan-le*		
	he	ba	teacher	POSS	word	listen–bored with–ASP		
	'He listened to the teacher's words and as a result he was bored with them.'							
30.	*ta*	*ba*	*xiaoshuo*	*kan-lei-le*				
	she	ba	novel	read–tired–ASP				
	'She read the novel and as a result she was tired.'							
31.	*ta*	*you*	*zhongyu*	*ting*	*le*	*zhe*	*shou*	*ge*
	he	again	finally	listen	ASP	this	CL	song
	'Finally he listened to this song again.'							
32.	*ta*	*ba*	*zhuozi*	*ca-ganjing-le*				
	he	*ba*	table	wipe–clean–ASP				
	'He wiped the table clean.'							

Thank you again for your cooperation!

The sentences (Survey 2)

Rating

1. *ta* *xi* *yifu* *xi-lei-le*

he wash clothes wash–tired–ASP

'She washed the clothes and as a result she was tired.'

2. *ta* *ba* *wo* *da* *le*

she *ba* I hit ASP

'He beat me.'

3. *ta* *ting* *le* *you* *zhe* *shou* *ge*

she listen ASP again this CL song

'He listened to this song again.'

4. *ta* *ba* *shoujuan* *ku-shi-le*

he *ba* handkerchief cry–wet–ASP

'She cried the handkerchief wet.'

5. *ta* *ting-fan-le* *laoshi* *de* *hua*

he listen–bored with–ASP teacher POSS word

'He listened to the teacher's words and as a result he was bored with them.'

6. *ta* *jiangshu* *xizhi* *le* *zhe* *jian* *shi*

she talk detailed ASP this CL event

'She talked about this event so as to make it very detailed.'

7. *ta* *ba* *na* *shou* *ge* *chang-hong-le*

she *ba* that CL song sing–popular–ASP

'She sang that song and as a result the song was popular.'

8. *ta* *xiang-qingchu* *zhe* *ge* *wenti*

he think–clear this CL question

'He thought about these questions and as a result he was clear about them.'

Rating

9.	*ta*	*ba*	*Xiaoyu*	*de*	*hua*	*dong*	*le*
	she	*ba*	Xiaoyu (name)	POSS	word	understand	ASP

'She understood Xiaoyu's words.'

10.	*ta*	*ca*	*zhuozi*	*ca-ganjing-le*
	he	wipe	table	wipe–clean–ASP

'He wiped the table clean.'

11.	*ta*	*xiang-qingchu*	*zhe*	*ge*	*wenti*
	he	think–clear	this	CL	question

'He thought about these questions and as a result he was clear about them.'

12.	*ta*	*ba*	*zhe*	*ge*	*wenti*	*xiang-mingbai-le*
	he	*ba*	this	CL	question	think–understand–ASP

'He thought about this question and as a result he understood it.'

13.	*ta*	*ting-dong-le*	*Xiaokai*	*de*	*hua*
	she	listen–understand–ASP	Xiaokai (name)	POSS	word

'She listened to Xiaoyu's words and as a result understood them.

14.	*ta*	*ba*	*cai*	*chao-xian-le*
	he	*ba*	dish	fry–salty–ASP

'He fried the dish and as a result the dish was salty.'

15.	*ta*	*ting*	*laoshi*	*de*	*hua*	*ting-fan-le*
	he	listen	teacher	POSS	word	listen–bored with–ASP

'He listened to the teacher's words and as a result he was bored with them.'

16.	*ta*	*ti-pian-le*	*qiu*
	he	kick–aside–ASP	ball

'He kicked the ball aside.'

Rating

17. *ta* *ba* *yifu* *die-zhengqi-le*

she *ba* clothes fold–neat–ASP

'She folded the clothes and as a result the clothes were neat.'

18. ta *nong-huai-le* *xiao* *huoche*

he do–broken–ASP small train

'He played with the model train and as a result it was broken.'

19. *ta* *ba* *beizi* *die-hao-le*

she *ba* quilt fold–well–ASP

'She folded the quilt well.'

20. *ta* *ca-ganjing-le* *zhuozi*

he wipe–clean–ASP table

'He wiped the table clean.'

21. *ta* *ba* *Xiaoming* *de* *hua* *ting-dong-le*

she *ba* Xiaoming (name) POSS word listen–understand–ASP

'She listened to Xiaoming's words and as a result understood them.'

22. *ta* *nong-le* *toufa*

she do–ASP hair

'She did her hair.'

23. *ta* *ba* *zhe* *shou* *ge* *lian-hui-le*

he *ba* this CL song practice–can–ASP

'He practiced this song and as a result he could sing it.'

24. *ta* *xiang* *zhe* *ge* *wenti* *xiang-mingbai-le*

he think this CL question think–understand–ASP

'He thought about this question and as a result he understood it.'

Rating

25.	*ta*	*die-zhengqi-le*	*yifu*			
	she	fold–neat–ASP	clothes			

'She folded the clothes and as a result the clothes were neat.'

26.	*ta*	*ba*	*toufa*	*ca-gan-le*	
	he	*ba*	hair	wipe–dry–ASP	

'He wiped the table clean.'

27.	*she*	*ku-shi-le*	*shoujuan*
	she	cry–wet–ASP	handkerchief

'She cried the handkerchief wet.'

28.	*ta*	*die-le*	*yifu*
	she	fold–ASP	clothes

'She folded the clothes.'

29.	*ta*	*ting*	*Xiaoxia*	*de*	*hua*	*ting-dong-le*
	she	listen	Xiaoxia (name)	POSS	word	listen–understand–ASP

'She listened to Xiaoxia's words and as a result understood them.'

30.	*ta*	*ba*	*zhuozi*	*ca-ganjing-le*
	he	*ba*	table	wipe–clean–ASP

'He wiped the table clean.'

31.	*ta*	*shuo-qing*	*daoli*
	she	speak–clear	principle

'She explained the principle clearly.'

32.	*ta*	*ba*	*xiao*	*huoche*	*nong-huai-le*
	he	*ba*	small	train	do–broken–ASP

'He played with the model train and as a result it was broken.'

								Rating
33.	*ta*	*chao-xian-le*		*cai*				
	he	fry–salty–ASP		dish				
	'He fried the dish and as a result the dish was salty.'							
34.	*ta*	*ba*	*laoshi*	*de*	*hua*	*ting-fan-le*		
	he	*ba*	teacher	POSS	word	listen–bored with–ASP		
	'He listened to the teacher's words and as a result he was bored with them.'							
35	*ta*	*chang-hong-le*		*na*	*shou*	*ge*		
	she	sing–popular–ASP		that	CL	song		
	'She sang that song and as a result the song was popular.'							
36.	*ta*	*shengzi*	*la*					
	he	rope	pull					
	'He pulled the rope.'							
37.	*ta*	*ca-gan-le*		*toufa*				
	she	wipe–dry–ASP		hair				
	'She wiped her hair dry.'							
38.	*ta*	*ba*	*zhe*	*ge*	*wenti*	*xiang*	*le*	
	he	*ba*	this	CL	question	think	ASP	
	'He thought about this question.'							
39.	*ta*	*fan*		*le*	*laoshi*	*de*	*hua*	
	he	bored with		ASP	teacher	POSS	word	
	'He was bored with the teacher's words.'							
40.	*ta*	*die-hao-le*		*beizi*				
	she	fold–well–ASP		quilt				
	'She folded the quilt well.'							

Thank you again for your cooperation!